NEW STUDIES IN BIBLI

Unceasing kindness

NEW STUDIES IN BIBLICAL THEOLOGY 41

Series editor: D. A. Carson

Unceasing kindness

A BIBLICAL THEOLOGY OF RUTH

*Peter H. W. Lau and
Gregory Goswell*

APOLLOS

INTERVARSITY PRESS
DOWNERS GROVE, ILLINOIS 60515

APOLLOS (an imprint of Inter-Varsity Press, England)
36 Causton Street
London SW1P 4ST, England
Website: www.ivpbooks.com
Email: ivp@ivpbooks.com

InterVarsity Press, USA
P.O. Box 1400
Downers Grove, IL 60515, USA
Website: www.ivpress.com
Email: email@ivpress.com

InterVarsity Press®, USA, is the book-publishing division of InterVarsity Christian Fellowship/USA® and a member movement of the International Fellowship of Evangelical Students. Website: www.intervarsity.org.

Inter-Varsity Press, England, originated within the Inter-Varsity Fellowship, now the Universities and Colleges Christian Fellowship, a student movement connecting Christian Unions in universities and colleges throughout Great Britain, and a member movement of the International Fellowship of Evangelical Students. Website: www.uccf.org.uk. That historic association is maintained, and all senior IVP staff and committee members subscribe to the UCCF Basis of Faith.

First published 2016

Set in Monotype Times New Roman
Typeset in Great Britain by CRB Associates, Potterhanworth, Lincolnshire
Printed and bound in Great Britain by Ashford Colour Press Ltd, Gosport, Hampshire

USA ISBN 978-0-8308-2642-1 (print)
USA ISBN 978-0-8308-9175-7 (digital)

UK ISBN 978-1-78359-448-1 (print)
UK ISBN 978-1-78359-453-5 (digital)

British Library Cataloguing-in-Publication Data

A catalogue record for this book is available from the British Library.

Library of Congress Cataloging-in-Publication Data

A catalog record for this book is available from the Library of Congress.

P 25 24 23 22 21 20 19 18 17 16 15 14 13 12 11 10 9 8 7 6 5 4 3 2 1

Y 37 36 35 34 33 32 31 30 29 28 27 26 25 24 23 22 21 20 19 18 17 16

Contents

Series preface

New Studies in Biblical Theology is a series of monographs that address key issues in the discipline of biblical theology. Contributions to the series focus on one or more of three areas: (1) the nature and status of biblical theology, including its relations with other disciplines (e.g. historical theology, exegesis, systematic theology, historical criticism, narrative theology); (2) the articulation and exposition of the structure of thought of a particular biblical writer or corpus; and (3) the delineation of a biblical theme across all or part of the biblical corpora.

Above all, these monographs are creative attempts to help thinking Christians understand their Bibles better. The series aims simultaneously to instruct and to edify, to interact with the current literature and to point the way ahead. In God's universe, mind and heart should not be divorced: in this series we will try not to separate what God has joined together. While the notes interact with the best of scholarly literature, the text is uncluttered with untransliterated Greek and Hebrew, and tries to avoid too much technical jargon. The volumes are written within the framework of confessional evangelicalism, but there is always an attempt at thoughtful engagement with the sweep of the relevant literature.

Many a small-group Bible study has focused on Ruth, partly because the book is short, partly because it has a romantic element with a happy ending, partly because the last few lines tie the book to the Davidic dynasty and hence to Jesus. But I know no full-length study that has read it closely and patiently through the lens of biblical theology (though see the admirable contribution of Barry Webb in *Five Festal Garments* in this series). Peter Lau and Greg Goswell have wonderfully filled that gap. They read Ruth in the context of its nearest Old Testament books ('nearest' both culturally and historically), and then in the context of the entire Christian canon. There can be little doubt that pastors committed to expository preaching and who choose to work their way through Ruth will gladly stand on the shoulders of Drs Lau and Goswell.

D. A. Carson
Trinity Evangelical Divinity School

Authors' preface

One sunny afternoon in Sydney we were sitting in a café enjoying a coffee and chatting about our common interests in the Old Testament. We hit on the idea of working on a book project together and a biblical theology of Ruth was an obvious choice for us both. This book is the outcome of what has been brewing since then. We hope you find it fresh, stimulating and, most of all, invigorating in your walk with the Lord Jesus.

Peter's nascent interest in Ruth began as an undergraduate, as he toiled over translating Ruth in a Hebrew class. The book became the focus of his postgraduate studies but, after completing his doctorate, his interest in Ruth was still not quenched, so further pieces were written. Yet a nagging thought remained: the most important approach to reading Ruth – using biblical theology – needed to be pursued. Peter would like to thank those who have endured his teaching and preaching on the book of Ruth, and his lecturing on biblical theology. Those furrowed brows spurred me to express myself more clearly, and those insightful questions forced me to think more widely and deeply. Peter would also like to thank students who provided feedback on some chapters of this book, as well as his 'in-house' proofreader, Ruth Wong.

Greg is grateful to all those who have influenced his thinking on Scripture and on the book of Ruth in particular. The study of the Bible is necessarily a cooperative exercise. We stand on the shoulders of those who have studied and written about the Bible before us (and I have done my best to acknowledge my debt by means of footnotes). The influence of our teachers is often more subtle and subliminal, and no doubt some of what I am quite convinced are my own 'good ideas' originally belonged to others, but I have forgotten the conversations of long ago and the off-the-cuff comments in lectures that were not written down but sank into my subconscious. Only on the Last Day will we realize how much we owe to others.

We wish to thank Don Carson for accepting this book into the New Studies in Biblical Theology series, one which we have both been enriched by and whose volumes have been added to textbook and reading lists for our students. We also thank Philip Duce for guiding us through the publishing process, and Steven Foong for compiling the indexes.

We dedicate this book to our children. Peter dedicates it to Zachary, Jeremy and Sophie. Greg dedicates it to his three daughters Geraldine, Katherine and Louise, whose favourite books of the Bible are (of course) Ruth and Esther. By God's grace, may they continue to 'grow in the grace and knowledge of our Lord and Saviour Jesus Christ. To him be the glory both now and to the day of eternity' (2 Pet. 3:18).

Peter Lau
Greg Goswell
January 2016

Abbreviations

AAR	American Academy of Religion
AB	The Anchor Bible
ABR	*Australian Biblical Review*
AcT	*Acta Theologica*
ANE	Ancient Near East
Ann.	Tacitus, *Annals*
Ant.	Josephus, *Jewish Antiquities*
AOTC	Apollos Old Testament Commentary
AYB	The Anchor Yale Bible
BBB	Bonner biblische Beiträge
BBR	*Bulletin for Biblical Research*
BDB	*Hebrew and English Lexicon of the Old Testament*, F. Brown, S. R. Driver and C. A. Briggs, Oxford: Clarendon, 1907
BECNT	Baker Exegetical Commentary on the New Testament
BETL	Bibliotheca ephemeridum theologicarum lovaniensium
BHK³	*Biblica Hebraica*, R. Kittel (ed.), Stuttgart: Württembergische Bibelanstalt, 1937
BHS	*Biblia Hebraica Stuttgartensia*, K. Elliger and W. Rudolph (eds.), Stuttgart: Deutsche Bibelstiftung, 1983
BHQ	*Biblia Hebraica Quinta*, Stuttgart: Deutsche Bibelgesellschaft, 2004–
Bib	*Biblica*
BibInt	*Biblical Intrerpretation*
BibSac	*Bibliotheca Sacra*
BKAT	Biblischer Kommentar: Altes Testament
BST	The Bible Speaks Today
BT	*The Bible Translator*
BTB	*Biblical Theology Bulletin*
BT Ber.	*Babylonian Talmud Berakot*
BZAW	Beihefte zur Zeitschrift für die alttestamentliche Wissenschaft

CB OT	Coniectanea biblica (Old Testament Series)
CBQ	*Catholic Biblical Quarterly*
CC	Concordia Commentary
CEV	Contemporary English Version
EJL	Early Judaism and Its Literature
ESV	English Standard Version
EQ	*Evangelical Quarterly*
FAT	Forschungen zum Alten Testament
GKC	*Gesenius' Hebrew Grammar*, E. Kautzsch (ed.), rev. and tr. A. E. Cowley; Oxford: Clarendon, 1910
HALOT	*The Hebrew and Aramaic Lexicon of the Old Testament*, L. Koehler, W. Baumgartner and J. J. Stamm, tr. and ed. under the supervision of M. E. J. Richardson, 4 vols., Leiden: Brill, 1995, 2004
HAR	*Hebrew Annual Review*
HAT	Handbuch zum Alten Testament
HCSB	Holman Christian Standard Bible
Heb.	Hebrew versification
Hist. eccl.	Eusebius, *Ecclesiastical History*
HSM	Harvard Semitic Monographs
HSS	Harvard Semitic Studies
HTKAT	Herders theologischer Kommentar zum Alten Testament
HUCA	*Hebrew Union College Annual*
IBC	Interpretation: A Bible Commentary for Teaching and Preaching
Int	*Interpretation*
IVBS	International Voices in Biblical Studies
JBL	*Journal of Biblical Literature*
JESOT	*Journal for the Evangelical Study of the Old Testament*
JETh	*Jahrbuch für evangelikale Theologie*
JETS	*Journal of the Evangelical Theological Society*
JJS	*Journal of Jewish Studies*
JNES	*Journal of Near Eastern Studies*
JPS	Jewish Publication Society
JR	*Journal of Religion*
JSOT	*Journal for the Study of the Old Testament*
JSOTSup	*Journal for the Study of the Old Testament, Supplement Series*

JSS	*Journal of Semitic Studies*
JTI	*Journal of Theological Interpretation*
LHBOTS	Library of Hebrew Bible/Old Testament Studies
LXX	Septuagint
Midr. Ruth Rab.	*Midrash Ruth Rabbah*
MT	Masoretic Text
NAC	New American Commentary
NASB	New American Standard Bible
NB	*nota bene*
NCB	New Century Bible
NICNT	New International Commentary on the New Testament
NICOT	New International Commentary on the Old Testament
NIGTC	New International Greek Testament Commentary
NIV	New International Version
NIVAC	The NIV Application Commentary
NJPS	New Jewish Publication Society (Bible version)
NLT	New Living Translation
NRSV	New Revised Standard Version
NSBT	New Studies in Biblical Theology
NT	New Testament
NTS	*New Testament Studies*
OBO	Orbis Biblicus et Orientalis
OBT	Overtures to Biblical Theology
OT	Old Testament
OTL	Old Testament Library
PNTC	Pillar New Testament Commentary
RB	*Revue biblique*
RSV	Revised Standard Version
RTR	*Reformed Theological Review*
SBJT	*Southern Baptist Journal of Theology*
SBL	Society of Biblical Literature
SBLDS	Society of Biblical Literature Dissertation Series
SBLMS	Society of Biblical Literature Monograph Series
SBS	Stuttgarter Bibelstudien
SBT	Studies in Biblical Theology
SJOT	*Scandinavian Journal of the Old Testament*
SNTSMS	Society for New Testament Studies Monograph Series

TDOT	*Theological Dictionary of the Old Testament*, ed. G. J. Botterweck, H. Ringgren and H.-J. Fabry; tr. J. T. Willis, G. W. Bromiley and D. E. Green. 15 vols., Grand Rapids: Eerdmans, 1974–2006
Them	*Themelios*
THOTC	Two Horizons Old Testament Commentary
TOTC	Tyndale Old Testament Commentaries
TrinJ	*Trinity Journal*
TynB	*Tyndale Bulletin*
UNHCR	United Nations High Commissioner for Refugees
USQR	*Union Seminary Quarterly Review*
VT	*Vetus Testamentum*
VTSup	Vetus Testamentum Supplements
WBC	Word Biblical Commentary
WTJ	*Westminster Theological Journal*
WUNT	Wissenschaftliche Untersuchungen zum Neuen Testament
ZAW	*Zeitschrift für die alttestamentliche Wissenschaft*

Chapter One

Introduction

In the church, the book of Ruth is understandably a firm favourite, a heart-warming tale of loyalty and love, a satisfying story of famine to fullness. As such, it is one of the Old Testament narratives that is studied in small groups and is preached from the pulpit. In the academy, the book of Ruth has been a testing ground for the whole gamut of hermeneutical approaches, a book through which any and every interpretive lens has been applied. These approaches include historical-critical, literary, social-scientific, feminist, cultural/contextual, missional, post-colonial and more.[1] Various lenses have highlighted different aspects of the rich narrative of Ruth, but the single lens missing is the one that is most beneficial for the church: the biblical-theology lens. There have been commentaries that have adopted a biblical-theological approach, of one form or another, to exegeting or interpreting the text,[2] but there has not been a detailed monograph treatment of the themes in the book of Ruth from a biblical-theology perspective.[3] This book aims to fill this gap.

Volumes in the New Studies in Biblical Theology series focus on one or more of the following areas: the nature and status of biblical theology; the exposition of the structure of thought of a particular biblical writer or corpus; the delineation of a biblical theme. Our approach in this volume is primarily thematic, so we do not make a significant contribution to the second area, namely, articulating the structure of thought found in the book of Ruth. Instead, we seek to make contributions to the first and third areas. *Regarding the first area*: we will read the book of Ruth focusing on the meaning of the text as intended by the author for original hearers, but mindful of the fact that the book as we have it is set within a wider context of Scripture.

---

[1] References for the first three approaches can be found in Lau 2011: 12–18. For feminist readings of Ruth, see Bauckham 1997; Brenner 1993b; and Brenner 1999; for cultural/contextual and post-colonial approaches, see Havea and Lau 2015; and Lau 2012; for missional approaches, see Thomas 2002 and chapter 9.

[2] E.g. Ulrich 2007; McKeown 2015. For an outline of the range of approaches that have been labelled 'biblical-theological', see Klink and Lockett 2012.

[3] Webb (2000) devotes one chapter to Ruth in his reflections on the *Megillot*.

We affirm that it is important to read each passage and book of the Bible on its own terms, deriving the meaning from each specific text, understood within its immediate literary, historical and cultural contexts.[4] Yet we also acknowledge that each book of the Bible, including those in the Old Testament, is nestled within a wider context, the consideration of which is essential for a complete understanding of a particular biblical text.

For Christians, this wider context includes not only the books surrounding it in the canon(s), or even a particular section of Scripture (either the historical books or the Writings for the book of Ruth), but the rest of the Old Testament, and right through to the New Testament. As Dempster has demonstrated in relation to the Hebrew canon,[5] the ordering of biblical books can highlight patterns and themes, from which one can discern a central narrative storyline. Indeed, different canons of Scripture, Greek as well as Hebrew, can provide different insights into the meaning of particular biblical books and Scripture as a whole. We will show that reading the book of Ruth alongside Judges and Samuel, as in the Christian canonical order (which follows the Greek), yields certain insights, and reading Ruth alongside Psalms and Proverbs, as in some Jewish canonical orders, yields further insights. Additionally, we will read the book of Ruth alert to its inner-biblical interrelationships and resonances.[6] These intra-biblical connections are pertinent for texts that might be dated later than Ruth, and with an element of authorial intent on the part of the later human author. However, since we hold that God, through the Holy Spirit, is the divine author superintending the writing of the whole of Scripture, we will also identify other inner-biblical links and developments within the canon.

Moreover, since the Old Testament points forward to and is fulfilled in Christ (e.g. Luke 24:27; John 5:39; 2 Cor. 1:20),[7] a Christian reading of any portion of Scripture must also consider the difference that Jesus makes to the interpretation of any particular text. That is, from

---

[4] This is especially important for us as authors, since our primary area of teaching is the Old Testament.

[5] Dempster (2003: 33–34) follows the ordering of the canon described in *Baba Bathra* 14b, a portion of the Talmud. On the book of Ruth's place in the Hebrew canon, see chapter 4.

[6] We try to avoid using the term 'intertextuality' because of the philosophical baggage it carries with it; cf. Beale 2012: 39–40. See also our argument in chapter 5. For recent discussions that aim to define inner-biblical exegesis, allusion, echo and intertextuality, see Stead 2009: 18–27; Meek 2014; Sommer 1996.

[7] See chapter 3 for further discussion of these passages.

a Christian perspective a complete reading of the Old Testament must have an eschatological element to it, since Christ is the midpoint and endpoint of salvation history: in his life, death, resurrection and ascension, and in his return to consummate salvation history. It is only after a consideration of how a passage relates to Christ and the gospel that application can be made to our contemporary Christian contexts, not before.[8] In this book we will consider not only the immediate and broader Old Testament canonical contexts, but also the context of the whole sweep of Scripture, including the New Testament.

Regarding the third area: we will discuss some themes in the book of Ruth within the context of the whole Scripture. As we examined the book of Ruth, we found that themes emerged which, within the context of the whole Bible, might be considered 'major' or 'minor'. One of the challenges of the discipline of biblical theology is faithfully to enunciate the unity within the diversity and the diversity within the unity.[9] Sometimes there is a focus on unity (e.g. the search for a thematic centre to Scripture; in other words, a search for *the* major theme or centre of biblical theology),[10] and at other times there is a focus on diversity (e.g. the delineation of minor themes or motifs).[11] In this book we explore both the 'major' and 'minor' themes in the book of Ruth. Some of the 'major' themes we will explore are redemption, kingship and mission, while some of the 'minor' themes or motifs are kindness, wisdom, famine, refuge, seed, doxology, and the hiddenness of God and human agency. Since our starting point is the book of Ruth, some themes that might be considered 'major' are discussed within other themes; for example, 'judgment and salvation' are treated within 'famine', 'land' is treated within 'redemption', and 'covenant' is mentioned in 'mission' and 'kingship'.

In terms of method, we will consider what the book of Ruth contributes to a certain biblical theme overall, as well as how a canonical

---

[8] Goldsworthy (2000: 113) is most insistent on this point: '[T]he application of the meaning of any text must proceed theologically via the application it has to Christ.'

[9] Cf. Martens (1977: 123): 'Biblical theology attempts to embrace the message of the Bible and to arrive at an intelligible coherence of the whole despite the great diversity of the parts. Or, put another way: Biblical theology investigates the themes presented in the Scripture and defines their interrelationships.' See also Carson 1995: 17–41; Hafemann and House 2007; Köstenberger 2012: 445–464.

[10] On which see Hamilton 2006: 57–84. He proposes 'the glory of God in salvation through judgment' as the central theme; see also Hamilton 2010.

[11] A 'motif' has the concrete sense of a recurrent image or object (e.g. famine), whereas 'theme' is broader, and various related motifs may contribute to the one theme. An example of an approach that focuses on the diversity in the OT is Brueggemann 1997.

understanding of the theme impacts the interpretation of specific aspects of the book of Ruth. Although we treat the themes in separate chapters, attentive readers will notice a degree of overlap in the treatment of these themes. This reflects the close interconnection of the themes; in general, themes do not exist in isolation in Scripture. Indeed, within the overarching narrative of the Bible, all the way from Genesis to Revelation, these themes can be viewed as different threads within the same cloth, or can be heard as different instrumental 'voices' within a symphony. Some may be more dominant than others, but each theme contributes to, interacts with and makes an essential contribution to the whole.

So to a roadmap of what is ahead in this book: although all the chapters in this book take into account both the nearer canonical context (within the OT) and the wider canonical context (whole of Scripture), in general terms chapters 3 to 5 focus more on delineating a theme in relation to the former (the OT context), while chapters 6 to 9 focus more on delineating a theme in relation to the latter (the context of the Bible as a whole). Chapter 2 is similar to but also different from the rest of the chapters: it is similar in that it reads the book of Ruth within the context of another Old Testament book, Ezra–Nehemiah; it is different in that it compares and contrasts a few themes, not just one. Chapter 10 will present a summary and some conclusions from our discussions undertaken in this book.

Chapter Two

Reading Ruth in the early restoration period

There is much debate about when the book of Ruth was written. The historical setting of the narrative is the time of the judges, but internal evidence reveals that the book was written, or at least edited, for a later audience. The mention of 'the days when the judges ruled' (1:1) at the beginning of the narrative implies that the era of the judges already lay in the past. The narrator's explanation of the sandal custom (4:7) indicates that the custom had changed or was no longer active, so a considerable amount of time had passed. The genealogy leading to King David (4:17, 22) provides the earliest time for the composition of Ruth: the early monarchy.[1] In scholarship, the two most popular periods for dating the book of Ruth are the monarchic and post-exilic periods. Different types of arguments have been adduced in support of each position,[2] but for the discussion at hand we will focus on the perceived purposes of the book of Ruth.

On the one hand, many who argue for a monarchic date view the purpose of the book as supporting the choice of David as king.[3] In this view, the strong element of God's providence in the book points to the choice of David as part of God's plan. The assumption is that David's Moabite ancestry is a hindrance to his dynasty, so the book is viewed as promoting Ruth's suitability as an ancestor of David: her conversion to Israel's God, her virtuous character and her acceptance into Israelite society. On the other hand, many who argue for a post-exilic date view the purpose of the book as a polemic against the ban of interracial marriages. Ezra and Nehemiah determined that those Israelites who had married foreign wives must divorce them

---

[1] For an argument that the genealogy is part of the original composition and not a later insertion, see chapter 3.

[2] The types of arguments can be classified as historical-chronological, theological-ideological, literary-stylistic and linguistic-philological, all of which have a subjective element. For details and references for each type, see Lau 2011: 47–53.

[3] E.g. Campbell 1975; Hubbard 1988; Gow 1992; Weinfeld 1996; Nielsen 1997; Block 1999. Scholars vary in their identification of a specific historical setting for such an apology, from during David's lifetime, to the reign of Solomon, to the time of Josiah.

(Ezra 10; Neh. 13:23–27). In this context, the book of Ruth is viewed as resisting this exclusivist stance. This second view is popular in recent commentaries.[4]

Despite all the scholarly debate and all the evidence that has been marshalled for each side, there has been no unanimous decision about the date of composition of Ruth. Since the author and date of composition are not stated, it is best to remain agnostic about when it was written. In any case, securing a date is not crucial to our discussion in this chapter, although the dating has implications for how to view our discussion. If one holds that Ruth was written earlier than Ezra–Nehemiah, our discussion would primarily be an exploration of how a person living in the early restoration period would understand the text within his or her own historical context. Moreover, the analogies between the two books enhance the relevance of Ruth in the early restoration period, a time in which Israel was a colony of the Persian Empire. Both the book of Ruth and Ezra–Nehemiah are narratives of 'return': Ruth and Naomi return from Moab; a group of Yehudites return from Babylon.[5] It is a period of adjustment for the characters in both narratives. Naomi's situation, as an Israelite repatriate, parallels that of the 'returnees' who were exiled to Babylon but now return to their ancestral lands. Ruth's experience as a newcomer to the land of Israel most closely parallels the experience of those Yehudites born in Babylon and returning to a foreign 'home' for the first time. If one holds that the book of Ruth was written around the time of Ezra–Nehemiah, our discussion would primarily be an exploration of the social, political and ideological factors that influenced the writing of the book of Ruth, and to which the book of Ruth is partly a response. We will take the former position in the following discussion.

To anticipate our findings, it is right and proper that the books of Ruth and Ezra–Nehemiah enter into dialogue with each other as constituent parts of Old Testament canon, and the book of Ruth can be understood to address issues in the early restoration period. However, since the book of Ruth probably comes from an earlier age, it is not surprising to discover that there is a lack of exact fit between the thematic foci of the story of Ruth and the chief issues of the period as reflected in Ezra–Nehemiah.

---

[4] E.g. LaCocque 2004; Matthews 2004; Zevit 2005; Eskenazi and Frymer-Kensky 2011; Hawk 2015.

[5] The return or restoration theme fits into the creation–sin–exile–restoration narrative pattern suggested by some biblical theologians, e.g. Pate, Duvall, Hays et al. 2004; Ciampa 2007: 254–308.

Inclusion or exclusion

In Ezra–Nehemiah the repatriates found themselves in a situation of threat to Israelite identity and existence. This threat derived not only from Persian imperialism, but also from 'the people of the land' (Ezra 4:4 [*'am-hā'āreṣ*]). Although the term is used neutrally or positively elsewhere in the Old Testament,[6] in Ezra–Nehemiah it has taken on a pejorative tinge,[7] referring to the resident population in Yehud (Judah). They are in contradistinction to Ezra–Nehemiah's view of 'true Israel', namely those who have returned from exile under the mandate provided by the decree of Cyrus (Ezra 1:2–4; 4:3).[8] The expression 'the people [sing.] of the land' occurs nowhere else in Ezra–Nehemiah. Elsewhere, either 'the peoples of the land' or 'the peoples of the lands' is used. The singular may be used in Ezra 4:4 to stress the contrast at this point with 'the people of Judah' in the same verse (a shorthand for Judah and Benjamin, 4:1), with both expressions looking back to 'his people' in Ezra 1:3.[9] In Nehemiah 9:24 the phrase 'the peoples of the land' is to be interpreted by the phrase which precedes it in the sentence: 'the inhabitants of the land, the Canaanites'. The plural 'the peoples who practise these abominations' in Ezra 9:14 follows the earlier reference in 9:1 in which 'the peoples of the lands' is expounded by a listing that includes people groups both inside (Hittites, Perizzites, Jebusites, Amorites) and outside the land (Ammonites, Moabites, Egyptians). Other references in which 'people' (*'am*) refers to foreign people are Nehemiah 1:8; 9:10, 22; 13:24. All other references to 'people' in Ezra–Nehemiah are to the people of Israel. The 'people(s) of the land(s)' in Ezra–Nehemiah always refers to foreigners, and the related phrase 'the nations [*gôy*] of the land' in Ezra 6:21 (our translation) confirms that foreigners are in mind. Within this context of foreign threat to Israel's integrity,

---

[6] On *'am-hā'āreṣ* in the Hebrew Bible, see Japhet 2006; Nicholson 1965.

[7] For a suggested diachronic development of the phrase, see Lipiński 2001: 175.

[8] According to Ezra–Nehemiah there is only one Israelite community in Yehud: the returned exiles (Ezra 2:1; Neh. 7:6; cf. Ezra 4:1; 6:19–20; 8:35; 9:4; 10:6–8, 16).

[9] Here is a listing of the relevant passages: 'the peoples of the land' in Ezra 10:2, 11; Neh. 9:24; 10:30, 31 (Heb. 31, 32), and 'the peoples of the lands' in Ezra 3:3; 9:1, 2, 11; Neh. 9:30; 10:28 (Heb. 29). Together with the reference in Ezra 4:4, there are twelve occurrences of these related terms. Blenkinsopp (1988: 108) seems to be right in saying that they 'are used for all practical purposes interchangeably. They refer to the inhabitants of either Judah or neighbouring provinces (Samaria, Idumea, etc.) who are outside the returned community and are therefore by definition religiously suspect.'

the book of Ruth can be read as promoting a worldview that preserves some elements of Israelite identity and freedom, but at the same time it resists other elements of Israelite identity and imperial rule.

Read in the context of the return from exile, the book of Ruth provides a subtle protest against ethnocentrism as central to Israelite identity. Some propose that the prohibition of intermarriage in the Persian period mainly served the interests of imperial social control.[10] According to these scholars, genealogical purity was a way of establishing land tenure for the returnees, thereby asserting control of land and property. If this was a factor, then the book of Ruth would undermine this aspect of Persian policy; however, the need to protect Israelite identity was probably the driving influence.[11] Whichever factors were involved, the book of Ruth resists a simplistic ideology of Israelite ethnic purity.

Although, in the book of Ruth, marriage to a non-Yahweh-fearing foreigner can lead to punishment (if the deaths of Mahlon and Chilion are interpreted in this way [1:4–5]), marriage to a Yahweh-fearing foreigner *is* permitted.[12] The crucial aspect of Israelite identity is a right (and exclusive) relationship with Yahweh expressed in acts of *hesed*, not one's ethnicity. In fact, although muted, a hint of an inclusive outlook may be detected in the mention in Ezra–Nehemiah of foreigners participating in the Passover (Ezra 6:19–21; v. 21: 'and also by everyone who had joined them and separated himself from the uncleanness of the peoples of the land to worship the LORD, the God of Israel'). An inclusive outlook may also be detected in the community pledge to follow the Torah (Neh. 10:28 [Heb. 29]), for those making the pledge included 'all who have separated themselves from the peoples of the lands to the Law of God'.[13] In other words, even in Ezra–Nehemiah, exogenous marriages are only outlawed if foreign spouses fail to commit themselves to the God of Israel and

---

[10] Seminally, Hoglund 1992.

[11] See the arguments provided by Lau 2011: 159–165.

[12] Deuteronomy prohibits marriage to foreign women because of the risk of apostasy (Deut. 7:3–4). Reading the book of Ruth in dialogue with this text leads to the possible conclusion that Mahlon and Chilion's marriage to foreign women led them to suffer Yahweh's punishment. Judgment did not befall Boaz because Ruth had already turned to Yahweh (Ruth 1:16–17; cf. 2:12). The Ruth narrative itself is silent about whether the deaths were an act of divine judgment, and their deaths remain an unexplained tragedy; so McKeown 2015: 17–18. See also the relevant discussion in chapters 6 and 9.

[13] See Lau 2009. Eskenazi and Frymer-Kensky (2011: lxxi n. 41) note that 'Ezra 6:21 could be read as referring to a loophole in this exclusionary policy'.

to practices consistent with that commitment.[14] A third possible hint of ethnic inclusiveness may be found, paradoxically, in the passage describing how Ezra dealt with the mixed-marriage problem (Ezra 10:16–44).[15] Many scholars hold that Ezra's actions in this passage contradict the laws against mixed marriage (e.g. Deut. 7:3). For example, Williamson (1985: 161) comments that it 'misinterprets the principle of the law along racist lines'. Scholars also note the prolonged period of time it took to settle the matter (three months) and the relatively small number of cases eventually found (about 110).[16] A careful case-by-case inquiry into the religious beliefs of the foreign wives would explain both of these features in the narrative, with only those wives who were found not to have faith in Yahweh expelled. Thus, the book of Ruth supports ethnic inclusiveness and its concern would help to draw the reader's attention to these three passages in Ezra–Nehemiah (Ezra 6:19–21; 10:16–44; Neh. 10:28).

On the other hand, the book of Ruth fails to address the specific concerns of the early restoration period (e.g. the issue of children speaking the foreign language of their mother [Neh. 13:23–24]; what to do with foreign wives who are not like Ruth), and so it is hardly the case (*pace* Eskenazi and Frymer-Kensky) that the story of Ruth 'provides an alternative or a solution to the problems that Ezra–Nehemiah seeks to address'.[17] In Nehemiah 13:23–28 it is plain that Nehemiah was opposed to marriages to women who retained their foreign languages and traditions, whereas Ruth the Moabitess is portrayed as adopting the God of Israel.[18] We cannot, therefore, follow Hawk when he views the book of Ruth as recording dissent to these reforms, for the reforms were not opposing marriage to foreign women like Ruth, namely women who had left their foreign gods behind and embraced the Israelite faith. It is just not true that Ezra and Nehemiah wanted 'to redefine Israel along lines of genetic

---

[14] Sweeney (2012: 433): 'Although Ezra–Nehemiah stipulates no procedure for conversion of a foreigner to Judaism, there is no indication in the book that foreigners who adhere to Yahweh were an issue.'

[15] There is a vast amount of literature on the mixed-marriage problem in Ezra–Nehemiah, tackling the problem from various perspectives. See, recently, Frevel 2011; Moffat 2013; Southwood 2012.

[16] The marriages involved priests, Levites and the laity of Israel (Ezra 10:18–44). The list of offenders is small compared with the overall numbers provided in Ezra 2 and Neh. 7.

[17] Eskenazi and Frymer-Kensky 2011: xxv.

[18] The contrast is noted by Sweeney 2012: 433. In fact, Ruth's Hebrew speech does not display any linguistic peculiarities, in contrast to the speeches of the native Hebrew speakers Boaz and Naomi; cf. Campbell 1975: 25.

purity'.[19] Hawk (like many others) fails to note references to the acceptance of proselytes in Ezra 6:21 and Nehemiah 10:28 (Heb. 29). We are in danger of turning one part of the Bible against another if we say, as Hawk does, that the author of Ruth is 'writing in opposition to the cleansing programme of Ezra and Nehemiah',[20] for it is plain that the canonical book of Ezra–Nehemiah approves the reform efforts.

There is no evidence, therefore, that the book of Ruth contradicts or implicitly condemns the policy of breaking up foreign marriages. On the other hand, what is only alluded to in two places in Ezra–Nehemiah (the ready reception of proselytes) is the focus of attention in the book of Ruth. Put simply, the book of Ruth and Ezra–Nehemiah are about different things. In terms of biblical theology, this is an example of how different canonical books supplement and balance each other, enabling a fuller presentation and application of God's variegated truth.

The law and the practice of *ḥesed*

Closely allied to its ethic of inclusiveness is the book of Ruth's promotion of an expansive application of the Torah as integral to Israelite identity. By contrast, in Ezra–Nehemiah, at least as commonly understood, the Torah is characteristically used as an instrument of prohibition and restriction. The law's application with regard to intermarriage reinforces this perception (Ezra 9 – 10; Neh. 13:1–3, 23–31).[21] Both accounts specifically name Moabites as among Israel's archetypal enemies (Ezra 9:1; Neh. 13:1; cf. 13:23), drawing on Deuteronomy 7 and 23:3–6.[22] Those infringing God's laws were threatened with state-sanctioned punishment in the decree of Artaxerxes (Ezra 7:26), though, in actual fact, the subsequent narrative in Ezra–Nehemiah fails to depict Ezra using the draconian civil powers given to him by the Persian king (Ezra 9 – 10). For example, it was appropriate that the threat to those who did not come to an assembly was to be 'banned [*bādal*] from the congregation' (10:8) as the problem of the assembly was that they had not 'separated themselves' (*bādal* [9:1]) from the

[19] Hawk 2015: 36.
[20] Hawk 2015: 39.
[21] Differences between the two accounts are also noted; see e.g. Smith-Christopher 1994: 243–265.
[22] On the use of Deuteronomic laws in Ezra 9 – 10 and Neh. 13:23–31, see, inter alios, Fishbane 1975: 115–128; Saysell 2012.

peoples of the lands.[23] It was 'the officials and the elders' who issued the order (10:8), and the issuing of the proclamation is not ascribed to Ezra.[24] Nowhere did Ezra use (or threaten to use) the plenipotentiary power that Artaxerxes gave him. Rather it was the community, acting on the authority of Scripture as interpreted by them, which addressed the problem of mixed marriage (9:1–2; 10:3). Ezra taught the law (note the didactic and hortatory tone of his recorded prayer in Ezra 9), as expected from what is recorded about him in 7:10, but the king's decree was apparently useless in reforming the life of the people.[25] Scholars puzzle over the lack of fit between the royal decree and what Ezra actually did,[26] but the point is that Ezra did not use the considerable powers it conferred upon him. With regard to the threat of confiscation of goods in 10:8, this recalls the Joshua conquest situation, with the word used ('all his property should be *forfeited* [*ḥāram*]'[27]) being the same as that in the ritual destruction of goods and foreign peoples depicted in the books of Deuteronomy and Joshua (e.g. Deut. 20:16; Josh. 10:1, 37). In other words, those returned exiles who failed to turn up to the assembly would be treated like foreign nationals. This radical procedure is not to be related to the powers alluded to in Artaxerxes' decree in Ezra 7:26, despite a superficial correspondence to the wording of the decree.

The book of Ruth does not display a strict, ethnocentric application of the law. It presents instead a generous application of the law according to the principle of *ḥesed* and focuses on the moral logic underlying the law. This would reinforce the application of the law found in Nehemiah 5. Here Nehemiah's call for an immediate cancellation of debts and return of property goes beyond the strict requirements of the 'release' (5:11–12; cf. Deut. 15:1–6; Exod. 23:10–11) or the jubilee (Lev. 25:8–55).[28] Instead, Nehemiah appeals to the Jewish nobles' and officials' sense of morality –'The thing that you are doing is not good' (5:9). They were not accused by Nehemiah

---

[23] See Blidstein 1974.

[24] As correctly noted by Clines (1984: 128), 'By summoning an assembly of the returned exiles who themselves call for the dissolution of mixed marriages, Ezra withdraws from the limelight, and refuses to impose his views by force of authority.'

[25] For this interpretation, see Goswell 2014b.

[26] See, for example, Janzen 2000.

[27] All emphasis in Scripture quotations is ours.

[28] Lowery 2000: 46–51. Some suggest that the legislation in Lev. 25 had not yet been formulated; rather, the laws in Lev. 25 were drafted in response to situations like that found in Neh. 5; so e.g. Rogerson 2010. The canonical ordering of the material does not support such a critical rearrangement.

of charging interest, despite some English versions (e.g. 5:7 RSV: 'You are exacting interest'),[29] but of lending money to the needy in order to confiscate their sons and daughters, fields, vineyards and houses when the loan principal could not be repaid.[30] The accusation of 'coercing a pledge' (*maššā' . . . nōšîm*) was made (5:7). The Hebrew root for the verb and noun (either *nš'* or *nšh*) has no intrinsic connection with the charging of interest, an illegal practice according to the law (Exod. 22:25 [Heb. 22:24]; Lev. 25:36–37; Deut. 23:19–20 [Heb. 20–21]).[31] The handing over of what was pledged alludes to the biblical injunction 'Do not act towards him as a coercer [*nōšê*]' (Exod. 22:25 [Heb. 22:24], our translation; cf. Deut. 24:10),[32] with this verse prohibiting a creditor from exerting pressure on the borrower to force repayment (cf. Neh. 5:7 NJPS: 'Are you pressing claims on loans made to your brothers?').[33] The thrust of Nehemiah's words (whether viewed as a statement or a question) was the unfairness of insisting on the repayment of loans or the impounding of property at a time of economic hardship. Nehemiah showed them the absurdity of what as creditors they were doing (5:8), for to the best of their ability Nehemiah and others had been buying back Jews who were slaves to neighbouring nations (cf. Lev. 25:47–48), enabling their repatriation from exile, and the creditors were undoing their good work. The creditors had nothing to say in defence of their actions (5:8b).

Nehemiah's main concern was the underlying morality of the creditors' behaviour rather than strict legal observance. Righteous behaviour in accordance with the law's perceived intentions, rather than its specific stipulations, is presented as a key manifestation of Israelite identity. Nehemiah heard complaints about the actions of some of the nobles and rulers towards their brother Jews (5:7), that they were exploiting their vulnerable fellow citizens (5:1–5). Nehemiah appealed to the creditors on the basis of common brotherhood (note the sevenfold occurrence of the term 'brother[s]' in vv. 1, 5, 7, 8 [x2], 10, 14. The demand for social justice was made on the basis of their status as 'brothers', which picks up what is also a key term in Leviticus 25 (vv. 25, 35–36, 39, 46–48). The use of Leviticus 25 shows that

---

[29] For the common view, see Fensham 1982: 195; Levering 2007: 156.
[30] According to the commentary on Ezra–Nehemiah attributed to Rashi.
[31] Gross 1997.
[32] For a discussion of this term, see Neufeld 1955: 375–376.
[33] There is no formal indicator of the question in the Hebrew text, but the NJPS version credibly translates Nehemiah's words as an incredulous and accusing rhetorical question.

Nehemiah was deploying a hermeneutic in which the law was applied in accordance with its intentions rather than its specifics, and proper behaviour was marked by right motivation.[34] The book of Ruth would reinforce such an approach wherein behaviour moves beyond the limits of strict legal responsibility, for it presents an ethic of generosity (*ḥesed*) as the behavioural norm in Israelite society.

God's sovereignty and human initiative

More briefly, there are three other areas where the book of Ruth provides pertinent input on the issues of the era of Ezra–Nehemiah. The book of Ruth's presentation of Yahweh's sovereignty has implications for Israelite identity in the restoration period. It reinforces dependence upon Yahweh as an appropriate response for an Israelite. In the face of an apparently unstoppable and ever-present Persian Empire,[35] within which Yehud was but one province, the book of Ruth affirms that God is in fact sovereign and omnipresent to act. That he can act even in the everyday affairs of his people – apart from overt displays of power – would be germane to an Israelite living at a time when the Persian military advance on Egypt was probably an important imperial influence (539–522 BC).[36] With the book of Ruth's affirmation of Yahweh's behind-the-scenes providential ordering of events,[37] Israelites can confidently place their trust in Yahweh. They do not need to live a life of uncertainty or of divided allegiance. Like the book of Ruth, Ezra–Nehemiah is free of overtly miraculous interventions, but the reality of God's favour towards his people is asserted at several points in its story of return and resettlement (e.g. Ezra 1:1; 6:22; 8:31; Neh. 6:16). In other words, the two books mutually reinforce their common view of God's providence.

Additionally, without at all requiring readers to set human action and divine action in opposition to each other, the book of Ruth contains an implied ethic of diligence and commends the use of intelligence and resourcefulness to overcome difficulties (with Ruth herself the chief model). Such initiative is appropriate where it is expressed in generous action (*ḥesed*). In this way the book of Ruth presents a paradigm for members of the Yehudite community to combine their meagre resources and to face and overcome their desperate situation.

[34] Lau 2011: 173.
[35] Berquist 2008: 44.
[36] Cf. Berquist 2008: 47.
[37] God's direct intervention is announced by the narrator at only one point (4:13).

The book of Esther is also set in Persian times and has a similar ethic of initiative and risk-taking. Its author uses the surprising procedure of excluding God from the story (though not, of course, denying his involvement),[38] with this noticeable divine absence helping to foreground human action and initiative, with the implied ethic that Jewish men and women should act with courage and wisdom in a situation of national crisis. Although the lot of a reader in the restoration period might seem dismal, the book of Ruth gives hope of progress and deliverance through the exercise of initiative, using whatever scanty resources might be available.[39]

The temple and prayer

Yahweh's sovereignty in the book of Ruth decentres the temple as fundamental to Israelite identity in the restoration period. The temple was important in this period, as underlined in Ezra–Nehemiah by its continuity with the Solomonic temple, priests and temple personnel,[40] and by its pivotal position to the overall movement of Ezra–Nehemiah.[41] However, the book of Ruth demonstrates that it is possible for Yahweh-fearers to express their faith without the state-sponsored temple and cult. Yahweh is still present in the lives of Israelites in the absence of a physical sanctuary (as also demonstrated in the book of Daniel).[42] The 'house of God' is a theme that pervades and unites Ezra–Nehemiah.[43] The people go up to 'rebuild the house of the LORD' (Ezra 1:3), with this house, at first, equated with the temple. The house is the goal of the journey (2:68), and the first six chapters of Ezra are taken up with the temple-building programme. However, the digression of Ezra 4:6–24, with its paralleling of (opposition to) wall-building and temple-building, hints at a wider definition of the 'house'.[44] When Ezra goes up, he too is concerned for the house and the proper ordering of temple worship and provision for it (7:27). The reformation of the life of the people in Ezra 9 – 10 is brought into relationship with the house of God (10:1, 6, 9), for the character of the people rebounds upon the house. Another hint of the wider

---

[38] Goswell 2010.
[39] Lau 2011: 166.
[40] E.g. Ezra 2:36–58; 6:18; Neh. 12:24, 45–46. Cf. Williamson 1985: 82–84.
[41] Eskenazi 1988: 38–39.
[42] Goswell 2012b.
[43] Dumbrell 1986: 66: 'This temple emphasis, in fact, is maintained throughout the entire Ezra–Nehemiah complex.'
[44] For this thematic development, see Eskenazi 1988.

definition of the house comes in Ezra's prayer, when Judah and Jerusalem seem to be called the 'holy place' (9:8–9).

When we pass over into the Nehemiah part of the joint book, the concern for the wall and gates of Jerusalem (Neh. 1:2–3) confirms the earlier hints of a wider definition of the house. It is plain from Nehemiah 2:20 what the wall is intended to do, namely shut out all sources of uncleanness from the sacred place, the city. The entire city is now as holy as the temple, as the consecration of the first section of the wall by the priests makes clear (3:1). The appointment of (temple) gate-keepers, (cultic) singers and Levites to guard the *city* gates (7:1–3) shows the sacral character of the city, and situating the assembly 'in the square before the Water Gate' does the same (8:1). The city is designated 'the holy city' (11:1, 18) and at the dedication the priests 'purified the people and the gates and the wall' (12:30). Lastly, in 13:22 it is the Levites who guard the city gates, which again bespeaks the expansion of the sanctity from the temple to the city as a whole. Though the people had earlier depended on royal patronage for the support of the temple cultus,[45] this is finally viewed as unsatisfactory, and the community pledge of Nehemiah 10 records that the people promised to provide the needed support (10:32–39 [Heb. 33–40]; summarized in 10:39b [Heb. 40b]: 'We will not neglect the house of our God'). The many prayers of the hero Nehemiah, likewise, are unconnected to the temple cultus (Neh. 1:5–11; 2:4; 4:4–5, 9, 14b [Heb. 3:36–37; 4:3, 8b]; 5:19; 6:9b). In line with this, as John Berquist points out, the efficacy of the many prayers in the book of Ruth (1:8–9; 2:12, 19–20; 3:10), independent of the temple and intermediaries such as priests, can be viewed as promoting a form of resistance,[46] encouraging post-exilic readers to look to God for help rather than continue their servile dependence on the help of the Persian kings. By demonstrating alternative religious practices, the book of Ruth could be viewed as undermining the hegemony of the Persian Empire and encouraging the returnees to jettison their economic dependence on their Persian overlords.

The kingdom of God and the Davidic kings

Finally, the presentation of Yahweh's sovereignty in the book of Ruth raises the hope for native imperial rule as a component of Israelite

---

[45] Persian patronage for temple and cult can be found in Ezra 3:7; 6:9; 7:15–17, 22; Neh. 2:8.
[46] Cf. Berquist 2008: 55. That is not to say that the priests function purely as agents of the Persian Empire.

identity. It is a reminder that Israel's ideal ruler is a Yahweh-installed king 'from among your brothers' (cf. Deut. 17:14–20). The book of Ruth alerts Israelites living in the early restoration period that they are heirs of the Davidic promise (4:18–22),[47] perhaps igniting aspirations for the re-establishment of the Davidic monarchy. On the other hand, no overt Davidic hope is on show in Ezra–Nehemiah itself. For example, nothing is said of any possible Davidic connection for Sheshbazzar (Ezra 1:8); likewise, the Davidic pedigree of Zerubbabel is ignored (cf. 1 Chr. 3:19); there is also the failure to make any mention of the Davidic dynasty or covenant in the historical review provided by the Levites' prayer in Nehemiah 9.[48] Within Ezra–Nehemiah, the only person to whom Davidic descent is ascribed is Hattush (Ezra 8:2), and he plays no real role in the book. This is another example of the book of Ruth's lack of exact fit with the early restoration period, in which there was no particular stress on messianic expectations. Notwithstanding this difference, the narrative of the restoration of Naomi's decimated family (culminating in Ruth 4) encourages confidence that, through God's enabling, the nation will be rebuilt after the devastation of exile.[49]

Without discounting the David link made in Ruth 4 (as well as other connections to David elsewhere in the book of Ruth),[50] the hope for the future of Israel embodied in the events of that chapter are not so tied to the person of David that there is no other basis of hope, for the sovereign good purposes of Yahweh for his people can be traced back to the patriarchal period (with the mention of Rachel, Leah and Tamar in 4:11–12). Consistent with this, the importance of Abraham in the theology of the prayer in Nehemiah 9 is signalled by the fact that this is the only time in the Old Testament that the verb 'to choose' (*bāḥar*) is used in relation to Abraham (9:7).[51] God was faithful in establishing his promise to Abraham to give 'his offspring' the land (9:7–8), and the covenant with him is elaborated in terms of the gift of the land. God's covenant with Abraham ('the covenant') is the only covenant specifically mentioned in the prayer. There are references to the 'land' throughout the prayer,[52] and the gift of the land to Israel

[47] See chapter 3.
[48] Goswell 2012a.
[49] Fentress-Williams 2012: 118. For a reading of Ruth 4 as an image of eschatological hope (with its vision of wholeness in human community), see Sakenfeld 1999b.
[50] See the arguments of chapter 3.
[51] Rendtorff 1997: 112, 115.
[52] Bliese (1988: 209) identifies 'land' as the key word in the prayer. Gilbert (1981: 310) says that no other biblical text uses the term so frequently.

as an inalienable possession is the theme that dominates the prayer.[53] The land theme culminates in the plea of 9:36–37 ('in the land that you gave to our fathers to enjoy its fruit and its good gifts . . . its rich yield').

Ezra–Nehemiah represents the voice of the ruling urban elite installed by Persia, as embodied in Ezra, Nehemiah, the priests and governors, but at the end of the communal prayer, a suppressed challenge to Persian rule is placed in the mouths of the Levites, who lament the nation's suffering under the control of a foreign king (9:36–37; 'we are slaves this day'). There is the longing for God to return them to a time of his direct rule, with the Israelites 'serving' him (9:35) rather than being 'slaves' of the Persian kings.[54] In other words, a 'kingdom of God' theology is on show in this prayer.

A negative portrayal of Persian rule can also be found in the two other major prayers in Ezra–Nehemiah (Ezra 9; Neh. 1). In the prayer of Ezra 9, Ezra confesses that their guilt remains 'to this day' (v. 7a) and that their punishment is that they are given over 'into the hand of the kings of the lands . . . as it is today' (v. 7b). The Persian kings are placed in the category of 'the kings of the lands', wording that echoes the widespread phrase 'the peoples of the land[s]' (used most recently in 9:1), so that the desire for emancipation from their Persian overlords is implicit. In Ezra's prayer, the time phrases, 'to this day' (v. 7a) and 'as it is today' (v. 7b), express the perspective that the Israelites were still (in some sense) in exile, namely, they were still, like their ancestors, suffering for their (persistent) sins by being under the yoke of foreign sovereigns. At most, Ezra sees Persian rule as providing 'a little reviving' (v. 8). The period of time specified by 'for a brief moment' (v. 8) in the wider context of the book means since the decree of Cyrus. The implication of the partial and fleeting nature of the relief may be that it would be lost unless they repented.

With regard to the prayer of Nehemiah, it climaxes with the words 'today' and 'this man' (Neh. 1:11), and 'Now I was cupbearer to the king' (in the second half of the same verse) prepares for the court scene in 2:1–8. In Nehemiah 2, the reader comes to realize that 'this man' is none other than the Persian king. The phrase reveals what Nehemiah thought of his royal master. The demonstrative adjective 'this [man]' (*zeh*) is often used in the Old Testament to express

---

[53] Ackroyd 1976: 155.
[54] Cf. Smith-Christopher 2002: 44–45. The Hebrew root *'ābad* is used in both cases.

contempt and it clearly has such force here.[55] Nehemiah needed the favour and permission of this king to do anything to help the city of Jerusalem and its people, but it irked Nehemiah to have to ask for his permission. The negative characterization of the Persian monarch in the prayer is plain. In this way, the main prayers of Ezra–Nehemiah subvert the grip of imperial power, so that overall Ezra–Nehemiah has a negative stance towards the Persian administration.[56]

Conclusion

We have discussed the relevance of the book of Ruth to the early restoration period. The book's stress upon ethnic inclusiveness would assist readers to notice the two passages in Ezra–Nehemiah that mention the incorporation of proselytes into Israel (Ezra 6:21; Neh. 10:28 [Heb. 29]), along with another that might also hint at inclusiveness (Ezra 10:16–44). Despite the marked difference in thematic focus, we found no evidence that the book of Ruth opposes or condemns the policy of breaking up exogenous unions. The book of Ruth emphasizes that relationship with Yahweh is expressed in acts of generosity and kindness (*ḥesed*). In line with this, Nehemiah's call for an immediate cancellation of debts and return of property does not follow strict legal stipulation but is certainly in accordance with the law's intention that Israelites should treat each other as 'brothers'. The books of Ruth and Ezra–Nehemiah, each in its own way, affirm a theology of Yahweh's behind-the-scenes providential ordering of events, but also encourage the exercise of courage and initiative to overcome the problems besetting the community. In both narratives the efficacy of prayer is independent of the temple and mediation of cultic personnel, and they encourage God's people to look for divine assistance in answer to prayer. Finally, the Davidic hope on show in the book of Ruth is not echoed by Ezra–Nehemiah, though in both books the fundamental basis of hope is the sovereign good purposes of God for his people.

---

[55] For this pejorative usage, see BDB 260 1a; *GKC* §136b cites 1 Sam. 10:27; 21:16 (Eng. 15); 1 Kgs 22:27; and Isa. 6:10 as examples of *zeh* 'with a secondary sense of contempt'.

[56] Goswell 2011.

Chapter Three

Ruth and the house of David

The Old Testament is a canonical corpus pointing forward to Jesus Christ. We have this on the authority of Jesus himself. That does not mean, however, that this is *all* the Old Testament does. It is sometimes assumed that a kind of 'nothing but' hermeneutic is required of a Christian reading of Scripture, but a consideration of the texts commonly relied upon places a question mark over this approach.[1] The claim by Jesus in John 5:39 ('it is they [the OT Scriptures] that bear witness about me') is hardly intended as a global hermeneutical principle, but refers to the Old Testament as one among a number of 'witnesses' to him, which include his own words (5:31), his Father (5:32, 37), John (5:33), Jesus' works (5:36) and Moses (5:46). There is nothing in the context that would indicate that verse 39 provides an *all-inclusive* test by which the validity of Old Testament interpretations are to be judged. It does not assert that *all* the Old Testament does is point forward to Christ. A second text, Luke 24:27, need mean no more than that in different parts of the Old Testament ('beginning with Moses and all the Prophets . . .') there are things concerning Jesus, and Luke 24:44 likewise ('everything written about me in the Law of Moses and the Prophets and the Psalms') is not a *comprehensive* statement of what the Old Testament is (now) to believers. Paul's statement in 2 Corinthians 1:20 ('all the promises of God find their Yes in him [Christ]') does not mean that the Old Testament is *nothing* but promises fulfilled by Christ. Another key Pauline text, 2 Timothy 3:15, says that the Scriptures 'are able to make you wise for salvation through faith in Christ Jesus', but this does not purport to state the *only* function performed by the Old Testament. Finally, 1 Peter 1:10–11 ('predicted the sufferings of Christ and the subsequent glories') is not saying that this is *all* that the prophets did, or that all a Christian should look for in the Old Testament is intimations of the person and work of Christ.

Biblical theology cannot be limited to just one theme, even one as important as messianic expectation, though, of course, this theme

---

[1] For insightful comments on this issue, see Wilson 2015: 318–320.

will take pride of place in any Christian evaluation and use of the Old Testament. Properly understood, the study of ethics is part of theology, and a biblical-theological approach does not need to deny or downplay the ethical import of Old Testament texts;[2] the ethics of the book of Ruth will be the focus of discussion in the next chapter.

Royal promise

That having been clarified, it can be reasserted that it is right and proper for Christians to seek and find Old Testament passages that point forward to and throw light on Jesus Christ. Such passages are not exhausted by a few classic texts in the Prophets (e.g. Isa. 9; 11; 53) and Psalms (e.g. Pss 2, 110).[3] In fact, the expectation of a future *king* (= Messiah) is pervasive and can be found in Old Testament narrative as well.[4] God's instructions and promises to Abram in Genesis 12:1–3 play a major role in setting the agenda for the books Genesis through to Kings that record selected events from creation to the demise of the Davidic monarchy at the time of the Babylonian exile. The focus of the first half of this key passage (12:1–2a) is on the promise of nationhood (i.e. land and descendants), and the fulfilment of nationhood is later guaranteed through the divine covenant made with Abraham in Genesis 15 (focusing on descendants [15:1–6] and land [15:7–21], in that order). The second half of the key passage promises universal blessing through the patriarch (12:2b–3) and this aspect is confirmed by covenant in Genesis 17, in which there is the promise that Abraham will be the 'father of a multitude of nations' (17:4–5). The divine oath of Genesis 22:16–18 ratifies the covenant promised in Genesis 17 and promises that the 'seed [= offspring]' (*zera'* [singular]) will be God's agent of universal blessing.[5] The term 'seed' is a keyword (*Leitwort*) in Genesis (used some fifty-nine times) and the line of Abraham's seed will give rise to royal descendants (17:6, 16; 'kings shall come from you'). The royal dimension of the Abrahamic promise is reiterated to Jacob (35:11: 'kings shall come from your own body'). It is noteworthy that at the close of Genesis, kingship is associated with the tribe of Judah (49:8–12; 'The sceptre shall not depart from Judah'). Later in the Pentateuch, the theme resurfaces in Balaam's oracle in Numbers 24:17–19 ('a sceptre shall rise out of Israel') and in Moses' instructions

---

[2] See the helpful approach of Wenham (2000).
[3] Berlin 1983: 110; cf. Howard 1990, 1998.
[4] For what follows, see Alexander 1998a, 1998b.
[5] Alexander 1997; Collins 1997; Williamson 2000.

about kingship in Deuteronomy 17:14–20. We could go so far as to say that the recurring theme of royal promise gives the entire Pentateuch a messianic shape.

Though not royal figures themselves,[6] both Moses and Joshua defeat many foreign kings (as summarized in the listing of Josh. 12). The book of Judges anticipates the era of the kings (esp. Judg. 17:6; 18:1; 19:1; 21:25), though this book cannot be read as a blanket endorsement of kingship. For example, when Gideon is offered the kingship, he refuses, and his refusal sounds like an in-principle rejection of human rulership in favour of God's rule (Judg. 8:23: 'I will not rule over you, and my son will not rule over you; the LORD will rule over you').[7] In addition, the subsequent reign of Abimelech is hardly a recommendation for the institution (Judg. 9). The book of Ruth provides a story about David's ancestors, and the genealogy in Ruth 4:18–22, in effect, picks up the storyline from Genesis and *via* *Perez* connects David to the Genesis 'seed' theme (cf. Gen. 38:29; Ruth 4:12).[8] The request for a king in 1 Samuel 8 displeases Samuel the judge and is exposed by God as an attempt to break away from his rule (8:4–9), but God accedes to their request. The first king, Saul, is anointed and fails (1 Sam. 9 – 15), but David succeeds, and Yahweh makes a covenant with David in which he promises to establish his dynasty for ever (2 Sam. 7). The subsequent kings mostly prove unfaithful and bring the nation to ruin (1, 2 Kgs). The divine promise of a royal deliverer runs through Genesis to Kings, but the last king in David's line, Jehoiachin, is a pathetic figure of royal impotence (2 Kgs 25:27–30), so that God's promise of a royal saviour remains unfulfilled by the end of the book of Kings. What can be said is that the entire Genesis–Kings narrative (Ruth included) is interested in the coming of a divinely promised king, but he has not yet come. The post-exilic period plotted in Ezra–Nehemiah fails to provide the expected king in David's line. On that basis, the Old Testament is an 'unfinished story', a story in search of a satisfying conclusion, and it is easy to see why the first Christians saw in Jesus Christ the fulfilment of Old Testament hopes and the conclusion of the Old Testament story.

---

[6] It would be a grave theological error to view them as kings; see Goswell 2013.

[7] Gideon's words were theologically correct, but his actions hint that he did not live out his declaration: he names his son 'my father is king' (Abimelech; 8:31), he takes royal items as loot (8:21) and he keeps a sizeable harem (8:30; cf. Deut. 17:17).

[8] McKeown (2015: 72–77) provides an extensive discussion of the relation of the book of Ruth to Genesis.

The view that the book of Ruth is a late work, written to counteract the reforms of Ezra and Nehemiah banning exogamous marriages (Ezra 9 – 10; Neh. 13), continues to find many supporters.[9] This chapter does not try to demolish that approach so much as bolster the case for an alternative way of reading the book of Ruth. The aim is to show that the Ruth narrative can be read in relation to the house of David, namely that one of its main points is the providential preservation of the family that produced King David and the implications for the Judean royal house. The arguments are as follows:

1. None of the canonical positions assigned to the book of Ruth suggest that ancient readers understood it as a critique of restrictive views of intermarriage, whereas two of them assume a connection between the book and David.
2. The genealogy in Ruth 4:18–22 is not easily removed from the book and forges an explicit link between the family history of the book of Ruth and David. The link with David is more than an endorsement of the message of the book that does not as such relate to David.
3. The theme of God's control of events and that of his 'kindness' towards the ancestors of David prefigure God's dealings with David and his house.
4. Scenes that depict turning points in the plot in chapters 1 and 3 (Ruth's refusal to part from Naomi, and Ruth's appeal to Boaz) find later parallels in the life of David.

In other words, the book of Ruth fits neatly in the trajectory of Davidic hope found in the Old Testament historical books. It is highly appropriate, therefore, to find that the one reference to the name of Ruth in the New Testament is as an ancestress of Jesus Christ in the genealogy in the opening chapter of Matthew's Gospel (1:5).

The differing canonical positions of the book of Ruth

The book of Ruth is one of a number of Old Testament books that are placed in more than one position in various biblical canons (other prominent examples being Chronicles, Lamentations and Daniel),

---

[9] E.g. Korpel 2001: 230–233; Eskenazi and Frymer-Kensky 2011: xxiv, xxv; Amit 2000: 84–87; Matthews 2004. Chapter 2 has addressed this issue.

but the purpose of the present discussion is not to discover its *original and right* position, if such a concept has any meaning,[10] for the positioning of biblical books is a paratextual phenomenon that reflects the varying perceptions and evaluations of later generations of readers (not of the biblical authors themselves), and no one canonical position need be privileged above the others.

In Hebrew canonical orders, Ruth is found in the third canonical division (Writings) and put either before Psalms as a kind of biography of the psalmist David, or, more often, placed after Proverbs, making the heroine Ruth an example of 'an excellent wife/worthy woman' (cf. Prov. 31:10–31).[11] In Greek orders, Ruth comes after Judges, in an apparent effort to put it in its historical setting, because the story is set 'in the days when the judges ruled' (Ruth 1:1).[12] Are we to read the book of Ruth as a lead-up to David the chief psalmist, as providing a wisdom model in the person of Ruth, or as a historical book following Judges? There may be no right or wrong answers to that question; rather the point is that the differing canonical positions make a difference to how one views and reads a book. Different sorts of questions arise out of distinct literary contexts.[13] The fact that a book like Ruth can be placed in quite different positions in the Hebrew Bible and Greek Old Testament shows that book order reflects readerly perception of what a book is about.[14] The positioning of a book due to thematic considerations means that alternative placements are possible, for any book is likely to have more than one theme. We will argue that Ruth appears to work well in all three canonical positions. To start with, in this chapter, we will focus on the meaning of the book of Ruth when placed after the book of Judges.

---

[10] See Wolfenson 1924: 171–175; Steinberg 2006: 125–129; Stone 2015. For a different view, see Dempster 2015. For the general issue of biblical book order, see Goswell 2008: 673–688. For a more detailed discussion of the biblical paratext, see the opening of chapter 4.

[11] For an analysis of the book of Ruth following Proverbs, see chapter 4.

[12] Jerome states that this is the reason for this placement (*Prologus Galeatus*); for a translation, see Beckwith 1985: 119–20. In Josephus (*Ant.* 5.318–337), the story of Ruth follows that of the judges. So, too, in the list of Melito (Eusebius, *Hist. eccl.* 4.26.13–14), Ruth follows Judges, and in Origen (Eusebius, *Hist. eccl.* 6.25.2), Ruth is joined to Judges as one book.

[13] As noted by Fentress-Williams (2012: 20), 'Each of these locations within Scripture offers a different conversation partner for the book of Ruth.'

[14] With regard to books like Ruth and Lamentations found in the Writings in the Hebrew canon, Seitz (2009: 101) speaks of their later (according to him) migration in the Greek canon 'toward other books with which they have intentional literary or theological affiliation'.

Ruth between Judges and Samuel

Ruth 1:1 locates the action in Bethlehem in the period of the judges, and the Ruth narrative forms a sharp contrast with the story of the Levite from Bethlehem (Judg. 17:8–9) and that of the Levite's concubine who comes from Bethlehem (19:1–2), and with the drastic method used to provide wives for the surviving Benjaminites (Judg. 21).[15] Judges 21 concerns the preservation of an Israelite tribe (Benjamin) threatened with extinction (Judg. 21:6), and the book of Ruth depicts God's providence in preserving the Bethlehemite family that eventually produces David (Ruth 4:5, 10, 18–22).[16] Supporting the postulated thematic connection, the rare idiom 'to take [nāśāʾ] wives' used in Judges 21:23 recurs in Ruth 1:4.[17] Despite the variety in the ordering in Greek lists of Old Testament books,[18] what we can say is that the books Genesis–Ruth are a set grouping of eight books (Octateuch) and Ruth is always placed after (or joined to) Judges.[19] In other words, in the Greek Bible Judges serves as a foil for the following book of Ruth.

In the forward direction, there are connections between the figures of Ruth and Hannah as the latter, through her offspring Samuel (the anointer of the first two kings), is also related to the coming monarchy (1 Sam. 1 – 2). The marriage of Boaz and Ruth and the birth of a son thematically prepare for Elkanah and Hannah and their (at first) childless relationship. In the Greek canon, Ruth 4:15 and 1 Samuel 1:8, with their similar but different expressions about being better than seven/ten sons, are only a dozen verses apart.[20] In addition, the book of Ruth covers much the same ground as do the books of Samuel, namely, the period from 'the days when the judges ruled' (Samuel being the last judge; 1 Sam. 7:15) to David.[21] The book of Ruth may, therefore, be treated as a 'prehistory' of the Davidic house, for, according to the genealogy provided by Ruth 4:18–22, Ruth and Boaz are the great-grandparents of David.[22] Without insisting

---

[15] For a reading of the book of Ruth in light of Judg. 17 – 21, see chapter 7.

[16] Campbell 1975: 35–36. Moore (2001: 27–41) tries to interpret Ruth in continuity with and in contrast to Judges; cf. Gale 1989: 369–375.

[17] Zakovitch 1999: 33, 79. The phrase is elsewhere found only in 2 Chr. 11:21; 13:21; 24:3; Ezra 9:2, 12; 10:44; Neh. 13:25.

[18] There is no uniform Greek order; see Botte and Bogaert 1996: 541–543.

[19] Swete 1968: 226–227.

[20] Jobling 1993: 133–134.

[21] Jobling 1993: 131. The transitional character of the book of Ruth between Judges and Samuel is argued for by Linafelt 1999: xvii–xxv; cf. Stone 2013a: 119–130.

[22] Sasson 1979: 250–251.

that the *only and proper* position for Ruth is following Judges, in this chapter the reading of the Ruth narrative takes that canonical positioning of the book as its starting point and looks for possible connections between the story of Ruth and the house of David.

The David connection

The interpretation of the book of Ruth in recent scholarship has made little of the David connection that is explicit in the final form of the book, but what this chapter offers is a kind of *backwards* reading, viewing the David connection as fundamental to the elucidation of the book's theme and purpose.[23] The habit of readers establishes the principle that a consideration of the end of a book transforms how one reads the book as a whole,[24] for a book's content and action must lead up to its finale. The uncovering of the link to David in the last number of verses of the book (4:17–22) requires the reader to reread the story and to discover what might have been missed on the first reading. As stated by Jonathan E. Dyck, 'Reading the ending first is simply a shortcut to a critical reading of the text.'[25]

According to F. W. Bush, the final resolution of a plot, and especially the dénouement (outcome or consequences of the resolution) and any accompanying coda of a complex narrative, are important indicators of theme.[26] In the case of the narrative of Ruth, the plot centres on the filling of Naomi's emptiness (1:21). All the other characters – her husband, her sons, her two daughters-in-law, Boaz, even the son whom Ruth bears – stand in relation to Naomi (see 1:3, 5–6; 2:1; 4:17).[27] All this tends to focus the story from Naomi's perspective. Her loss of family (husband and sons) at the beginning of the book (1:5b: 'so that the woman was left without her two sons and her husband') is compensated for by the provision of a son (through Ruth) at its end (4:13–17a). Though the son is born to Boaz and Ruth (4:13), 4:17a underlines the significance of the son for Naomi ('A son has been born to Naomi'). This does not have to be taken as meaning that the issue of an heir for the line of Elimelech is only a secondary concern (*pace*

---

[23] Material in this chapter has been adapted with permission from Goswell 2014a.
[24] Dyck 1998: 77–78.
[25] Dyck 1998: 78.
[26] Bush 1996a: 48–49. Bush is dependent on Beekman, Callow and Kopesec 1981: 135, 137.
[27] Berlin 1983: 83–84.

Bush),[28] for the dénouement moves beyond the temporal needs of Naomi and shows that the son turned out to be an ancestor of illustrious David (4:17b: 'They named him Obed. He was the father of Jesse, the father of David'), and the connection with David is reinforced by the genealogy given in the coda (4:18–22).

Katharine Doob Sakenfeld would see the David connection acting only as 'an imprimatur' on the implied ethic of the book about the need for the Israelite community to adopt a generous view of outsiders.[29] She states: 'Because of David's stature in Judean tradition, just the mention of his name is sufficient to drive home the storyteller's point of view.'[30] While Sakenfeld's view by no means denies the canonical link to David, its effect is to minimize that link's significance for the message of the book, since its role is only as *support* for its controversial implied ethic of inclusion of foreigners rather than being part of the message of the book as such. Likewise, for André LaCocque, 'the authority of the interpretation of the law presented in the book of Ruth finds its foundation in the person of David'.[31] Again, on this interpretation, the unquestionable prestige of David is used as support for the provocative message of the book about the reception of foreigners but makes no further contribution. The connection with David is more than this, for, as noted by Adele Berlin, the canonical link to David not only 'tends to elevate the status of the story', but 'tends to elevate David'.[32]

The genealogy leading to David

An examination of the genealogy is necessary, for the originality of 4:17b–22 is commonly rejected in recent scholarship, with 'all but universal agreement' that the verses are a later *appendix* to the story proper;[33] the case is, however, anything but decisive.[34] We do not need to discount the genealogy as a later addition and in so doing reject any *original* Davidic connection. The Ruth narrative has a symmetrical design, with a series of parallels found between chapters 2 and 3 and between chapters 1 and 4.[35] The chiastic balance of the story requires

---

[28] Bush 1996a: 51: 'his significance relates entirely to Naomi.'
[29] Sakenfeld 1999a: 4–5.
[30] Sakenfeld 1999a: 84.
[31] LaCocque 2004: 12.
[32] Berlin 1983: 110.
[33] Campbell 1975: 172.
[34] See the detailed review and critique of the majority position provided by Hubbard 1988: 15–21.
[35] Porten 1978: 23.

some kind of 'family history' at the end matching what is found at the beginning (1:1–5), and that is exactly what the genealogy provides.[36] Shimon Bar-Efrat has commented on the chiastic structure of this book,[37] noting that the book opens with information about (three) people who died before the beginning of the main action (Elimelech, Mahlon, Chilion, 1:1–5) and ends with a list of the (three) generations that were born after the conclusion of the main action (Obed, Jesse, David), with the matching numbers supporting the point made by Bar-Efrat.[38]

The name of Perez begins the genealogy (4:18: 'Now these are the generations of Perez: Perez fathered . . .') and he has already been named in the body of the book (4:12: 'and may your house be like the house of Perez'). The portrait of Perez as ancestral head is common to both 4:12 and the genealogy, which, therefore, suits its context and was presumably tailored to fit the narrative it caps. So too, whatever the exact relation between the genealogy in Ruth 4 and the genealogy provided in 1 Chronicles 2:5–16, both passages give special prominence to the line of Perez, and the linear genealogy in Ruth 4 may be crafted to highlight the names of Boaz (seventh generation) and David (tenth generation).[39] The effect of the genealogy is to link the story of Ruth with the Bible's 'main narrative' (= Primary History), namely Genesis to Kings, in which, as we briefly noted at the start of this chapter, kingship is a major concern; in fact, the theme of kingship is sounded immediately before the Ruth narrative in the refrain that punctuates the last chapters of Judges: 'In those days there was no king in Israel' (Judg. 17:6; 18:1; 19:1; 21:25). The name Perez takes the reader back into the patriarchal stories (*Vätergeschichten*) of Genesis (notably the circumstances of the birth of Perez in ch. 38), then we move forward to David (whose final years are recorded in 1 Kgs 1 – 2); thus the genealogy helps to establish continuity between earlier Israelite history and the beginning of the Davidic monarchy.[40]

[36] Bertman 1965.

[37] Bar-Efrat 1980: 156–157.

[38] *Pace* Hubbard 1988: 17 n. 46: 'Against Bar-Efrat, however, one notes that only the last three members of the list fit that description.'

[39] This is the thesis of Sasson (1979: 183–184, 186), and it is evaluated by Sakenfeld 2004: 410–416; cf. Porten 1978: 47–48.

[40] Johnson 1969: 78; cf. Fisch 1982: 435; Gerleman 1981: 10–11. Cf. Prinsloo (1980: 340), who says the genealogy 'adds a new and wider dimension to the book'. For linear genealogies as a way 'to support the political claims of the kings', see Wilson 1977: 195; cf. Wilson 1984: 60, 61.

In other words, the genealogical material in Ruth 4:17b, 18–22 indicates the wider significance of the story. In support of this, the blessing provided by the family to Israel as a whole has already been suggested by 4:11–12. The blessing uttered in 4:11–12 speaks of the future fame of the house (*qĕrā'-šēm*), and this is picked up and widened in verse 14 ('and may his name be renowned [*wĕyiqqārē' šemô*] in Israel'). The blessing also speaks of multiple 'offspring' (*hazzera'* read as a collective) and this finds its fulfilment in the family genealogy leading to David. The blessing that likens Ruth to Rachel and Leah, 'who together built up the house of Israel' (4:11), and the hyperbolic commendation of Ruth in 4:15b ('[she is] more to you than seven sons') also hint that she will be an ancestress of a famous figure with pan-Israelite significance.[41] Likewise, the analogy of resourceful Tamar, who becomes an Israelite matriarch (4:12)[42] – and we might add a reference to another exemplary foreigner, Rahab (Josh. 2, 6; cf. Matt. 1:3)[43] – supports the thesis that Ruth's role will affect the destiny of the nation as a whole.

The only paragraph marking for Ruth in the Tiberian Masoretic tradition is at 4:17, before the genealogy of David in 4:18–22,[44] and in the Leningrad Codex the genealogy is set out in such a way that nine lines each begin with 'he begat' (*hôlîd*). This arrangement sets this paragraph off from what precedes. The genealogy has often been considered a late addition to the book,[45] but those responsible for the paragraphing cannot have been entering into such critical debates. It marks the boundary between story and genealogy and, if anything, highlights the genealogy as being of special significance for the meaning of the preceding family history, linking it into God's wider purposes for Israel, which will be blessed through the house of David.

Scholars have problems with 4:17b because there seems to be no connection between the name Obed (v. 17b) and what is said by the local women: 'A son has been born to Naomi' (v. 17a), but the assigning of the name 'Obed' (= he who serves) is appropriate for one who will serve the needs of Naomi in her old age (the role assigned

---

[41] Hubbard 1988: 21–22.

[42] E.g. van Wolde 1997: 127–131; Nielsen 1997: 13–17. It is not clear from Gen. 38, but most commentators suggest that Tamar is a Canaanite, e.g. Waltke and Fredricks 2001: 508; Hamilton 1995: 434.

[43] Donaldson 1999: 138–139.

[44] Korpel says that the lack of other major divisions may be due to the fact that the tradition 'may rest on . . . a "purged" manuscript' (2001: 46). As noted by Korpel, several Hebrew manuscripts have an open or closed paragraph after 3:7 (2000: 134).

[45] Korpel 2000.

to him in 4:15 by the Bethlehemite women who name him).[46] In addition, as suggested by Hubbard, the importance of the birth of Obed is more than just signifying the survival and future of the threatened family, for Yahweh's intervention strongly implies that the child has a special destiny (cf. Samson and Samuel in the surrounding books).[47] This is supported by the fact that 4:13 is the only time in the book of Ruth that *the narrator* describes God as active in events ('the LORD gave her [Ruth] conception, and she bore a son').[48]

The hidden polemic of the book of Judges

It has been recently argued that the book of Judges presents a polemical view of early Israelite history that promotes the interests of the tribe of Judah, and specifically the Davidic dynasty, by exposing the flaws of the judges originating from the northern tribes.[49] On this theory, the success of the tribe of Judah (1:1–20) is set over against the failures of the northern tribes (1:21–36) in order to demonstrate the benefits of Judean (= Davidic) rule.[50] Othniel (from Judah) could be viewed as the model judge (3:7–11), whereas the judges from the other tribes appear in a less favourable light. Marc Brettler suggests that most of the body of the book of Judges (3:7 – 16:31) should be read *allegorically*, so that the supremacy of southern leadership emerges as the clear theme of the central section of the book. There is polemic against Benjamin (1:21; chs. 19–21) and against the towns of Gibeah and Jabesh-gilead in particular (19:14–30; 20:9; 21:10). The first was Saul's home town and the second was his burial place (cf. 1 Sam. 11:4; 31:11–13). Using this approach, Judges 17 – 18 is read as polemic against the later Danite sanctuary established by Jeroboam (1 Kgs 12:29–30) and Judges 19 – 21 is viewed as critical of the emergent kingship of the Saulide dynasty. At least a couple of stories

[46] See Bush 1996b: 13; Porten 1978: 47; Beattie 1994: 32 (the Targumic rendering of 4:21b connects the name Obed with his later wholehearted service of God); Beattie 1977: 131.

[47] Hubbard 1988: 20, 97.

[48] Ruth 1:6 is not, despite the assertion of some (e.g. Campbell 1975: 29), another instance of the storyteller directly asserting God's involvement, for it only states what Naomi *heard* (from whom? on whose authority?), namely 'that the LORD had visited his people and given them food'.

[49] Sweeney 1997; McKeown 2015: 79. There is, however, the Judahite failure to destroy Canaanites in their allotted land (Judg. 1:16, 19); and the incident involving men of Judah handing Samson over to the Philistines may put that tribe in a less favourable light (15:9–13).

[50] Brettler 1989; O'Connell 1996: 305–329.

display a non-Ephraimite (Judean) viewpoint (8:1–3; 12:1–6) and behind this may lie the later use of 'Ephraim' as an epithet for the Northern Kingdom (cf. Isa. 7:2; 11:13; Ezek. 37:16 and frequently in Hosea).

The weakness in this approach, however, is that it involves a lot of reading in, and Yairah Amit is frank in admitting that it is *hidden* polemic.[51] The most that can be said with certainty is that the presentation in Judges puts a question mark over Saul's kingship from the first (cf. 1 Sam. 9:21). This is different in principle from viewing the events of the book of Ruth as relevant to the fortunes of the house of David, for the final genealogy makes *explicit* the Davidic connection of the Ruth narrative (4:17b–22), and so the reader is invited to discern what the story says or implies about later Davidic rule.

Rereading the book of Ruth

The connection of the family with David is hinted as early as Ruth 1:2, which specifies the Ephrathite lineage of Elimelech and family ('They were Ephrathites from Bethlehem'), this being the clan name for a section of the population of Bethlehem (cf. 4:11).[52] From the start, therefore, the biblically literate reader of the narrative of Ruth would suspect that there is a link to the family of David, for in 1 Samuel 17:12 David is said to be the son of 'an Ephrathite of Bethlehem in Judah'.[53] The reader's suspicion that the story might have some connection with the family of David finds specific confirmation at the close of the book (4:17b, 18–22).

Likewise, the refuge taken by Elimelech and family in neighbouring Moab during the time of famine (1:1–5) is later replicated when David leaves his parents in the safekeeping of the king of Moab during the period when he is on the run from Saul (1 Sam. 22:1–4). In other words, an episode in the early history of the family (the sojourn in Moab) foreshadows what will happen in the experience of its most famous descendant. This is in line with Israelite storytelling generally, wherein typological parallels drawn between earlier and later historical events support a belief in the providential ordering of history (e.g. the description of what is, in effect, an Egyptian sojourn and exodus

---

[51] Amit 1994: 38–40; 2009: 319–320.
[52] See the discussion provided by Bush 1996a: 64–65, 67.
[53] Cf. Mic. 5:2: 'But you, O Bethlehem Ephrathah, who are too little to be among the clans of Judah'; Ps. 132:6: 'Behold, we heard of it in Ephrathah.'

of Abram in Gen. 12:10 – 13:1).[54] Kirsten Nielsen views the book of Ruth as written 'to champion the right of David's family to the throne', such a realpolitik defence being needed because of his dubious Moabite ancestry.[55] This view may find support in the repeated reference to Ruth's Moabite heritage (e.g. 1:22; 2:2, 6, 21), but we have no other indicator in the Old Testament that the part-Moabite ancestry of David was an embarrassment to the ruling house of Judah. The discovery of these intertextual links in the opening section of the book of Ruth encourages the reader to look for other connections with the later history of David.[56]

Divine providence

As noted already, God's direct involvement is stated by the narrator only once (4:13), but God is repeatedly referred to by characters within the story (1:6, 9, 16–17, 20–21; 2:12, 20; 3:10, 13; 4:11–12, 14).[57] This creates an expectation of how God will (or should) act to remedy problems or reward right behaviour. As noted by Campbell (1975: 29), a striking feature of the story is the way in which each of the three main characters acts in the way that God is expected to act, the correspondence implying that they are divine agents.[58] Naomi asks that God might provide her daughters-in-law with 'rest' (1:9), but later it is she who seeks 'rest' for Ruth (3:1) (*měnûḥâ* in both instances). Boaz calls on God to recompense Ruth as one who has taken refuge under God's 'wings' (2:12, *kānāp*), but later Ruth, in effect, calls on Boaz to act as God's agent by spreading his 'wings' (= edge of garment; *kānāp*) over her (3:9). Above all, God's 'kindness' (*ḥesed*) towards the family (2:20) is shown in part by Ruth's 'kindness' (*ḥesed*) in thinking of the needs of the family and being willing to marry Boaz (3:10).[59] It is highly significant that these examples of human characters as divine agents (3:1, 9, 10) are found in the lead-up to or within what might be viewed as the key scene in the book: the

[54] See the discussion by Cassuto 1964: 334–337.

[55] Nielsen 1997: 23–29; cf. Gow 1992: 130–139, 203–210.

[56] E.g. Berger (2009: 433–452) makes an inner-biblical connection between Ruth and Bathsheba.

[57] See Hals 1969.

[58] On which see chapter 7.

[59] We have chosen the translation 'kindness' for this admittedly difficult-to-translate Hebrew word because, as demonstrated by Andersen (1986: 41–88), *ḥesed* denotes non-obligatory generous action. He examines the three uses of the term in the book of Ruth (59–60).

clandestine meeting between Ruth and Boaz on the threshing floor (3:7–13).

In line with this, the rise of David to the throne in the books of Samuel is shown to be providential (1 Sam. 16:13, 18; 18:12, 28, etc.). What is more, the term 'wing' (*kānāp*) recurs in two important episodes in 1 Samuel concerning the rise of David to the throne.[60] In 1 Samuel 15, Saul's act of tearing the 'skirt' (*kānāp*) of Samuel's robe (15:27) is turned by Samuel into a prophetic sign (15:28: 'The LORD has torn the kingdom of Israel from you this day and has given it to a neighbour of yours, who is better than you'). Likewise, in 1 Samuel 24, David deftly cuts off the 'corner' (*kānāp*) of Saul's robe (24:5), with David's restraint in not slaying Saul acknowledged by Saul himself as proof that David is more righteous than him and will receive the kingdom (24:16–22). Another connection between the scene at the threshing floor in Ruth 3 and events in David's life is Ruth's deferential self-reference as Boaz's 'servant' (3:9 ['āmâ x2], specifically female servant). Abigail repeatedly uses the same term about herself in her meeting with David in 1 Samuel 25 (vv. 24–25, 28, 31, 41), and that meeting also leads to marriage (25:42).[61] Just as Boaz invokes a divine blessing on Ruth (3:10), so David blesses Abigail, whom he views as God's agent, because her initiative in intercepting him on the way to kill Nabal saved him from bloodguilt, which would have imperilled his rise to the throne (1 Sam. 25:32–33). By their courage and resourcefulness, Ruth and Abigail, each in her own way, play a vital role in securing the welfare of the Davidic house.[62] In what amounts to a record of the prehistory of the Davidic house, the author of Ruth shows that the workings of divine providence (through human agency) on behalf of David began during the lives of his ancestors.

Kindness, human and divine

It is widely recognized that the entwined themes of divine and human 'kindness' (*hesed*) are important in the book of Ruth (1:8; 2:20; 3:10). In being willing to return with Naomi, the two daughters-in-law show 'kindness' to their deceased husbands and to her (1:8), and this quality

---

[60] Only the first connection is noted by Eskenazi and Frymer-Kensky (2011: xxiv).

[61] Zakovitch 1999: 61; for further allusive links between Ruth 3 and 1 Sam. 25, see Berger 2009: 259, 267–269.

[62] Cf. Feeley-Harnik (1990: 179): 'the book of Ruth depicts women's work as essential to creating the Davidic monarchy.'

is confirmed in the case of Ruth by her adamant refusal to part from Naomi (1:16–17). In line with this, Boaz later blesses Ruth for her 'kindness' (3:10). This verse actually speaks of her *two* acts of kindness ('You have made this last kindness greater than the first'). The first was her loyalty to Naomi and the family (cf. Boaz's praise of Ruth in 2:11–12), and the second is her willingness, for the sake of the family, to marry a relative of her deceased husband, though Boaz is an older man.[63] Naomi asks that God might repay the kindness of her daughters-in-law with kindness (1:8: 'May the LORD deal kindly [*ḥesed*] with you'), and she sees in the new development reported by Ruth (Boaz's favourable treatment of Ruth in the field) a signal that God is acting in kindness towards the family (2:20). The sentence in 2:20 is ambiguous ('whose kindness has not forsaken the living or the dead'), with the pronoun's antecedent either Yahweh or Boaz ('May he [Boaz] be blessed by the LORD'). The second alternative is the one most often favoured by scholars, namely, that it refers to Boaz's kindness, but if the ambiguity is deliberate (the most likely scenario), the reference is to God's kindness shown through that of Boaz.[64]

As noted by Sakenfeld, a remarkably similar scene to that in Ruth 1:8–18 is found in 2 Samuel 15:19–23, which depicts David leaving Jerusalem and attempting in vain to discourage someone from going with him.[65] What is more, foreign (Philistine) Ittai's forceful declaration in the form of an oath that he will be with David 'whether for death or for life' (15:21) is close to that of Ruth (cf. Ruth 1:16–17).[66] David urges Ittai the Gittite, who has served him for only a short while, to go back and not go with him, concluding with an invocation of divine kindness (15:20 MT: 'and take back your brothers with you in kindness [*ḥesed*] and faithfulness'). This difficult text is commonly amended using the Septuagint (positing missing words dropped out by homoioteleuton) to read: 'and take your brothers with you, and may the LORD show steadfast love and faithfulness to you' (cf. NRSV).[67] Even without textual repair, however, the reference must be to *divine* kindness (cf. David's use of the word pair 'kindness and faithfulness' in 2 Sam. 2:5–6). The texts in Ruth 1 and 2 Samuel 15 both depict an aborted leave-taking in which someone not in a position to repay kindness (Naomi, David) asks God to do what he or she cannot do.

---

[63] See Sakenfeld 1985: 32; Lau 2011: 107–109.
[64] Cohen 1997; Glueck 1967: 41–42; Bush 1996a: 134–136; Hawk 2015: 86.
[65] The parallel is noted by Sakenfeld 1985: 34; cf. Hubbard 1988: 103.
[66] Eskenazi and Frymer-Kensky 2011: 18–19.
[67] For repair of the text using the Septuagint, see Driver 1913: 314.

There is a close relation between God's 'kindness' and the Davidic covenant tradition,[68] whose fountainhead is the dynastic oracle in 2 Samuel 7, wherein God promises (through Nathan) that he will not take his 'kindness' (*ḥesed*) from David's son (7:15; cf. 22:51). Solomon said that God showed 'great kindness' to David (our translation) in giving him an heir to sit upon the throne (1 Kgs 3:6; 2 Chr. 1:8). Behind the special position given to the house of David stands God's kindness. The word 'kindness' (*ḥesed*) is used seven times in Psalm 89 (vv. 1–2, 14, 24, 28, 33, 49).[69] The psalm opens with praise of Yahweh's acts of kindness (*ḥasdê*, v. 1), for God's kindness is firm and enduring (v. 2), as illustrated by his covenant with David (vv. 3–4). God's kindness enabled David to defeat his enemies (vv. 22–23). It is expected that the covenant will stand firm because of God's kindness (v. 28), even in the face of disloyalty among David's descendants (v. 33; cf. 2 Sam. 7:11b–16), but the unthinkable has happened and it appears that God has renounced the covenant (vv. 38–51). Compared with either 2 Samuel 7 or Psalm 89, Psalm 132:11–12 places greater stress on the conditionality of the covenant arrangement with the Davidic house.[70] The Ruth narrative can be understood as giving hope for the future of the Davidic house. Despite the ancestors of David experiencing a time of extreme peril, God's kindness did not fail the family, and likewise (by implication) God's kindness will not fail the dynasty of David. In other words, the story of Ruth read in the context of the historical books (Genesis–Kings) amounts to a strong assertion of God's providential upholding of the Davidic house, with the implication that the Messiah will indeed come.

Conclusion

If the Ruth narrative is read as addressing the issue of political legitimacy, it might be viewed as reflecting the vested interests of a pro-David or pro-Judahite party (e.g. aiming to answer those who cast aspersions on the Davidic house because of the Moabite ancestry of its founding king). We have instead provided a theological reading of the book that interprets it within the wider story of God's purposes for Israel, with divine providence and kindness upholding the dynasty of David for the benefit of Israel as a whole. A number of factors

---

[68] This paragraph depends upon Sakenfeld 1985: 52–63; 1978: 139–147.

[69] See Steussy 1999: 137–143.

[70] Pomykala (1995: 13) notes that it is an explicitly conditional version of the dynastic promise; cf. Cross 1973: 233.

point to the conclusion that the book of Ruth is best read as preparatory to God's dealings with David and his house. None of the canonical positions assigned to the book in Hebrew and Greek canons (before Psalms, after Proverbs, or between Judges and Samuel) suggest that ancient readers viewed it as written to promote a more generous view of foreigners. If its placement after Judges in the Greek Old Testament (and subsequent Christian canon) is allowed to have an impact on reading, the events in the book of Ruth are to be seen as preparing for David. The symmetrical design of the book requires the presence of the genealogy in 4:18–22, and the genealogy explicitly connects the family history given in the book of Ruth with David. The link with David is more than a commendation of the message of the book that does not as such have anything to do with the house of David, and evidence for this is that key scenes in Ruth 1:8–18 and 3:7–13 have significant parallels in the life of David. The later history of David and his house is anticipated by the Ruth narrative's depiction of the workings of divine providence on behalf of the family that produced David and by its exploration of human and divine 'kindness' in the lives of his forebears.

Chapter Four

Ruth as a wise woman

The meaning of a literary portion or work is in large measure dependent on its context, and in the case of a biblical book one of the contexts for its interpretation is the other canonical books among which it is situated. This phenomenon is an aspect of the biblical 'paratext' (a term coined by Gérard Genette),[1] which includes such features as book titles, book order and internal divisions within books (e.g. paragraphs). These elements provide a frame of reference for the text and exercise a powerful influence on its reception.[2] In other words, an effect is produced on readers by placing biblical books in a particular sequence.[3] Timothy J. Stone uses the phrase 'compilation consciousness' to refer to the way in which books are associated with neighbouring books in the canon.[4] The paratextual elements embody the evaluations of ancient readers and set up certain expectations for future readers.[5] Having already considered the book of Ruth in its position after Judges, in this chapter the discussion focuses on the Proverbs–Ruth sequence found within the Hebrew canonical tradition.

Physical contiguity is regularly understood by readers to indicate that there must be a significant connection between books. This readerly habit forms the basis of the following analysis of the book of Ruth, a book that is put in more than one position by the different interpretive communities that lie behind the various biblical canons and so, in terms of the history of interpretation, has been read in more than one context. There is also the possibility that the

---

[1] See Genette 1991: 261–262; Genette 1988: 63; Genette 1997.
[2] For the 'framing' function of paratext, see Maclean 1991: 273–275; den Hollander, Schmid and Smelik (2006: vii): 'The paratext frames the text and thereby informs perception of the text by the reader.' Cf. MacLachlan and Reid (1994: 39): 'But frames are not just borderlines; as we have seen, they also have the potential to carry meta-messages about how to interpret what they enclose.'
[3] For a recent discussion of this phenomenon, see Spellman 2014: 108–123, esp. 109: 'Where an individual writing is positioned in relation to other writings in a collection (either materially or conceptually) has significant hermeneutical ramifications.'
[4] Stone 2013a: 12.
[5] See Tannen (1993: 14–56), who speaks in terms of 'structures of expectation' (15, 21).

37

contemporary reading of biblical books in a prescribed canonical sequence will lead to fresh interpretive insights into their meaning, and that, indeed, is what we seek to demonstrate in this chapter which focuses on the book of Ruth in its Hebrew canonical setting.

It is not likely to be the case, however, that different canonical settings will produce wildly different (let alone contradictory) interpretations of the same book; for instance, the prominent role of Ruth herself in the book named after her will be recognized by all readers, whatever canonical position is given to the book.[6] The book received the title 'Ruth' in both the Greek and Hebrew traditions, despite the fact that the central character is Naomi. The book depicts Naomi's crisis, moving from her emptiness (1:21) to her fullness (4:17), yet the book is named 'Ruth' for it is the figure of Ruth who captures the reader's interest, since she features in every scene in the book except that at the city gate in 4:1–12, where, however, she is the subject of conversation in that all-male situation. The theme of the book is the manner and method by which Naomi's hopeless condition is reversed, but it is through loyal and active Ruth that the reversal takes place. This makes Ruth the *main* character in the narrative (the main character need not always be the central character) and so the book is aptly named.

The placing of the book of Ruth between Judges and Samuel (in the Greek canonical tradition) reinforces a reading that gives prominence to the character and actions of Ruth, for women are conspicuous in both books as capable figures or in a heroic pose. Examples include the theologically perceptive Hannah (1 Sam. 2:1–10) and Abigail (1 Sam. 25:23–31), and women specifically described as wise are the 'wise woman' of Tekoa (2 Sam. 14) and that of Abel of Beth-maacah (2 Sam. 20). A listing of women who help rescue others must include Deborah and Jael (Judg. 4 – 5), Michal (1 Sam. 18:20–29), and once again Abigail (1 Sam. 25).[7] This chapter seeks to demonstrate that reading the book of Ruth in the Hebrew canon (in the position following Proverbs 31) takes this interpretive move in a certain direction and encourages an appreciation of its heroine as an example of the wisdom ethic taught in the book of Proverbs.

---

[6] Berlin 1983: 83–110. We acknowledge our dependence on Berlin for the discussion in this paragraph.

[7] See Ackerman 1998; Klein 2003: ch. 1. Klein looks at Achsah, Deborah, Jephthah's daughter and Manoah's wife, and says: 'all four are resourceful, undertaking actions but deferring to the authority of males' (12); cf. Pigott 2002: 145–173.

The book of Ruth in the Writings

The modern Bible reader is used to reading the book of Ruth following Judges (its position in the Greek canon),[8] but in the Hebrew canon (Tanak) Ruth is found in the third and final section of the canon, the *Ketuvim* (Writings). This chapter explores the hermeneutical implications of placing the book of Ruth in the Writings. Due to some fluctuation in the order of the individual books within the Writings,[9] the book of Ruth is found in two canonical positions. As previously noted, according to the Babylonian Talmud (*Baba Bathra* 14b), Ruth comes at the beginning of the Writings, presumably because of the early setting of the story, for the events narrated belong to the time of the judges (Ruth 1:1: 'In the days when the judges ruled . . .').[10] In that Talmudic quotation, 'Ruth and Psalms and Job and Proverbs' are linked together, with Ruth (ending with the genealogy of David) positioned as a preface to Psalms, and Psalms–Job–Proverbs forming a tripartite wisdom collection. 'Qoheleth' is the next book in line, unconnected by a conjunction to books either before or after it, though it is strategically placed between books also viewed as Solomonic compositions.[11] Next, we find three *pairs* of books, namely 'Song of Songs and Lamentations' (a genre grouping of songs, romantic and mournful), 'Daniel and Esther' (both court tales wherein the safety of Jews is under threat), and lastly the books 'Ezra (–Nehemiah) and Chronicles' (with their obvious similarities explaining their juxtapositioning).[12]

In some medieval Hebrew manuscripts, Chronicles comes at the beginning of the Writings; however, the sequence that has Chronicles in last position became established in the printed editions of the Hebrew Bible: at the beginning is the group of 'three great writings' (*BT Ber.* 57b), Psalms, Job and Proverbs, in order of decreasing length. In all the varying sequences for Writings, Psalms, Job and Proverbs are always found together, either in that order or as Psalms–Proverbs–Job. The little group of *Megillot* ('scrolls') that includes Ruth is placed next, and finally Daniel, Ezra–Nehemiah and Chronicles. The order

---

[8] For analysis of the book in this canonical position, see chapter 3.
[9] A tabulation of eleven alternative orders is provided by Ginsburg 1966: 7.
[10] Rendtorff 1985: 245.
[11] Pope 1977: 18.
[12] *Pace* Steinberg 2006: 144–151. Steinberg's explanation of the order in *Baba Bathra* is less than convincing, one reason being that he ignores the way in which books are coupled (often in pairs).

of the five books of the *Megillot* in the Leningrad Codex (B 19ᴬ, the base text of the scholarly Hebrew Bibles *BHK*³, *BHS* and *BHQ*) and in Sephardic codices appears to be based on the principle of chronology: Ruth, Song of Songs (written by a young Solomon?), Ecclesiastes (by Solomon when he was old?), Lamentations and Esther.[13] It is usually said that these five books are grouped together for liturgical reasons, due to their public reading at the five main festivals; however, this rationale has recently been questioned by Timothy J. Stone, who argues that the process was the reverse: namely, it was due to the five-book grouping that Ruth, Song of Songs and Lamentations in particular began to be read at feasts.[14] Certainly, the associations of Ruth with Weeks and Song of Songs with Passover are not strong and could be viewed as contrived. In other Hebrew Bibles (especially those used by Ashkenazic Jews) the order reflects the sequence of the major Jewish festivals in the calendar (assuming the year starts with the month Nisan): Song of Songs (Passover), Ruth (Weeks), Lamentations (Ninth of Ab), Ecclesiastes (Booths) and Esther (Purim).[15] The liturgical use of the *Megillot* explains their placement directly after the Pentateuch in the editions of the Hebrew Bible in the fifteenth and sixteenth centuries,[16] for the Pentateuch and the *Megillot* are the only portions read in their entirety in the lectionary of the synagogue.

Ruth read at the Feast of Weeks, during the wheat harvest, picks up on the barley and wheat harvests featured in the book (1:22; 2:23; cf. Lev. 23:15–21; Num. 28:26–31).[17] The book of Ruth followed by Song of Songs in the *Megillot*, or preceded by it according to the order of the annual festivals (assuming the year starts with the month Nisan: Song of Songs [Passover], Ruth [Weeks], etc.),[18] emphasizes the love-story aspect of Ruth, most prominent in the public meeting of Boaz and Ruth in chapter 2 and their clandestine meeting in chapter 3. The Ruth narrative, for its part, gives an agrarian setting for the pastoral images of Song of Songs. In the order of books Proverbs, Ruth and Song of Songs (Leningrad Codex), both Ruth

---

[13] There is, however, some minor variability in the codices; see the tables provided by Dukan 2006: 67; Steinberg 2006: 133, 152; Beckwith 1985: 452–464; Brandt 2001: 151–171. The Aleppo Codex appears to have the same order as the Leningrad Codex, but because of damage, leaves are missing after several words in Song 3:11a.

[14] Stone 2013a: 105–111.

[15] Wolfenson 1924: 157.

[16] For details, see Ginsburg 1966: 3–4; Wolfenson 1924: 155 n. 13.

[17] Daube 1956: 48–49; Koosed 2011: 121–126.

[18] Wolfenson 1924: 157; Bauer 1963: 116, 119.

and Song of Songs develop the picture of the virtuous and assertive woman pictured in Proverbs 31,[19] and it is worth noting that the female lover is the first and main speaker in the song.[20] When followed (or preceded) by Song of Songs, the romance aspect of the book of Ruth is highlighted.

Ruth as the first of the *Megillot* follows immediately upon the book of Proverbs (in the Leningrad Codex), presumably because of a link in their subject matter.[21] Proverbs closes with an alphabetical acrostic poem of twenty-two lines (31:10–31), with each verse starting with a successive letter of the Hebrew alphabet.[22] It celebrates the 'worthy woman' (*'ēšet ḥayil*), with this expression occurring in the opening line (31:10, 'An *excellent wife* who can find?'), and the juxtaposed book of Ruth can be understood as going on to describe just such a woman. The thematic linkage between the books of Proverbs and Ruth is supported by the fact that in Ruth 3:11 Boaz calls Ruth 'a worthy woman' (*'ēšet ḥayil*). The phrase 'worthy woman' occurs only once elsewhere in the Old Testament, namely Proverbs 12:4 ('An *excellent wife* is the crown of her husband'). The wording in Proverbs 31:31 fits the woman Ruth ('let her works praise her in the gates'), for in Ruth 3:11 Boaz, in praising Ruth, says: 'all my fellow townsmen [lit. 'all the gate of my people'] know that you are a worthy woman', and the people at the gate and the elders who meet there are recorded as praising Ruth (4:11–12). So, also, Proverbs 31:23 applies to Boaz ('Her husband is known in the gates when he sits among the elders of the land'), for this sounds like an allusion to the scene at the city gate depicted in Ruth 4. The canonical placement next to Proverbs suggests that Ruth the Moabitess is to be viewed as a real-life example of the piety taught in Proverbs and embodied in the exemplary woman of Proverbs 31.

The book of Ruth is not usually considered to be a wisdom work, and we are not arguing that it should be classified in this way. Certainly none of the *dramatis personae* are identified as 'wise' and the story makes no use of what may be viewed as exclusively wisdom terms. On the other hand, the narrative provides in the person of Ruth a

---

[19] Cf. Longman 2001: 2.
[20] See the statistics provided by Brenner 1993a: 88.
[21] As suggested by Campbell 1975: 34, 125; McCreesh 1985: 38–40; Hubbard 1988: 216; Bush 1996a: 173–174; Zakovitch 1999: 31–32; Fischer 2001: 101–102. The link between Prov. 31 and Ruth was noted by medieval Latin commentators; see Smith 1996: 23, 49, 52.
[22] The Hebrew alphabet contains twenty-two consonants.

paradigm,[23] namely a pattern of behaviour worthy of emulation by readers (e.g. an ethic of hard work [2:7, 17; cf. Prov. 6:6–11; 10:26; 13:4]), and the book of Ruth contains themes that find a place in acknowledged wisdom books (e.g. marriage to a suitable wife, theodicy, providence, the care of the poor and reward).

Similarities and differences

It would appear that thematic considerations are responsible for the positioning of the book of Ruth after Proverbs, though any book is likely to have a number of major themes, such that alternative placements are possible on this basis. There are differences between the portrayal of Ruth and the ideal woman of Proverbs 31 (e.g. their markedly different social status); however, that does not undermine the positing of a connection between the two portraits, but simply confirms that in interpreting the book of Ruth we must not allow the interpretation to be exclusively controlled by Proverbs 31. We should expect a thoughtful consideration of the juxtapositioning of Ruth and Proverbs to throw light on the meaning of Ruth and to enable us to see things that might otherwise have remained unnoticed. On the other hand, this paratextual connection will not exhaust the reading of the book of Ruth.

There are both similarities and differences between the heroine Ruth and the 'good wife' of Proverbs 31.[24] In regard to similarities, both women are energetic and active (e.g. Prov. 31:15, 27; Ruth 2:2, 7, 17); both work to supply the needs of their households (Prov. 31:15, 21; Ruth 2:18); both show 'kindness' (*hesed*; Prov. 31:26; cf. 31:20; Ruth 3:10); both are praised as superior by their husbands and by others (Prov. 31:28–29; Ruth 3:10–11; 4:15); both work hard (Prov. 31:13, 27; Ruth 2:2, 17, 23); and both women are God-fearing (Prov. 31:30; Ruth 1:16; 2:12).

As for differences between the two women, these include their race and class, for the woman of Proverbs 31 is an upper-class Israelite.[25] This would support the view that neither text has influenced the other, but the two are of entirely separate origins. There is nothing to suggest that the author of Proverbs 31 had Ruth in mind, nor is there evidence that the book of Ruth was influenced by the portrait of Proverbs

---

[23] Scott 1971: 85–87.
[24] For similarities and differences, see Goh 2014. In what follows we acknowledge our dependence on Goh.
[25] Perdue 2000: 275, 279.

31. The canonical juxtapositioning of Proverbs and Ruth in the Hebrew canonical tradition is a *post-authorial* phenomenon, with biblical book order reflecting the perceptions and views of ancient readers, who were right, however, to detect the presence of significant thematic connections between these two canonical portions. They were placed side-by-side because they were viewed as belonging together and believed to be mutually enriching, and this prescribed order of reading was intended to be a hermeneutical guide for future generations of readers.

The differences are not to be overemphasized, however, for the idealized portrait of Proverbs 31 can be understood as describing what Ruth *became*, beyond the time frame of the canonical book that ends with the birth of her first child: she was fully integrated into Israelite society as the wife of a respected local dignitary; she left behind her life of poverty; she became the mother of more than one child (possibly); and she found wider scope for her obvious ability in the management of a large household.[26] In fact, putting the book of Ruth after Proverbs 31 strongly implies that Ruth did go on to achieve all that an Israelite wife and mother could and should do, and so this is one way in which juxtaposing Proverbs and Ruth shapes readerly evaluations.

Reading Ruth alongside Proverbs 31

When the book of Ruth is read with Proverbs as its canonical conversation partner, a number of themes come into prominence: Ruth's worth, her praiseworthy character, her foreign status, theodicy, providence, the practice of kindness, diligence, the use of intelligence and reward.[27] Each of these themes will now be explored in turn.

The book of Ruth read in conjunction with Proverbs 31 serves to highlight the term 'worth' (*ḥayil*), for this is a key descriptor for both women. Certainly the presence of this word in the opening line of the poem establishes its thematic importance ('An *excellent* wife who can find?'). In the case of the book of Ruth, Boaz's declaration of Ruth's

---

[26] So also Sakenfeld (1999a: 62): 'It is easy to imagine, based on what is known of Ruth so far, that as Boaz's wife she would become the epitome of the wife described in Proverbs.'

[27] According to McKeown (2015: 4), 'many of the themes in the book [of Ruth] relate to practical problems and issues similar to those discussed in the other books that are usually classified as wisdom literature'. He does not, however, develop this insight.

'worth' occurs at a crucial turning point in the plot (3:11),[28] when he commits himself to do the part of the next of kin (involving marriage to Ruth). This Hebrew word has a wide semantic range, such that the exact nuance of the epithet applied to Ruth ('a *worthy* woman' [*'ēšet ḥayil*]) may be disputed, but the basic idea is that of *strength*, whether physical strength, competence, efficiency, wealth, social standing, military heroism, moral substance or mental capacity.[29] In Proverbs 31, the mother of Lemuel advises him not to give his strength (*ḥayil*) to women who destroy kings (31:3), whereas in the book that follows, Ruth, the 'woman of worth' (*'ēšet ḥayil*), builds up the Israelite kingdom (via her descendant David).[30] In the final poem of Proverbs, the initial use of the key word in 31:10 and its reuse in 31:29 ('Many women have *done excellently* [*'āśû ḥayil*]') bracket the actual description of the model woman (31:10–29), this being another sign of the importance of this term in Proverbs 31.[31] Lying outside the main body of the poem, 31:30–31 is differentiated as a coda. To designate these two verses a coda is not to deny that they are integral to the poem, but rather identifies them as of special significance. These final verses emphasize the woman's praiseworthy character (*hālal* ['to praise'] x2, picking up its use in v. 28). In addition, it is in verse 30 that the prime virtue featured in the motto of the book of Proverbs ('the fear of the LORD'; Prov. 1:7; 9:10) is ascribed to the woman, and in verse 31 the poet calls on male readers to 'Give her of the fruit of her hands', namely a share of what she has earned as a reward for her virtuous behaviour.

In the case of the book of Ruth, there is the earlier use of the matching expression for a male in application to Boaz as 'a worthy man' (*'îš gibbôr ḥayil*, Ruth 2:1). This refers to his social standing as one who has an important place in the community and to his material wealth as an owner of fields and servants (2:3–4, 8, 15, 21, 23). A comparable use of this phrase is found in 1 Samuel 9:1 in regard to Saul's father, Kish, who has asses and servants (cf. 2 Kgs 15:20, 'all the wealthy men' [*kol-gibbôr haḥayil*]). There is, however, sufficient elasticity in the meaning of the term to enable its reapplication to

---

[28] As noted by Stone 2013a: 133.

[29] See e.g. Scott 1985: 185–186 ('a capable wife'); Waltke 2005: 520–521; Murphy 1998: 243; Szlos 2000: 97–103, esp. 98: 'how strikingly physical and powerful a depiction it is'; Yoder 2003: 427; Yoder 2001: 76–77; Kosmala 1975: 374; Eising 1980: 350–351; Kwon 2012: 171, 173.

[30] Goh 2014: 498–499.

[31] Lichtenstein 1982: 205–206; who is followed by McCreesh 1985: 32.

Ruth, who has none of these things (3:11) but whose moral gravitas earns her the equivalent female epithet. In the case of the Moabitess, sojourner and gleaner, the complimentary description of her as a 'woman of worth' cannot refer to social standing, but 'emphasizes the quality of Ruth's person'.[32] It is Ruth's devotion to her mother-in-law and loyalty to the family that causes Boaz to speak of her in such terms (2:11–12; 3:10). His kindly treatment of her in chapter 2 enables the reader to come to a recognition of Boaz's own moral worth (for *'îš ḥayil* denoting *moral* worth, see 1 Kgs 1:42). The description of Boaz in 2:1 means that he is in a position of influence and wealth to render assistance to the two widows, Naomi and Ruth, if he is willing to do so, and the account in chapter 2 shows that he exceeds any formal obligation to help them, as recognized by the expressions of gratitude by Ruth (2:10, 13) and Naomi (2:19–20).[33] The fact that Ruth is 'a worthy woman' (using the matching expression for a woman) means that Boaz and Ruth are ideally matched and suited as marriage partners.[34]

In addition, the elders of Bethlehem express the following wish for Boaz's welfare: 'May you act worthily [*wa 'ăśê ḥayil*] in Ephrathah and be renowned in Bethlehem' (4:11), an expression that is matched in Proverbs 31:29 ('Many women have done excellently [*'āśû ḥayil*]'). What is in mind is clarified by the continuation of the speech of the Bethlehemite elders in the adjoining verse (4:12), namely the building up of his house through the progeny provided through Ruth. The final praise of Ruth placed on the lips of the women of Bethlehem (4:15) also speaks of her great worth ('[she] is more to you [Naomi] than seven sons'). This is high praise in a culture that placed great value on male progeny and in a story whose plot was initiated by Naomi's loss of husband and sons (1:5), which loss has only now been compensated for by the male descendant provided through Ruth (4:13–17, esp. v. 17b: 'A son has been born to Naomi [through Ruth]').

In praise of Ruth

According to Al Wolters, the genre of the poem in Proverbs 31 is that of hymn, namely a song of praise for a heroic woman ('Song of the Valiant Woman'),[35] but Michael V. Fox is probably right to prefer

---

[32] Campbell 1975: 125.
[33] Bush 1996a: 43.
[34] This is also noted by Davis 2006: 14.
[35] Wolters 1988: 451; Wolters 2001.

the category *encomium*, seeing that 'hymn' is a generic category more properly used of the praise of God and Proverbs 31 lacks the usual hymnic Hebrew participles, except for 31:27a (*ṣôpiyyâ*).[36] As noted by Fox, parallels are found in biblical psalms that praise the righteous man who 'fears the LORD' (Pss 112; 128),[37] and extrabiblical examples are Sirach 38:34b – 39:11; 44:1 – 50:24; 1 Maccabees 3:3–9; 14:4–15. In the same way, Ruth is repeatedly praised by other characters in the book named after her (1:8; 2:11; 3:10–11; 4:15), and the association with Proverbs 31 assists the reader to notice this feature in the book of Ruth. The regular praising of Ruth signals that her character and actions (notably her kindness [*ḥesed*] to family and her diligence) are meant to be viewed by readers as exemplary and this anticipates that she will receive her due reward.

Reading the book of Ruth within a wisdom frame

The preponderance of feminine imagery in Proverbs 1 – 9 and 31 suggests to Claudia Camp that these two sections were chosen to frame the book as a whole.[38] Whether Proverbs 31:10–31 is part of an editorial frame around the book is open to dispute, but what cannot be gainsaid is that the poem about 'the good wife' is a fitting end to the book, for the metaphor of *finding* a wife (= Lady Wisdom) forms the subtext of Proverbs 1 – 9. The 'excellent wife' of Proverbs 31 is the feminine embodiment of the wisdom ethic of Proverbs, but in contrast to Lady Wisdom depicted in Proverbs 1 and 8–9, she is a real-life woman and is realistically portrayed.[39] The poem about the 'excellent wife' forms a bridge between the teachings of Proverbs and the story of Ruth in which a man finds a suitable wife,[40] and the link encourages the reading of Ruth within a wisdom framework.[41]

In the book adjoining Proverbs, Ruth the 'foreigner' becomes a model of proper behaviour and the appropriate wife. Ruth is repeatedly designated 'the Moabitess' by the narrator and by other characters

---

[36] Fox 2009: 902–905.

[37] Longman (2014: 386–389) finds various links between Ps. 112 and Prov. 31.

[38] Camp 1985: 187–191; so, too, Whybray 1994: 161–162.

[39] As emphasized by Lang 2004; and Yoder 2001: 75–91.

[40] We should not understand the opening line of the poem ('An excellent wife who can find?') to mean that it is an impossibility (cf. Prov. 20:6b: 'a faithful man who can find?'). Finding a suitable wife is a theme touched on in 18:22 ('He who finds a wife finds a good thing').

[41] Cf. Stone (2013a: 16): 'When Ruth is read in conjunction with Proverbs, certain aspects of the book move into the foreground, while others recede into the background.'

within the story, underlining her outsider status (1:22; 2:2, 6, 21; 4:5, 10; cf. 1:4: 'These [the two sons of Naomi] took Moabite wives'). Ruth acknowledges that she is a 'foreigner' (2:10, *nokriyyâ*), and her self-designation is highlighted in her speech to Boaz by means of Hebrew wordplay[42] when she asks him: 'Why have I found favour in your eyes, *that you should take notice of me* [*lĕhakkîrēnî*], since I am a foreigner?' In Proverbs, the female foil for Lady Wisdom and the competitor for the young man's affections is pejoratively designated a 'foreign woman' (*nokriyyâ*, our translation; 2:16; 5:20; 6:24; 7:5; 23:27),[43] but, in this case, it is probably not an ethnic label (given 2:17: '[she] forgets the covenant of her God [= Yahweh]'),[44] instead painting the unchaste wife as a moral 'outsider', that is, one who behaves in ways inconsistent with membership in the covenant community.[45] This woman is an Israelite who acts like an outsider, but, in a variation on the theme, Ruth is an ethnic outsider who acts as a true Israelite (e.g. her Abraham-like oath to leave home and country [1:16–17; 2:11; cf. Gen. 12:1–3]),[46] and she is shown to be a suitable wife for noble Boaz.[47] To have a 'foreigner' as a model of virtue is in line with the *internationalism* of wisdom (cf. the figure of Job) and the acknowledgment in Israelite wisdom circles that individuals from other nations can possess wisdom that is compatible with Yahwism (Prov. 30:1; 31:1; 1 Kgs 4:29–34 [Heb. 5:9–14]).

Consistent with wisdom books (esp. Job), Ruth can be read as a theodicy: namely, it seeks to justify the mysterious ways of God. Proverbs also makes clear that the events of life often defy human understanding (Prov. 16:1–2, 9; 19:14, 21; 20:24; 21:30–31). The book of Ruth opens with an inexplicable tragedy, for no reason is provided for the deaths of Naomi's husband and two sons (Ruth 1:1–5).[48] Naomi's accusatory statement that 'the LORD has testified against me'

---

[42] Wolfe 2011: 10, 35.

[43] Newsom 1989: 148. Carlos Bovell goes so far as to relate Orpah to the 'strange woman' of Proverbs: see Bovell 2003: 183–186.

[44] Fox 2000: 120.

[45] Waltke 2004: 121–122; cf. Maier 1995: 97–99, 262, 266, who notes the parallel with the terminology in Deut. 4:23, 31. Fox argues she is simply someone else's wife and so out of bounds (2009: 139–141); cf. 'forbidden woman' (Prov. 2:16 etc.).

[46] According to Stone, Ruth is 'in critical dialogue with Proverbs' at this point; see Stone 2013a: 136; also 139: 'her connection to wisdom's ideals in Proverbs logically brings to the fore her foreign status. Ruth embodies Proverb's ideals and yet is a foreigner.'

[47] Trible 1982: 168; Glover 2009: 308: 'In Ruth a Moabitess pledges herself to Israel and through various cultural transitions becomes an Israelite.'

[48] McKeown 2015: 15–16.

(1:21) should not be read as an admission of wrong on her part, as if to say that the tragedy was a divine judgment upon her for leaving the land or allowing her sons to marry foreigners.[49] She holds God accountable for the sad events and renames herself 'Mara' (Bitterness [*mārā'*]), with the explanation that 'Shaddai has dealt very bitterly [*hēmar*] with me' (1:20, our translation). This echoes Job, who also lost children, felt himself to be suffering unjustly and who swore 'by Shaddai who embittered [*hēmar*] me' (Job 27:2, our translation).[50] This way of reading Ruth is supported by its relation to Lamentations, a neighbouring book in the *Megillot* which alludes to destroyed Jerusalem's widow status (1:1: 'How like a widow has she become' [cf. 5:3]), and this forms a parallel to Naomi's situation (e.g. Ruth 1:3, 5). The two books, each in its own way, wrestle with the problem of theodicy,[51] given their recognition of God's involvement in distressing situations, the decimation of a family on the one hand and of the city of Jerusalem on the other (Ruth 1:20–21; Lam. 2:1–8). The family crisis of Naomi is brought to a happy resolution at the close of the book, when God acts to preserve the familial line (4:13b: 'the LORD gave her [Ruth] conception, and she bore a son').

The theme of divine providence is prevalent in wisdom literature and is also found in the book of Ruth. Neither overtly miraculous occurrences nor dramatic divine interventions are to be expected in the book of Ruth when read within a wisdom framework. Only once does the narrator mention God's direct involvement in events (4:13), though characters within the story repeatedly speak *about* God, such that the (largely) hidden nature of God's providence is a pervasive theme (1:6, 9, 16–17, 20–21; 2:4, 12, 20; 3:10, 13; 4:11–12, 14).[52] More subtly, the apparently *chance* event of Ruth entering the field of Boaz (2:3), together with the arrival of Boaz and of the unnamed close relation on the scene *at just the right time* (2:4; 4:1 [the implication of the *hinnê* clause]),[53] support a theology of the divine superintendence of events.[54] We may compare this perspective with the 'string of sayings on divine governance' in Proverbs 15:33 – 16:9.[55] According to Proverbs, even the chance outcome of casting a lot reflects divine

---

[49] Sakenfeld 2003: 136.
[50] Kalmanofsky 2014: 160.
[51] Noted by Korpel 2001: 230–231.
[52] See Hals 1969.
[53] Berlin 1983: 94: 'Just then'.
[54] Campbell 1975: 29, 93, 141; Eskenazi and Frymer-Kensky 2011: 71.
[55] Clifford 1999: 157.

control and therefore brings an end to arguments over what is the right course of action to take (16:33; 18:18).

The 'excellent wife' of Proverbs 31 speaks wisely and inculcates kindness (31:26: 'the *teaching of kindness* [*ḥesed*] is on her tongue').[56] This may refer to what she instructs her children and household servants, namely to treat the poor with kindness, such that her teaching is consistent with her own humane actions (cf. 31:20: 'She opens her hand to the poor and reaches out her hands to the needy'). As noted by Fox, this recalls the teaching of Lemuel's mother about the kingly responsibility of caring for the poor (31:6–9; cf. 20:28).[57] It also anticipates the 'kindness' (*ḥesed*) theme in the juxtaposed narrative of Ruth, and Ernst Würthwein goes so far as to claim that Ruth was written as a wisdom composition to illustrate the truth of Proverbs 21:21 ('Whoever pursues righteousness and *kindness* [*ḥesed*] will find life, righteousness, and honor').[58] Ruth and Boaz practise 'kindness', for their actions for the sake of the welfare of the family go beyond the formal obligations of a daughter-in-law or of the male relative who was not the nearest of kin (2:20; 3:12).[59] Just as Proverbs makes use of antithetical pairs of characters to describe behaviour and its consequences (e.g. wise/foolish, righteous/wicked, lazy/diligent, rich/poor),[60] so also does the book of Ruth. In two situations of choice – whether to go with Naomi or return to Moab (Ruth/Orpah), and whether to redeem the parcel of land (and marry Ruth) or not (Boaz/the unnamed nearer relative) – characters are depicted as coming to opposite decisions,[61] and the choices made have consequences for the characters concerned: Orpah leaves the story (1:15), the nearer relative remains without a name (4:1: 'Mr So-and-So' [*pělōnî 'almōnî*]),[62] and Boaz marries Ruth and she gives birth to a son (4:13).

Both Proverbs and the book of Ruth contain the theme of diligence and commend the use of intelligence and resourcefulness to overcome difficulties. Like Ruth the gleaner (ch. 2), the woman of Proverbs 31

---

[56] With the Hebrew genitive relation (*tôrat ḥesed*) indicating the content of her teaching (= teaching *about* kindness).

[57] Fox 2009: 897. This is one of a number of links between Prov. 31:1–9 and 31:10–31; see Waltke 2005: 501–503.

[58] Würthwein 1969: 5–6.

[59] According to Andersen, *ḥesed* denotes non-obligatory generous action; see Andersen 1986: 59–60.

[60] Clifford 1999: 22.

[61] Bush 1996a: 42.

[62] For an attempt to discern the reasons for Mr So-and-So's refusal, see Lau 2011: 74–80.

labours with her hands (31:13) and is hard-working (31:15, 18–19, 27). Reflecting this work ethic, Proverbs places side-by-side for comparison the industry of the ant and its consequences (6:6–8) and the sluggard's indolence and its consequences (6:9–11; cf. 24:30–34).[63] In the night scene at the threshing floor, Ruth departs from the script given to her by Naomi (3:4b: 'he will tell you what to do'),[64] for instead of waiting for instructions from Boaz she takes the initiative and instructs *him* what to do,[65] proposing marriage as the best solution for the family's problems (3:9), and Boaz sees the good sense and propriety of what she calls on him to do.

Lastly, the theme of recompense or reward plays an important role in both books. Actions have consequences, and the receiving of reward or punishment is integrally related to how people behave.[66] While it is not always explicit in Proverbs that God upholds the act–consequence nexus, in a number of passages God is said to be active in retribution (e.g. 5:21–23; 23:10–11; 24:11–12; 29:26).[67] There is an element of intrinsic retribution (e.g. 26:27), but it is not wooden or mechanical (e.g. the requirement to care for the poor, who presumably are destitute through no fault of their own [21:13; 22:22; 28:27]).[68] Turning to the book of Ruth, we find that Naomi and Boaz both express the wish that God might reward Ruth for her actions on behalf of the family (1:8–9; 2:11–12). Naomi makes mention of a correspondence between Ruth's action and the hoped-for response from God ('May the LORD deal kindly with you, as you have dealt [kindly] with the dead and with me').[69] For his part, Boaz specifically expresses the hope that God will recompense Ruth for what she has done ('The LORD repay you for what you have done'). In Naomi's mind the reward needs to take the form of Ruth finding 'rest' (*mĕnûḥâ*, 1:9), and for Boaz the hope is that Ruth will find shelter under God's 'wings' (*kānāp*, 2:12). They place upon God the obligation of rewarding Ruth, but, as it happens, each has an essential part to play in the process of reward, as indicated by the reuse of significant terms when Naomi

[63] Fox 2000: 218.

[64] As noted e.g. by Hubbard 1988: 212; Fewell and Gunn 1990: 52–53.

[65] Also noted by Adams 2014: 57.

[66] For this paragraph, we acknowledge our dependence on Fox 2000: 91–92.

[67] Böstrom 1990: 90–140, esp. 101, 136; Dell 2006: 90–124. For the same issue in prophetic texts, see Miller 1982: 121–139.

[68] See Van Leeuwen 1992.

[69] Hubbard 1988: 104: 'Here emerges a key theological assumption of the book: the intimate link between human action and divine action. In this case, human kindness has earned the possibility (even likelihood) of a God-given reward.'

sends Ruth to the threshing floor (3:1: 'Should I not seek *rest* for you?' [*mānôaḥ*]) and when Ruth calls on Boaz to marry her (3:9: 'Spread your wings [*kānāp*] over your servant'). The implication is that Naomi and Boaz are instruments through whom God ensures that Ruth receives her just deserts, but the subtle handling of this theme in the book of Ruth is consistent with the way in which the book of Proverbs depicts God's involvement in retributive justice.

Women as models of good behaviour in the New Testament

Consistent with the use of an idealized women as the embodiment of Wisdom in Proverbs 31 and the interpretation of the heroine Ruth as a real-life example of the wisdom ethic of the book of Proverbs, in the Gospels, both by his actions and in his teaching, Jesus shows that he places a high value on women.[70] Jesus speaks to women in public and private (John 4:9, 27); he teaches them and encourages them to learn (Luke 10:38–42); he openly commends them when they demonstrate faith (Matt. 15:21–28) and devotion (Luke 21:1–4). Jesus has women among his band of travelling companions (Luke 8:1–3). He treats men and women as equals, one indicator being his style of teaching in which he selects images for his parables that regularly pair a man and a woman: for example, the woman of Zarephath and Naaman the leper (Luke 4:25–27); the twin parables of the mending of a garment (the task of a woman) and the making of wine (the work of men) (Luke 5:36–39); the parable of the mustard seed (men do the farming) and the story of the woman kneading leaven into dough (Luke 13:18–21). It is women who are found by the cross (Mark 15:40–41) and witness the burial (Mark 15:47), and they are honoured by being the first to witness the resurrection and carry the news to others (Mark 16:1–8).

Likewise, in the apostolic letters, women are commended by Paul and listed among his co-workers (e.g. Rom. 16:1–5), and the letter to the Philippians is written (at least in part) to help two Christian women to be reconciled (Phil. 4:2). The behaviour of Ruth is never commented on as such in the New Testament, but, in line with our reading of the book of Ruth, in 1 Peter 3:3–6 Christian wives are instructed that beauty is more than outward appearance, and Peter invokes the example of 'the holy women' of the Old Testament period,

---

[70] For a perceptive survey, see Bailey 2008: 189–275.

with Sarah specifically mentioned. Though famed for her beauty (cf. Gen. 12:11), it is Sarah's submissive behaviour as Abraham's wife that is held up as a model.

Conclusion

The placement of Ruth after Proverbs 31 in the Hebrew canonical tradition reflects a perception by ancient readers that there are significant connections between the two texts. The similarities and differences between the passages are such that the link must be viewed as post-compositional. This canonical positioning encourages the reading of the book of Ruth within a wisdom frame, with Ruth modelling key aspects of the wisdom ethic of Proverbs. The outcome is that certain features of the narrative of Ruth are given greater prominence than might otherwise be the case. Nine themes in particular are highlighted: Ruth's moral worth, her praiseworthy character, her foreign status, the issue of theodicy, divine providence, the practice of kindness, diligence, the use of intelligence and recompense.

Recollection of the alternative placement of Ruth among historical books (between Judges and Samuel) in the Greek canonical tradition leads to important biblical-theological implications of reading Ruth alongside Proverbs 31. One is the compatibility of the wisdom ideal (exemplified in the figure of Ruth) and the salvation-historical focus of the narrative book of Ruth (given the David linkage), for there is no evidence that these are competing or incompatible ways of interpreting the book. That the same book was read from these two perspectives by different ancient interpretive communities means that wisdom ways of thinking are no 'foreign body' within Old Testament theology more generally. In addition, or to say the same thing in a different way, this shows the essential relation between ethics and biblical theology, and that a biblical-theological approach does not need to deny or downplay the ethical import of Old Testament narratives.

Chapter Five

Ruth and the Psalter

In this chapter we will examine the canonical enjambment of the book of Ruth and the Psalter in the listing of Old Testament books provided by the Talmud, arguing that this encourages an exploration of possible links between the two books. Indeed, it is probable that in doing that we are simply following the path already trodden by the ancient readers who placed them together for this very reason. We will tease out the thematic links between Ruth and Psalms that include the key terms 'refuge', 'wings' and 'kindness', comment on the movement from lament to praise in both books, and explore the significance for biblical theology of the relationship between narrative and poetry as affirmed by the juxtapositioning of Ruth and Psalms.

The order of the books in the Writings (or Hagiographa), the third section of the tripartite Hebrew canon, fluctuates significantly in Jewish canonical tradition. An earlier tradition preserved in the sixth-century Babylonian Talmud tractate *Baba Bathra* (14b) reads: 'Our rabbis taught that the order of the prophets is Joshua and Judges, Samuel and Kings, Jeremiah and Ezekiel, Isaiah and the Twelve . . . The order of the Writings is Ruth and the Book of Psalms and Job and Proverbs, Ecclesiastes, Song of Songs and Lamentations, Daniel and the Scroll of Esther, Ezra[–Nehemiah] and Chronicles' (our translation).[1] The pairing of books is a noticeable feature of the listing, but what is most pertinent for the present discussion in this way of organizing the Old Testament books is that Ruth immediately precedes the Psalter. Louis Jacobs argues that 'order' (*sēder*) in this Talmudic passage means the chronological order in which the compilers of the various books of the Writings lived.[2] The implication is that Ruth comes at the head of the Writings because of the chronological principle that the events narrated belong to an early period in the history of Israel, the time of the judges.[3] The Talmud links the books

---

[1] For the text, see Epstein 1976.
[2] Jacobs 1991: 34.
[3] Rendtorff 1985: 245.

of Judges, Ruth and Samuel to the prophet Samuel as author or compiler, but the presence of the ten-generation genealogy leading to David in the final chapter of Ruth (4:18–22) was undoubtedly another factor taken into account by those who ordered the biblical books in this way.[4]

In this *baraita*,[5] the relevant listing is 'Ruth and book of Psalms and Job and Proverbs' (coupled together in the way indicated), so that this is a four-book mini-collection, with Ruth (ending with the genealogy of David) positioned as a preface to Psalms. It may well be that the book of Ruth is being treated as a kind of 'Davidic biography', since Ruth and Boaz are the great-grandparents of David (Ruth 4:18–22).[6] In fact, the same Talmudic passage goes on to note that there issued from Ruth the person of David who 'delighted' God with 'songs and praises',[7] and a little further down it is stated that 'David wrote the book of Psalms'. Jordan M. Scheetz comments that 'it is not difficult to see this rationale as a thematic link between Ruth and the book that follows, Psalms'.[8] The Psalter is indeed closely connected to David, for seventy-three psalmic titles forge a direct link to David by means of the phrase 'Of David' that refers to him as author. Interpreting 'Of David' (*lĕdāwid*) as a *lamed auctoris* is supported by the expansive title of Psalm 18, which reads: 'A psalm of David [*lĕdāwid*], the servant of the LORD, who addressed the words of this song to the LORD', and this is connected to the body of the psalm by the words 'He said' (cf. 2 Sam. 22:1–2a).[9] In other words, the ordering of the books in the *baraita* stresses the connection of Ruth with her famous descendant who was in large measure responsible for the Psalter. A similar canonical rationale appears to be at work in an alternative arrangement of the biblical books found in certain early medieval Hebrew codices (Aleppo and Leningrad) which place Chronicles at the head of the Writings, with Psalms following

---

[4] Also Beckwith 1985: 158–159.

[5] A *baraita* is a quotation preserving a pre-AD 200 tradition of the Tannaim, the rabbinic scholars of the first two centuries.

[6] For the multiple connections of the book of Ruth with things Davidic, see chapter 3.

[7] The use of the verb meaning 'to saturate, refresh' and, by extension 'to delight' (*rāwâ*) suggests a connection by means of wordplay with Ruth's name, *rût* (cf. *BT Ber.* 7b) (Jastrow 1996: 1459).

[8] Scheetz 2013: 25.

[9] See the discussion provided by Cooper 1983: 125. While accepting that the Hebrew preposition *lĕ* can have a range of meanings, Johnson argues that it is best to understand the Davidic psalms as put in the mouth of David and imagined as uttered by him (2009: 4–6).

it.[10] In its retelling of Israelite history, Chronicles presents David as the founder of the Jerusalem cult and organizer of temple worship (esp. 1 Chr. 13 – 16; 23 – 26), so that placing Psalms after it makes perfect sense.

The earliest (and best) position for the book of Ruth?

Some recent scholars have argued that we should privilege the canonical arrangement found in *Baba Bathra* as the oldest and the one that makes most sense,[11] with Roger Beckwith going so far as claiming that 'the position of Ruth in the Hagiographa is only explicable if it immediately precedes the Psalms'.[12] Beckwith finds the canonical order in which Ruth is read as providing the prehistory of David the chief psalmist totally compelling. Building on the work of Beckwith, scholars such as Steinberg, Koorevaar and Dempster take the order of the books in *Baba Bathra* as their starting point in analysing the Writings.[13] In the process, they make some interesting observations on the possible macro-structural role of the book of Ruth in the organization of the Writings as a canonical unit. Julius Steinberg sees Ruth as an introduction to the Psalter (due to the David link) and posits that Psalms and Chronicles provide the Writings with a historico-theological frame (with key themes in both books being the house of David and the house of God). Hendrik Koorevaar, for his part, notices that the book of Ruth and Chronicles both have genealogies, a David connection, and foreigners (Ruth/Cyrus) who act as instruments of God's universal purposes, and therefore he views them as forming an *inclusio* around the Writings as a canonical unit.[14] Stephen Dempster explains the logic of the canonical arrangement in *Baba Bathra* in this way: 'Following this "little book of David" is a "large book of David"', the Psalter,[15] but the main focus of his reading of the book of Ruth is the way in which it gives hope after

---

[10] Cf. McIvor 1993: 13: 'the position of Chronicles just before Psalms in the St Petersburg Codex [= Leningrad B19a] may have been because Chronicles, in which David plays such a leading role, was regarded as a good introduction to the book attributed to him' (our addition).

[11] E.g. Beckwith 1985: 122–127, 154–166.

[12] Beckwith 1985: 156.

[13] Steinberg 2006: 87–89, 183–186, 193–194; Koorevaar 1997; Dempster 2003: 35; 1997: 38–39, 202.

[14] Koorevaar 1997: 68.

[15] Dempster 2003: 194.

the record of the exile and the demise of the house of David at the end of 2 Kings.[16]

We see no reason to dispute the observations made, but the difficulty arises when, following the lead of Beckwith, they trace the Talmudic arrangement of the canonical books back as far as the second century BC and perhaps even earlier. The earliest conclusive evidence of a canon structured in this way is the Talmudic *baraita*,[17] and Beckwith's arguments to the contrary are not convincing. Even less likely is the view of Koorevaar, who opts for a still earlier dating for the origination of the tripartite canon in the fifth century BC, relying on what is said in 2 Maccabees 2:13 about Nehemiah founding a 'library' (*bibliothēkēn*) and collecting the books about the kings and prophets, the books of David and the letters of kings about votive offerings.[18] This probably refers to Samuel–Kings, Psalms and Ezra–Nehemiah (NB Ezra 7:14–20), but the limited information available about this initiative in collecting sacred books means that this historical notice fails to provide evidence of the existence of the tripartite canon (Tanak) at this early stage. In addition, the reference to Judas Maccabeus 'collecting all the books that had been lost' (*c.* 160 BC; 2 Macc. 2:14) cannot be interpreted to mean anything as specific as a classification and organizing of the canonical books in the Prophets and Writings sections, despite what Beckwith says.[19]

Commonly rehearsed arguments for the existence of a tripartite canon at an early period include supposed allusions in the Prologue to the Greek version of the Wisdom of Jesus ben Sira (*c.* 132 BC),[20] wherein, it is claimed, the grandson of Jesus ben Sira three times differentiates the three sections of the canon, calling the first two sections 'the law and the prophets (or prophecies)', though using a different expression each time for the third section, this indicating to Beckwith that this section did not yet have an agreed title. The names used for the supposed third section are: (1) 'and others that have followed in their [the prophets'] steps'; (2) 'and the other books of the fathers'; (3) 'and the rest of the books'. Given the general (and variable) wording, it is far from established that these are in fact references to canonical books or even to a stable literary

[16] Dempster 2003: 91, 193; 1997: 204.
[17] After a review of the evidence, this is also the conclusion of Steinmann (1999: 140).
[18] Koorevaar 1997: 50–51, 66.
[19] Beckwith 1985: 152.
[20] Beckwith 1985: 211–222.

corpus.[21] According to Lim, these are references to 'a third category of miscellaneous books of ancient Israelite literature'[22] that, with Scripture, formed a curriculum for the education of scribes and included Ben Sira's own book.

Beckwith sees the threefold structure of the Old Testament canon also reflected in the post-resurrection saying by Jesus recorded in Luke 24:44: 'everything written about me in the Law of Moses and the Prophets and the Psalms [*psalmoi*] must be fulfilled.' Beckwith views the third division as now given its own title (named after the first book or the most important book within the division),[23] but the designation 'Psalms' may refer only to that individual book, Jesus singling out the Psalter as a particularly important biblical witness to him. The reading of 'Psalms' as a synecdoche for a third canonical division is, in fact, a retrojection of later evidence from the Talmud.

Beckwith sees another dominical saying as alluding to the three groups of canonical books, namely: 'that on you may come all the righteous blood shed on earth, from the blood of innocent Abel to the blood of Zechariah the son of Barachiah, whom you murdered between the sanctuary and the altar' (Matt. 23:35; cf. Luke 11:51). This could reflect a canonical arrangement that began with Genesis and ended with Chronicles, seeing that the murder of Abel is recorded near the beginning of Genesis (4:3–15) and that of Zechariah near the end of Chronicles (2 Chr. 24:20–22).[24] However, the same sweep of Old Testament history could be referred to even if Chronicles was placed after Kings (as in the Greek canonical tradition), and R. Laird Harris correctly points out that Luke's wording is *temporal* rather than literary ('the blood of all the prophets, shed from the foundation of the world . . . from the blood of Abel to the blood of Zechariah').[25] According to H. G. L. Peels, these two particular murders are chosen only because in each case there is a call for divine vengeance.[26]

The arguments rehearsed above amount to the fact that the ordering of the biblical books in the early list preserved in *Baba Bathra* 14b

---

[21] Barton 2007: 47–48. It is counter-challenged by Beckwith, but not convincingly in our view; see Beckwith 1991. For the view that these expressions refer to non-canonical works, including Ben Sira, see Carr 2011: 161–162.

[22] Lim 2013: 94; also 101: 'It is an open-ended way of referring to books other than the law and prophecies.' For his full argument, see Lim 2013: 94–102.

[23] Beckwith 1985: 111–115.

[24] Though in Chronicles it is 'Zechariah *the son of Jehoiada*', and so the two individuals are not necessarily to be identified.

[25] Harris critiques Beckwith's argument; see Harris 1990: 79.

[26] Peels 2001; cf. Gallagher 2014.

was carefully constructed and makes a great deal of sense, and Beckwith and those who follow him have made a valuable contribution to the effort to explain the logic behind the canonical order found in the *baraita*. This achievement does not, however, prove what they think it does, namely the *originality* of this particular order, such that other (deviant) orders are demonstrated to be later disturbances of this artistic original.[27] The fact of the matter is that each of the different canonical orders (e.g. Ruth after Judges, Ruth after Proverbs 31, and Ruth preceding the Psalter) has its own logic, and no one order of books can be proved to be earlier and (therefore) better than the others.

Dividing up the book of Ruth

As we have seen, the various canonical orders of the biblical books are, in effect, a paratextual commentary provided for Scripture by ancient readers who read and understood the books in a particular way. Another aspect of this interpretive frame is the differing schemes of textual division *within* the books in the manuscript tradition.[28] The book of Ruth in its medieval Christian dress (its familiar form in the English Bible) has four chapters that convincingly divide the book into four episodes: leaving and returning to Bethlehem (ch. 1), the public meeting between Ruth and Boaz (ch. 2), the private meeting between Ruth and Boaz (ch. 3) and the resolution of the story at the city gate (ch. 4).[29] According to Marjo C. A. Korpel, the credibility of these subdivisions is supported by a chain of responsions (or refrains) between the final verses of the first three chapters: 'at the beginning of barley harvest' (1:22), 'until the end of the barley and wheat harvests' (2:23), and 'unless he has finished the matter today' (3:18).[30] This way of dividing the text reveals the episodic nature of the storytelling technique of the biblical author.

In terms of the impact of textual divisions on readers, material is highlighted by placing it at the beginning or end of a textual unit. This factor gives a verse at the opening or close of a unit maximum visibility,

---

[27] Cf. Beckwith 1985: 165: 'The three sections of the canon are not historical accidents but works of art.'

[28] For the unfortunate ignoring of this feature of ancient manuscripts by modern critical editions of the Bible, see Olley 2014.

[29] The present-day chapter divisions (capitulation) are those provided by Stephen Langton (1150–1228), university teacher in Paris and later Archbishop of Canterbury, who annotated the Latin Vulgate; see Smalley 1952: 221–224.

[30] Korpel 2001: 221–222.

and a verse so marked is understood as announcing a key theme, disclosing an important piece of information or perhaps summarizing the content of the demarcated section of text.[31] In the Hebrew Masoretic tradition, the book of Ruth is bifurcated into reading portions by a division (*seder*) at the start of 2:12,[32] thereby highlighting the statement by Boaz, who unknowingly forecasts Ruth's future. This particular division is not indicated in the text of the Leningrad Codex but it is in the Masoretic list of the codex.[33] An alternative reading tradition places the *seder* division at 3:13, just after Boaz's statement again commending Ruth and now pledging to do all that she asks (3:10–12).[34] In other words, some ancient Jewish readers noted the importance of the statements made by Boaz in 2:12 (the head verse in the second *seder*) and in 3:10–12 (the final verses of the first *seder* in an alternative division of the book into *sedarim*). Ruth 3:11 is a key text linking the book of Ruth and Proverbs through the common expression 'worthy woman' (*'ēšet-ḥayil*; cf. Prov. 31:10),[35] and Ruth 2:12 and 3:10 have a similar linking function to the Psalter (see below).

The halfway point in the book is marked by the Masoretes at 2:21, immediately after Naomi tells Ruth of the connection Boaz has with the family (2:20). In other words, each division serves to accentuate a crucial stage in the plot of the book of Ruth. The Hebrew divisions would seem to highlight what are in effect programmatic statements by Boaz and in this way foreground the part played by him in the redemption of Naomi's family. In doing so they redress the balance, for Naomi is the central character of the book (it is *her* crisis) and Ruth its main character (she is present in almost every scene), but Boaz also has an essential part to play in the drama about the restoration of family fortunes. The chapter divisions at 2:1 and 4:1 also put a focus upon Boaz, with the first verse revealing the fact of his existence and his kinship to Naomi, and the second narrating his decisive step of going up to the gate to 'settle the matter' (3:18). What we are seeking to illustrate is that different ways of dividing the biblical text reflect ancient reading practices and are significant for interpretation (and frequently contain an exegetical insight).

---

[31] For the possible functions of divisions, see Goswell 2012c: 224–225.

[32] Marked by a large Hebrew letter *sāmek* (the first letter of *seder*) in the margin of Hebrew Bibles.

[33] The *BHS* brackets the symbol: [*sāmek*]. It is not included in *BHQ*.

[34] The fact that the *seder* division comes after 3:12 has a cliffhanger effect, with Boaz revealing to Ruth (and the reader) that there is, however, a kinsman nearer than him.

[35] See chapter 4.

God as a refuge

Returning to our main point, the division of the biblical text in the Masoretic tradition suggests that Ruth 2:12 (at the head of the second *seder*) is a particularly important statement, containing as it does a cluster of key terms that find fuller elaboration either in Proverbs (recompense, reward) or in the Psalter (wings, refuge). In line with Boaz's commendation of Ruth for 'taking refuge' in Yahweh (2:12 [Hebrew root *ḥāsâ*]), the Psalter goes on to portray God helping her descendant David in his troubles. David is shown to be one who 'takes refuge' in God just as did Ruth herself (2:12: 'under whose wings you have come to take refuge'),[36] so that it could be said that Ruth is an embodiment of the implied ethic of the Psalter.

Jerome Creach views the first occurrence of the refuge motif in the Psalter as strategically placed as an addendum to Psalm 2 (the last line of 2:11: 'Blessed are all who take refuge in him'), signalling the importance of this concept in the subsequent psalms and encouraging those who use the Psalter to adopt this ethic. In Book I of the Psalter the term is repeatedly used to characterize the righteous (5:11 [Heb. 12]; 17:7; 18:30 [Heb. 31]; 31:19 [Heb. 20]; 34:8, 22 [Heb. 9, 23]; 36:7 [Heb. 8]; 37:40), and the fact that it is placed in the opening verse of various psalms (7:1 [Heb. 2]; 11:1; 16:1) confirms that seeking refuge in Yahweh is 'a key organizing feature' for this part of the Psalter.[37] In addition, a series of psalms in Book I focus on the character of the righteous person (Pss 15; 24; 34; 37), such that 'it seems plausible that Book I of the Psalter should be read as an extended picture of true piety, seen as total reliance on Yahweh and exemplified by David'.[38]

Later in the Psalter, in response to the crisis represented by the apparent failure of the Davidic covenant (Ps. 89), there is in Book IV the reaffirmation of the older Mosaic theology of the kingship of God (NB the title of Ps. 90: 'A Prayer of Moses, the man of God'), and the godly way of dealing with such a crisis is to take refuge in Yahweh (91:2, 4, 9). Then, towards the end of the Psalter, Psalm 118:8–9 states: 'It is better to take refuge in the LORD than to trust in man. It is better to take refuge in the LORD than to trust in princes' (cf. 142:4–5 [Heb. 5–6]; 144:3–4; 146:3). Human rulership (even that exercised by the Davidic house) will fail, but God can be relied on to

[36] Steinberg 2006: 444–445; cf. Creach 1996. In this section we acknowledge our dependence on Creach.
[37] Creach 1996: 77.
[38] Creach 1996: 80.

help and protect his people. Therefore, when the book of Ruth is placed before the Psalter as a preface, it can be understood as alerting the reader to what will be a fundamental affirmation of the Psalter, namely the need to rely on God alone.

God's wings

In Ruth 2:12 Boaz evokes the image of the protecting 'wings' of Yahweh, the God of Israel, a metaphor that apparently is in no need of explanation or elaboration, with its meaning immediately understood; and, indeed, this motif is found a number of times in the Psalter (17:8; 36:7 [Heb. 8]; 57:1 [Heb. 2]; 61:4 [Heb. 5]; 63:7 [Heb. 8]; 91:4). In this way, the ancestress of the chief psalmist anticipates the piety of David, who calls on God to defend and help him in his troubles. The similarity of these psalmic texts to Ruth 2:12 is noted by Kwakkel, who includes this text in his study of the metaphor of Yahweh's wings.[39]

That the Hebrew word (kĕnāpayim) does mean 'wings' and not the other lexical possibility, 'skirt' (e.g. Num. 15:38; 1 Sam. 24:4 [Heb. 5]), is shown by the parallel in Psalm 91:4, where the synonymous term 'pinions' is used ('He will cover you with his pinions, and under his wings you will find refuge').[40] It is plainly a metaphor for God's protection of his people, as also is the figure of the 'shadow' (ṣēl) which precedes 'wings' in four of these psalmic texts (e.g. 17:8: 'hide me in the shadow of your wings'). This understanding of the metaphor is confirmed by the Hebrew verbs used in association with it, namely 'to find refuge' (ḥāsâ) and 'to hide' (sātar). In addition, what is said in the parallel poetic line often supports the idea that the metaphor refers to divine defence and help – see Psalms 17:8a ('Keep me as the apple of your eye'); 57:1 (Heb. 2) ('till the storms of destruction pass by'); 63:7 (Heb. 8) ('for you have been my help'); or else the wider context does the same – see 36:6b (Heb. 7b) ('man and beast you save, O LORD'); 61:3 (Heb. 4) ('for you have been my refuge, a strong tower against the enemy'); and the content of Psalm 91 as a whole. Furthermore, in all these psalms (except Ps. 91) God's 'kindness' (ḥesed) is mentioned either in the verse which refers to God's wings (Ps. 36:7 [Heb. 8]) or in its immediate context (Pss 17:7; 36:5, 10 [Heb. 6, 11]; 57:3 [Heb. 4]; 61:7 [Heb. 8]; 63:3 [Heb. 4]). Psalm 91 makes mention

---

[39] Kwakkel 2010: 143. In what follows we acknowledge our dependence on Kwakkel 2010.

[40] Cf. the same parallel in Ps. 68:13 (Heb. 14) and Deut. 32:11.

of God's 'faithfulness' (*'emet*) in verse 4b, and this term is also found in Psalms 57:3, 10 (Heb. 4, 11) and 61:7 (Heb. 8).

The metaphor possibly originates from the habit of hens and other birds protecting their young by gathering them under their wings, though this avian mode of behaviour is never referred to in the Old Testament itself (but see Matt. 23:37 and Luke 13:34). LeMon rejects the idea that the wings of Yahweh allude to the wings of the cherubim in the temple, for in the Psalter the wings always belong to God himself, not to any creature in the service of God.[41] A more likely explanation of its origin is Ancient Near Eastern iconography which depicts winged gods and goddesses as a way of asserting their protective powers,[42] such that the authors of Psalms are drawing on (and adapting in the service of orthodox Israelite theology) a common stock of cultural images. An appreciation of the meaning and force of the metaphor does not, however, depend on discovering the precise birthplace of the imagery. Pointing to multiple references to the wings of Yahweh in the Psalms, Hawk views its use in Ruth 2:12 as a metaphorical depiction of God as the mighty warrior who fights for and protects his people,[43] so that God's providential ordering is to be discerned behind the happy outcome in the book of Ruth. Again, this thematic link between Boaz's description of Ruth and the book of Psalms that follows in the book order in *Baba Bathra* presents the heroine Ruth as a model of the piety of the Psalter.

Divine kindness

Divine 'kindness' is on show in the actions of Ruth (and Boaz) that result in the preservation of the family line that leads to David (1:8; 2:20; 3:10). Just as the heroine Ruth embodies and experiences God's 'kindness' (*ḥesed*), so also in the Psalter David praises God as the one who 'shows kindness (*ḥesed*) to his anointed, to David and his seed for ever' (18:50 [Heb. 51], our translation).[44] In Boaz's second commendation of Ruth (3:10),[45] her first act of 'kindness' is her willingness to return with Naomi from Moab (cf. 2:11), and her second (and greater) act of 'kindness' is her proposal of marriage to Boaz instead of accepting an offer of marriage from a younger man

---

[41] LeMon 2010: 83–94.
[42] For the ANE motif of winged deities, see LeMon 2010: 27–58.
[43] Hawk 2015: 81–82.
[44] For the 'kindness' theme in Ruth, cf. Rendtorff 2005: 53–64; Mays 1986: 143–155.
[45] His first commendation of Ruth is recorded in 2:11–12.

unconnected to the family. In each case, Ruth chooses what is good for the family in preference to her personal welfare and ease.

In the Psalter, David rejoices that God shows kindness to 'the king', in that his patron God upholds him and gives him victory over his enemies (21:7 [Heb. 8]). This is a significant connection between the book of Ruth and the theology of the Psalter. As might be expected after what is depicted in the story of Ruth, God's kindness extends to ordinary Israelites and to Israel as a whole, not just to the king, and the formula 'His kindness endures for ever' (our translation) becomes a refrain in a number of psalms (e.g. 100:5; 106:1; 107:1; 118:1–4; and esp. twenty-six times in Ps. 136). The Hebrew term 'kindness' expresses 'God's free commitment to his people',[46] and its repeated use in Psalm 136 shows that it 'is broadened in generalized prayer and praise to encompass all manifestations of God's power in action for his people'.[47] The term 'kindness' (ḥesed) is found some 127 times in the Psalter,[48] so that it would be no exaggeration to claim that it is a key word expressing Israel's experience of God's special favour and help in a variety of trying circumstances.

In her study of the meaning of ḥesed, Sakenfeld finds that it denotes a loyal and gracious act that, though rooted in an established relationship with the person(s) in need, goes beyond strict obligation. It is action above and beyond the call of duty,[49] hence our decision to translate ḥesed as 'kindness'.[50] In the case of the book of Ruth, though Boaz is a relative of Naomi, he is not strictly required by law or custom to go to the lengths that he does in helping to restore family fortunes (even marrying Ruth). According to Kraus, God's kindness 'is his liberating, saving, helping, healing mercy extended to Israel and to the poor in Israel. It implies action that changes destiny, that rescues, that constantly arises anew out of the perfection of Yahweh's grace and mercy.'[51] By means of Ruth and Boaz, who model (and are instruments of) God's 'kindness', the biblical reader is helped to see the graciousness of God's dealings with his needy people. With regard to the Psalms, a difference compared with the book of Ruth is that it is almost invariably divine ḥesed that is spoken of, with the lone

---

[46] Sakenfeld 1978: 167.
[47] Sakenfeld 1978: 167–168.
[48] Kraus 1986: 43.
[49] Sakenfeld 1978: 24, 233–234; 1985: 13, 39–42, 83–98. We acknowledge our dependence on Sakenfeld's fine discussion.
[50] In preference, for instance, to the common English renderings 'steadfast love' and 'loyalty'.
[51] Kraus 1986: 44.

exception being in Psalm 109, wherein the imprecation is expressed: 'Let there be none to prolong *ḥesed* to him' (v. 12), for 'he did not remember to do *ḥesed*' (v. 16), the moral failure being that the person cursed took advantage of the weak.

With regard to God, in the Psalter *ḥesed* is most commonly connected to the request for deliverance from enemies (e.g. 143:12: 'And in your kindness cut off my enemies' [our translation]). In Psalm 107 God's 'kindness' repeatedly shows itself in acts of deliverance with which it is, in effect, equated, for it is in parallel with 'his wondrous works' (vv. 8, 15, 21, 31). More frequently, the term *ḥesed* is nuanced as the ability to deliver in response to pleas for rescue from enemies and persecutors (e.g. 31:16 [Heb. 17]: 'save me in your kindness'; cf. 109:26; 143:12). According to Sakenfeld, a third nuance of *ḥesed* is God's willingness to deliver, when the psalmist asks that his life be spared in accordance with God's *ḥesed* (119:88, 149, 159). A fourth nuance is of *ḥesed* as God's 'protective care' (32:10; 36:10 [Heb. 11]), and a special incidence of this sense is the promise of God's protection for the Davidic house (2 Sam. 7; Ps. 89).[52] The events of the book of Ruth are another (not unrelated) demonstration of this brand of divine *ḥesed*. Finally, in the context of the penitential psalms, God's *ḥesed* is experienced by the psalmist as forgiveness, and as a consequence of forgiveness he helps, restores or heals (e.g. 6:1, 4; 86:5). In this last instance, it is especially plain that God's 'kindness' goes beyond behaviour strictly required by the covenantal bond. In summary, therefore, the book of Ruth anticipates (and supports) the broader theology of divine 'kindness' on display in the Psalter, and Ruth and Boaz are presented as vehicles of God's kindness and mercy to the family in distress.

The movement from lament to praise

Another similarity between the book of Ruth and the Psalter – noticeable when the two books are placed side-by-side as they are in the canonical list in *Baba Bathra* – is that in each book there is the same movement from lament to praise. In the case of the Psalter, Norman K. Gottwald, thinking in form-critical terms of the relative distribution of psalm types, noted that the early part of the Psalter is dominated by individual laments (mostly by David) but that it concludes in communal praise (e.g. Pss 107; 118; 124; 136). Gottwald

[52] On this, see chapter 3.

summarizes his observation in this way: 'there is a dramatic shift from the lamenting individual to the praising community.'[53] Without reference to Gottwald, Walter Brueggemann has taken this observation further and investigated 'how one gets from one end of the Psalter to the other'.[54] He noted that the Psalter is framed by Psalm 1, which prefaces the collection with a strong affirmation of Torah piety (the axiom that obedience leads to well-being), and by Psalm 150, which closes the Psalter with an unqualified call to praise God. His thesis is that the way from Torah obedience to unbridled praise is 'by way of candid lament that gives full expression to suffering and rage'.[55] Brueggemann pays special attention to three psalms that, he argues, form a sequence: at the centre of the Davidic lament Psalm 25 is a threefold petition for and affirmation of Yahweh's 'kindness' (*ḥesed*; vv. 6–7, 10); Psalm 73 enables a re-perception and reorientation to take place; finally Psalm 103 affirms the reality of God's 'kindness' (vv. 4, 8, 11, 17). In other words, a drama of hard-won faith is played out in the final form of the Psalter.[56]

Brueggemann finds a similar pattern in the drama of the book of Job,[57] but it is also not difficult to see the same process taking place in the book of Ruth. In the face of an inexplicable family tragedy, Naomi lashes out in accusation against the God whom she holds responsible for the deaths of her husband and two sons (1:20–21). Later, because of the attention lavished on Ruth by Boaz, Naomi praises him (and probably also Yahweh) for his 'kindness' (2:20); and at the end of the book, with the family restored in the person of infant Obed placed in Naomi's bosom (4:17), the crisis has been happily resolved and God's kindness vindicated and displayed. What is more, just as the focus of the Psalter moves from the individual to the community, in the book of Ruth the transition is from a lamenting individual (Naomi) to the rejoicing Bethlehemite community (elders, women) speaking of the prospects for and restoration of the family (4:11–12, 14–15). Last of all, the theme of 'kindness' (*ḥesed*) plays a key role in both books (as already demonstrated).

The similarities just noted are remarkable and not at all contrived, but within what conceptual framework are these resemblances to be understood? The biblical canon marks out an interpretive space

---

[53] Gottwald 1985: 535.
[54] Brueggemann 1991: 64.
[55] Brueggemann 1991: 72.
[56] For comments on Brueggemann's scheme, see Wilson 1992: 134–136.
[57] Brueggemann 1991: 89 n. 1.

within which texts, recognized as authoritative, interact and mutually inform each other.[58] The canon of Scripture fosters the interaction of texts, but only within a prescribed set of texts whose connection one with the other is neither arbitrary nor merely imagined by the reader.[59] Operating within the bounds of the canon, reading a biblical book in relationship with other biblical books both narrows the range of meanings it can conceivably have and opens up new interpretive possibilities as the contents of one canonical text throw light on another.[60] Those who approach Scripture with evangelical presuppositions see a divine Author standing behind the human authors of the different biblical books, superintending what is written and providentially ensuring the preservation of the canonical corpus, so that the detection of connections between canonical books by later readers of Scripture (say, common themes and patterns in Ruth and Psalms) does not need to be limited to what the biblical authors may have consciously intended. On this basis, the juxtapositioning of books (e.g. Ruth–Psalter) or their clumping in canonical groupings (e.g. Pentateuch, Four Gospels) is an indication that ancient readers saw the conjoined material as closely related (in some way) in meaning. In addition, the inclusion of a text (e.g. Ruth) in the canon affects how it is read, by expanding the context of interpretation beyond the original historical context (in so far as that is recoverable) to a new literary context in the 'library' of Scripture (e.g. Job is placed among *other* wisdom books, and Luke becomes part of the Four Gospel corpus rather than placed beside Acts).

Such inner-biblical interrelationships and resonances (and the modes of exegesis suited to their discovery and analysis) are not the same as 'intertextuality', a term we avoid because of the philosophical baggage it carries with it. Intertextuality is the free association of *all* texts, and, as usually understood and practised, challenges the idea of canon as a *fixed* group of texts, viewing canon as an illegitimate fence around Scripture that gives a privileged status to certain texts over other texts. For intertextuality there are no boundaries, and the result is that there is no settled context from which to determine the stable meaning of a text, for it may be compared and associated

---

[58] For this and what follows, see Vanhoozer 1998: 134–135.

[59] The interpretation of these set texts takes the form of the exegetical analysis of common themes, motifs, typology, quotations, allusions and echoes, both within the OT and across the testamental divide (see e.g. Beale 2012).

[60] Cf. Broyles 2001: 157.

with any text at all.[61] Without the concept of canon, a text is hermeneutically equidistant from all other texts. By contrast, the biblical canon places a limit on the possible interpretations of a text, for priority is given to relations with other biblical texts over possible relations with extra-canonical material.[62]

Ruth and the historical psalms

The conjoining of the book of Ruth and the Psalter in the listing of the books in the Writings provided by *Baba Bathra* 14b suggests the compatibility of story and psalm, of discourse and praise, in the canon of Scripture. This is also affirmed by the presence in the Psalter of the so-called 'historical psalms' which uncover the historical dimension and roots of the Israelite faith on show in the modes of appeal and praise (e.g. Pss 77; 78; 105; 106; 136).[63] In this context, it is appropriate to draw special attention to Psalm 78, for this psalm rehearses 'the glorious deeds' of Yahweh (78:4), and its survey of salvation history reaches its climax in God's choice of David (78:70–72). In other words, as in the book of Ruth, God's earlier dealings with his people are viewed by the psalmist (Asaph) as reaching their culmination in the special place given to David in the plans and purposes of God. The didactic flavour of the opening verses of the psalm (78:1–4) makes it obvious that the aim of Asaph is to draw theological and ethical lessons from the history of Israel.[64]

In addition, in Old Testament narrative it is often in the praise recorded in 'insert hymns' that significant and insightful biblical-theological linkages are discerned and celebrated as God's people reflect on the meaning of past and future events (e.g. Exod. 15:1–21; Deut. 32; Judg. 5; 1 Sam. 2:1–10; 2 Sam. 22; Dan. 2:20–23).[65] These psalms 'emphasize God's role in the events recounted by the surrounding stories' and in this way they bring to the fore the theological dimension of the events.[66] It seems that story and psalm need each other fully to disclose the revelation of God in history. For example, a theology of the Divine Warrior is on display in the 'Song of the Sea'

---

[61] On the question of defining intertextuality, see Sommer 1996: 487; and Meek 2014: 283.

[62] See Schulz 2010: 30.

[63] For a wider discussion of theology and history in Psalms, see Bullock 2011: 99–118.

[64] Longman 2014: 289–290.

[65] This is amply demonstrated by Watts 1992.

[66] Watts 2005: 291.

in Exodus 15 (15:3: 'The LORD is a man of war'). In this song, God is praised in his capacity as King, Warrior and Creator, who, using wind and water as his weapons, overthrew the Egyptian enemy and rescued his afflicted people. By embedding such psalmic material in Old Testament narrative, historical events and theological 'commentary' on these events are conjoined and their separation is declared to be invalid from a canonical viewpoint (in contrast to the post-Enlightenment opposition of fact against faith). It is not surprising, therefore, that such 'historical' material is also to be found in the Psalter, thereby highlighting God's involvement in the events that made up the history of Israel and determined their destiny (e.g. the allusion to the miraculous events at the Red Sea in Ps. 77:11–20). Likewise, the interpretive move of placing the book of Ruth next to the Psalter is an act of recognition by devout ancient readers that the God whose 'kindness' is praised in the theology of the Psalms proved to be just such a God in the experience of the needy family of Naomi.

The historical superscriptions in the Psalter, specifying the circumstances which gave rise to them, also show the link between their poetic expressions of pious sentiment and historical events, in this case mostly happenings in the life of David as recorded in the books of Samuel (e.g. 2 Sam. 15 and the title of Ps. 3 [Heb. 3:1]: 'A Psalm of David, when he fled from Absalom his son'). The thirteen psalms that have historical superscriptions that depict David in times of peril are Psalms 6; 7; 18; 34; 51; 52; 54; 56; 57; 60; 63; and 142. Together they provide a portrait of David as one who turned to God and implored his help in dire circumstances. In that sense, they supplement (and adjust) the presentation of David found in the books of Samuel. For example, Psalm 51 fills out substantially the terse expression of penitence made by David in response to Nathan's rebuke for his adultery and recorded in 2 Samuel 12:13 ('I have sinned against the LORD'). It is not the case, however, that we are shown a completely different David in the Psalms from the one we find in the books of Samuel, though there is a shift in focus. For example, the one brief appeal by David to God in the account of Absalom's rebellion (2 Sam. 15:31: 'O LORD, please turn the counsel of Ahithophel into foolishness') is given much fuller elaboration in Psalm 3.[67] As noted by Johnson, rather than focusing on David as king, these psalms emphasize 'elements of David's history that would have been common

---

[67] See the connections drawn between the psalm and the account in 2 Sam. (e.g. the sleep motif) by Johnson 2009: 14–27.

to all',[68] namely when he was falsely accused (Ps. 7), guilty of adultery (Ps. 51) or feeling isolated (Ps. 142). By these means, David becomes a model of behaviour for the godly in general.

The same kind of thinking seems to lie behind the post-authorial move to place the story of Ruth in front of the Psalter, in effect making them canonical conversation partners. This is an example of 'canon logic',[69] wherein the placing of biblical books in a sequence reflects the interpretive evaluations of early readers, who placed particular Bible books in positions that made sense to them, and, subsequent to this, the canonical order(s) of the books became a guide for later readers.[70] A persistent problem for those attempting to construct a theology of the Old Testament has been the difficulty of meaningfully combining history and theology,[71] and behind this duality stands the old dichotomy of fact and faith. The implication we draw from the canonical shape of the Old Testament (our focus being the Ruth–Psalter collation) is that it implies a certain interpretation of the theology of the Old Testament,[72] one that includes the conviction that beliefs about God's character and his ways are not arbitrary or flights of human imagination but are generated and sustained by Israel's historical experience of God's 'kindness' (e.g. as exemplified in the story of Ruth). In this way, the 'ugly ditch' between fact and faith is bridged.

Conclusion

It is plain that the book of Ruth was read from (at least) three perspectives by different ancient interpretive communities, and there is no evidence that these are competing or incompatible ways of interpreting the canonical book. Chapter 4 demonstrated the compatibility of the wisdom ideal epitomized in the figure of Ruth with the salvation-historical focus of the narrative of the book of Ruth (given the David linkage). In the present chapter, in probing the relation of the book of Ruth to the Psalter, we have shown that the

---

[68] Johnson 2009: 4.

[69] The expression is that of Wall (2002: 26–27), who draws on Outler 1980.

[70] As recognized, for example, by Childs 1979: 564. Childs, however, explores only the possible significance of the Judges–Ruth sequence of the Greek Bible.

[71] For a survey that brings out this point, see Ollenburger, Martens and Hasel 1992.

[72] Likewise, Bockmuehl asks 'whether the shape of the New Testament itself may outline an implied interpretation of its own theology' (2006: 103). He goes on to argue that 'the macrostructure of the New Testament canon can be seen to give important pointers to its implied meaning as a received whole' (2006: 108–109).

prayer and praise of God's people recorded in the Psalter is rooted in the salvific experience of God as the refuge and protector of his people and the one who shows kindness to them. One result is that readers are influenced to view the heroine Ruth as a model of a piety of the same variety as her illustrious royal descendant who composed many of the psalms.

An ever-present danger in our reading of Scripture is that we may compartmentalize different aspects of God's truth that actually belong inseparably together. In this regard, an implication of what we have explored in this chapter is that we need a broad definition of biblical theology, namely one that is wider than simply a 'salvation history' approach and includes ethics and doxology. In summary: biblical theology is grounded in real historical events (including the 'small town' story of Ruth); it informs and empowers ethical living; and it leads to and finds expression in prayer and praise.

Chapter Six

Famine in Ruth

Since there is no explicit evaluation by the narrator, interpreters are divided over how to evaluate Elimelech's decision to take his family out of the Promised Land. Some commentators view Elimelech's actions as springing from a lack of trust in God and the subsequent tragedies as God's punishment.[1] Other commentators argue that the tragic events should be understood as incidental details that function to set the scene for the following plot.[2] In this chapter we will probe this conundrum from the perspective of biblical theology. We will first trace the motif of famine through the Old Testament and then we will apply this understanding to see what light it sheds on the events at the beginning of the Ruth narrative. Finally, we will follow the biblical-theological trajectory of famine and hunger to sketch some contemporary Christian implications.

Patriarchal responses to famine

Famine is an extreme scarcity of food affecting a large number of people usually caused by climate changes, especially drought.[3] In the Bible, other causes include hailstorms (Exod. 9:22–25), insects (e.g. Joel 1:4), enemy invasion (Deut. 28:49–51; cf. Judg. 6:3–5) and siege (e.g. 2 Kgs 6:24–25; 25:1–3). Along with pestilence and warfare, famine is one of the classical triad of catastrophes (e.g. 2 Chr. 20:9; Jer. 14:12; Ezek. 6:11; Rev. 6:8). Since the patriarchal narratives are prior to the Ruth narrative within the storyline of the Old Testament, they form part of the background to understanding Elimelech's decision. That the patriarchal narratives form part of the interpretive grid for a reader of Ruth is supported by the explicit references to characters and episodes from Genesis. Famine and infertility are motifs common to the Ruth narrative and most of the sojourn accounts in Genesis, and parallel phrases in the description

---

[1] E.g. Baylis 2004: 420–422; Block 1999: 624, 626–627; Younger 2002: 429.
[2] E.g. Bush 1996a: 67; Eskenazi and Frymer-Kensky 2011: 6, 8; Sakenfeld 1999a: 21; and for an extended defence of this position, see Chisholm 2013: 592–600.
[3] Material in this chapter has been adapted with permission from Lau 2012–2016a.

of Elimelech's sojourn and Abraham's first sojourn reinforce the connection.[4]

Both Abraham and Isaac migrated to escape famine (Gen. 12:10; 26:1). Scholars have noted the similarities between the two accounts, as well as the description of Abraham's sojourn in Gerar, which was not due to famine. These three sojourn accounts contain similar elements (see Table 1).[5]

Table 1: Comparison of sojourn accounts in Genesis

Element	Genesis 12:10–20	Genesis 20:1–18	Genesis 26:1, 7–17
Migration	Abraham sojourns in Egypt because of famine (v. 10)	Abraham sojourns in Gerar (v. 1)	Isaac sojourns in Gerar because of famine (v. 1)
Deception	Abraham tells Sarah to say that she is his sister (vv. 11–13)	Abraham tells Abimelech that Sarah is his sister (v. 2a)	Isaac tells men that Rebekah is his sister (v. 7)
Abduction	Pharaoh takes Sarah (vv. 14–16)	Abimelech takes Sarah (v. 2b)	No abduction
Deliverance	The LORD afflicts Pharaoh (v. 17)	The LORD rebukes Abimelech in a dream (vv. 3–8)	Abimelech sees Isaac caressing Rebekah (v. 8)
Confrontation	Pharaoh rebukes Abraham (vv. 18–19)	Abimelech rebukes Abraham (vv. 9–13)	Abimelech rebukes Isaac (vv. 9–16)
Conclusion	Abraham leaves with wealth (v. 20)	Abimelech rewards Abraham; Abraham prays for Abimelech (vv. 14–18)	Isaac separates from Abimelech (v. 17)

The main theological point of these similarities is to emphasize the continuity in the covenant from Abraham to Isaac. The common thread is a threat to the covenant, yet the covenant continues with Abraham's descendants, starting with Isaac. The lack of narratorial comment on Abraham's sojourn in Egypt (Gen. 12:10–20) makes it difficult to evaluate his actions with certainty. On the one hand,

---

[4] Block (1999: 626 n. 611) lists the parallel phrases: (1) announcement of famine (*wayhî rāʿāb bāʾāreṣ*, 'there was a famine in the land'); (2) description of departure (*wayyēlek*, 'and he went' [Ruth 1:1]; *wayyēred*, 'and he went down' [Gen. 12:10]); and (3) purpose in going (*lāgûr*; 'to sojourn').

[5] Adapted from Garrett 2000: 130.

that the famine was 'severe' (v. 10) suggests that Abraham had 'no other option'.[6] His intention to sojourn in Egypt for only a short time signals his intention to return to the Promised Land. On the other hand, the lack of God's direct intervention with Abraham by action or word suggests his disapproval.[7] This understanding is reinforced by the contrast of Abraham's rebuke by a pagan king, whereas in the past God favoured Abraham with his voice.[8] Abraham's subsequent actions born of fear instead of faith may indicate that his original motive for leaving Canaan was the same.[9] This latter reading views Abraham as faltering in the face of this stern trial from God.

Based on this understanding, it is noteworthy that when Isaac is about to leave the Promised Land for Egypt, God commands him to stay. Just like his father, Isaac is faced with a trial because of famine (26:1). God's command to stay is backed up with a promise: God vows his ongoing protection and provision (26:3a). God then re-iterates the promises he made in his covenant with Abraham: land, offspring, blessing (26:3b–4; 22:16–18). In obedience, Isaac remains in Gerar (26:6) and, despite his subsequent lapse of faith (26:7–11), God ultimately blesses him with abundant crops, flocks and herds (26:12–14).[10] In fact, the hundredfold yield from the crop demonstrates that Isaac didn't need to seek food in Egypt. Thus, the strong hint from God's command to Isaac to remain in the land is that the default location for his people is Canaan, the land that he promised to them. Indeed, although there might be a famine, God can still bless abundantly.

This understanding is affirmed in the episode with Jacob, which is the exception that reinforces the general principle. By this time Jacob is the elderly patriarch of a seventy-strong household (46:27). He has just received news that his favourite son, Joseph, is still alive and ruling in Egypt (45:25–28).[11] There is a famine in the land of Canaan but although Jacob sends his sons to gather food from Egypt, he himself

---

[6] Wenham 1987: 287.

[7] Waltke and Fredricks 2001: 212.

[8] Waltke and Fredricks 2001: 212.

[9] Cf. Janzen 1993: 24; Kidner 1967: 116.

[10] God's blessing despite some of Abraham's actions is highlighted by the commentators, e.g. Hamilton 1995: 200: 'These blessings are certainly not the divine response to model obedience by the patriarch.' However, Isaac's decision to remain in Gerar was an act of obedience deriving from faith.

[11] Of course, Joseph left the Promised Land, but he was taken against his will (Gen. 37:23–36).

is reluctant to leave the Promised Land.[12] So God appears to him in a dream, confirming his identity as the same covenantal God, and reassuring him that it is his will for him to go down to Egypt (46:2–4). God comforts Jacob by promising that he will continue to be with him, even outside the Promised Land, and will bring him back.

A comparison of the migrations of Jacob and Abraham is instructive. In both cases, famine is the trigger for migration. Abraham goes to Egypt without God's clear direction and the result is that his family is placed in jeopardy. Jacob goes to Egypt under God's guidance and the patriarch preserves his family.[13] In short, the general principle that can be drawn from the patriarchal narratives is this: the default location for God's people is the Promised Land unless God specifically instructs them to leave.[14]

Famine and God's purposes in the rest of the Old Testament

In contrast to Ancient Near Eastern beliefs in various gods who controlled rain and fertility, Israel understood Yahweh to be one who controlled the rains (e.g. Ps. 65:9–13) and hence also produce or famine. The one who created the world also controls nature, the seasons, and provides for all (cf. Deut. 28:12). Hence, famines are used by God for his purposes (e.g. Ps. 105:16–17).

One of these purposes is to punish his people for their disobedience to the covenant (Lev. 26:19–29; Deut. 28:23–24, 38–42; 32:23–24). During the reign of King David, there is a famine for three years (2 Sam. 21:1) because Saul had broken a vow (Josh. 9:15, 18–26) and put the Gibeonites to death. The famine is reversed after restitution is made for the killing (2 Sam. 21:1–14). The famine in Samaria during the time of Ahab is judgment against Israel's Baal worship, which was promoted by Ahab (1 Kgs 16:29–34). The description of neither rain nor dew falling to the earth points to the severity of the drought (1 Kgs 17:1; 18:2; cf. Luke 4:25). In this context the confrontation with the prophets of Baal proves that Yahweh is the true God (1 Kgs

---

[12] Wenham (1994: 441) explains: '[Jacob's] apprehension must . . . be assumed to arise out of the clash between the patriarchal promise of the land and his present necessity and desire to see Joseph.'

[13] Cf. Waltke and Fredricks 2001: 570.

[14] Baylis (2004: 421) argues this more strongly: 'While there were no warnings in the Mosaic Covenant about leaving the land, departure from the land was so unthinkable it was only mentioned as a judgment.'

18:20–40). God's sovereignty is underlined by his subsequent breaking of the famine (1 Kgs 18:41–46). The law also uses famine as a threat to encourage obedience to the requirements of the covenant (Deut. 11:13–17).

However, that is not to say that famine is always due to the disobedience of God's people. Sometimes the biblical account does not directly state that famine is punishment for sin. For instance, the famines in the time of the patriarchs are not specifically attributed to particular sins of God's people.[15] Within God's purposes, famine drives God's people to Egypt, where God's promise of offspring and nationhood is fulfilled (Gen. 46:3).[16] The sojourn in Egypt is 'part of the development of God's plan for this chosen family' (Gen. 12:1–3; cf. 15:13–14).[17] Even the parallel between Abraham's first sojourn and God's later deliverance of Israel from Egypt points to God's sovereignty.[18] Part of God's plan also includes judgment on Egypt and their gods during Israel's exodus (Gen. 15:14; cf. Exod. 6:6; 12:12).

Other sections of the Old Testament, especially the wisdom literature, loosen a strict correspondence between sin and suffering. Books such as Job, Proverbs and Ecclesiastes present a different angle on mechanistic retribution. Although an attentive reading of Proverbs will reveal that retribution is already flexible (e.g. Prov. 10:4; cf. 13:23), it is in Job that God's sovereignty over all creation is particularly prominent. Job's friends wrongly adhere to a mechanistic view of retribution but God's speech emphatically denies this (Job 38 – 41). God is intimately caring for all his creation and he will act justly. However, this does not mean that he will be bound to a 'reductionistic human concept of retributive justice in which he can do no more than reward righteousness and punish wickedness'.[19] The causes of famine and suffering are not always revealed to us; ultimately, God is free in his sovereignty.[20]

Indeed, another purpose of famine is that God may use times of scarcity to test his people (cf. Deut. 8:2–6). One response is to leave

---

[15] Some suggest that the famines could be due to the sins of the Canaanites; cf. McKeown 2008: 131.

[16] Sarna (1989: 313): 'A family visit is thereby transformed into an event of national significance with its preordained place in God's scheme of history.'

[17] Hamilton 1995: 591.

[18] For a list of similarities between Gen. 12:10 – 13:4 and Gen. 41:54b – Exod. 12:42, see Sailhamer 1992: 142.

[19] Wilson 2008: 154. Retributive justice is not the only principle that God uses to relate with people in his world.

[20] In his sovereign freedom God still acts consistently with his revealed character.

the Promised Land in search of food (e.g. Abraham and Isaac). However, the better response of his people in this situation is to remain in the land, continue to obey and fear God, and to trust God to provide (Deut. 8:1–20) – that is, unless God gives the word to leave the land. This exception was noted above in relation to the patriarchal narratives and is also seen in the time of the monarchy. Through Elisha, God directs the Shunammite woman to sojourn 'wherever you can' because God is going to bring a seven-year drought upon Israel (2 Kgs 8:1). She leaves for Philistine territory, returning to Israel at the end of the famine (2 Kgs 8:2).

Whatever the reason for famine, the general rule is that God will provide for his people. This theology is found in the Psalms. Even during famine, God will remain steadfastly faithful to those who fear him (Ps. 33:18–19). Similarly, the blameless will enjoy abundance in times of shortage (Ps. 37:19). In the book of Job, Eliphaz reinforces the idea that, although God might bring discipline through hardship, including famine, he will redeem his people from death (Job 5:17–27). God's provision for and preservation of the faithful is seen in the life of Elijah. Although there was a famine in the land, God still provided for him (1 Kgs 17:1–6).

There were many consequences of famine. Primarily, because for most of its history Israel was a subsistence agrarian society, famines were a threat to life itself. Those who were not able to store up excess produce in times of plenty were under greater threat during times of famine. Scarcity of food also led to increased demand and hence inflated prices (e.g. 2 Kgs 6:24–25). Hunger and physical weakness would leave populations vulnerable to external attack. The lack of food and the collapse of local economies would force people to sojourn elsewhere, as seen in the historical examples above. At an emotional level, despair was an understandable response to famine. Mourning, lamentation and distress are all found in Judah's response to drought (Jer. 14:1–6).

The extent to which people would avoid famine if at all possible is vividly illustrated in the interchange between King David and God. David had sinned by performing a census on his army instead of trusting God (2 Sam. 24:1–10; 1 Chr. 21:1–6). In response God gave him a choice of three years of famine, three months of the sword (attack by Israel's enemies) or three days of pestilence. David chose the one he considered to be the least harmful – pestilence (2 Sam. 24:13–15; 1 Chr. 21:12–14). The book of Lamentations suggests that those who perish by the sword are better off than those who suffer from famine (Lam. 4:9). Thus, famine was the most-feared catas-trophe, most likely because of the drawn-out and excruciating nature of the suffering. Famine can be so severe – especially during a siege – that it can lead to cannibalism (cf. Deut. 28:56–57; 2 Kgs 6:28–29; Jer. 19:9; Lam. 2:20; 4:10; Ezek. 5:10).

God also uses famine to draw his people back to himself. Haggai rebukes the people for disobeying God by neglecting to rebuild the temple. In response to their disobedience, God had withheld the dew, and the people experienced a lack of food (Hag. 1:10–11). God makes it clear that he sent the famine so that the people might repent from their sin (2:17). Once they obeyed God by starting to rebuild the temple, he would be keen to reverse the agricultural curses. The faithfulness of the people would lead to the blessing of harvests again (2:19).

In addition to repentance, prayer and supplication is another appro-priate response of God's people to famine. At the dedication of the temple, King Solomon envisaged a time of famine in the land as a result of lack of rain (1 Kgs 8:35). Again the cause is sin, and the correct response would be to repent. The people are also to pray to God, and Solomon pleads that God might listen to their prayers and respond by breaking the drought (8:36).

To summarize our understanding of famine in the Old Testament:

- It is often described as a judgment from God because of Israel's sin.
- It demonstrates God's superiority over other gods (esp. Baal).
- God uses famine to turn people back to him.
- Trust in God is essential during times of famine.
- In general, God's favour will rest on the righteous, even during famine.
- Yet the wisdom literature warns us that the general rule is not always applied mechanistically: God's will is supremely sovereign; his ways are beyond our understanding.

We'll keep these points in mind as we consider famine in the book of Ruth.

Famine in the book of Ruth

The historical setting for Ruth is the period of the judges. At this time, Elimelech and his family emigrated to Moab because of a famine.[21] The exact time during the period of judges is not specified.[22] The mention of this historical period is probably meant to recall the period in general. What in particular is the reader of the book of Ruth meant to recall? Two linked characteristics stand out. First, it is a time when there is 'no king' (Judg. 17:6; 18:1; 19:1; 21:25). This absence anticipates the narrative directly leading to King David (esp. Ruth 4:17–22). Second, it is a time characterized by what has been dubbed a 'Deuteronomic Cycle' (Judg. 2:11–19). Israel's obedience to God and his commands would lead to blessing, including productivity of crops and livestock, and defeat of their enemies (Deut. 28:1–14). Disobedience would lead to curses, including famine, infertility and defeat by their enemies (Deut. 28:15–68). With this background, it is likely that the beginning of the Ruth narrative is during a time of disobedience in the Deuteronomic Cycle, when Israel is suffering the covenant curse of famine.[23]

The verbs used to describe Elimelech and his family's progress indicate their intentions. Originally, it was meant to be a short stay or sojourn (*gûr*; Ruth 1:1) in Moab, but they end up settling there (*wayyihyû-šām*; v. 2) and ultimately living there (*yēšēbû šām*; v. 4) for at least ten years.[24] Since Elimelech chose to take his family out of the Promised Land, it seems likely that the food shortage affected the whole of Israel (Ruth 1:1). Climatically, Moab could have received more rain than Israel because the Transjordan plateau is higher than the Cisjordan in some sections. Hence, rain would fall on the western

---

[21] Historical climatology has found a general warming in Europe and the Near East from 1200 to 900 BC, approximating to the pre-monarchic and some of the monarchic period (Neumann and Parpola 1987). Just a 1°C rise in mean winter temperatures can reduce rainfall by up to 30 mm. Assyrian and Babylonian data from this time period record crop failure, famines and nomadic incursions (Neumann and Parpola 1987). The incursions are thought to result from a lack of food in the nomads' own lands.

[22] Jewish commentators place Ruth either in the period described in Judg. 17 – 21 or in the time of Ibzan (Judg. 12:8–10); so Malbim and Babylonian Talmud *Baba Bathra*, respectively.

[23] Yet the time of Judges is not presented as a never-ending cycle, but a downward spiral, which by the end of the book leads to moral and societal anarchy. This degeneration is attributed to the absence of an Israelite king. The degeneration of Israelite society is reflected in the degeneration of the cycle, with the last two cycles lacking rest from enemies altogether. The judges lead well enough to begin with, but their leadership degenerates so that the last judge, Samson, is almost unrecognizable as a judge. The book of Judges suggests that the time is ripe for a human king, under God the true King, to step in to recover the dire situation.

[24] The family could have stayed in Moab for ten years in total or the ten years could refer to the period after the sons were married. Since the Hebrew phrase is best taken as a summary, the former is more likely; see Bush 1996a: 94.

margins of Moab. However, as we discussed above, a lack of rainfall can also be interpreted theologically.

If famine was the result of Israel's disobedience, the correct response would have been to turn back to God. Understood within the context of our overview of famine in the Bible, Elimelech and his family should have remained in the Promised Land and repented or called for their fellow Israelites to repent. Continued trust in God to provide, coupled with supplication to God to end the famine, would have been another appropriate response. If Abraham's migration can be evaluated as springing from a lack of trust in God, then Elimelech's migration can be viewed similarly, considering the close parallels in the two accounts.[25] Moreover, the general rule that God would still provide for the righteous, those who feared him, is reflected in the survival of at least some who remained in Bethlehem (Ruth 1:19).[26] From a literary perspective, those who remained are a foil for the family who abandoned the Promised Land. Of course, we don't want to make too much of a gap in the narrative, but the silence about any direct word from God for Elimelech to leave Bethlehem is also consistent with our reading.

Nonetheless, as mentioned at the beginning of this chapter, this reading of Ruth within the covenantal background is not the only possible interpretation. Some readers might consider the proposed reading too mechanistic or reductionistic, and there may be some truth to this. Reading Ruth within the broader biblical-theological context warns us against holding too tightly to the proposed reading. Sections of the wisdom corpus urge us to leave room for God's free sovereignty. The lack of narratorial judgment about Elimelech's actions and the cause for the subsequent tragedies also allows for this line of reading. Moreover, the book of Ruth is closely tied to wisdom traditions in certain canons of the Old Testament.[27] Other wisdom elements could include:

1. the quiet providence of God, working behind the scenes;
2. the focus on daily life, its difficulties, and the use of cleverness to overcome obstacles;
3. the openness to other nations;

---

[25] The parallels are detailed in n. 4 above.

[26] In Ruth 1:19 some of the womenfolk of the town who knew Naomi before she left for Moab are amazed and almost in disbelief when they see her again upon her return to Bethlehem.

[27] See chapter 4.

4. the parallels between Proverbs 31:10–31 and Ruth (3:11);
5. the description of the character of Ruth, filling out the emphasis on character in Proverbs 1 – 4 and the sentence sayings.

Ruth is not a wisdom text, but these wisdom elements can be identified.[28] Hence, a weaker interpretation of retribution in Ruth is possible. On balance, however, since the covenantal context is more prominent in the book of Ruth, the stronger interpretation of retribution is the better reading.

Hunger in the book of Ruth

In the book of Ruth, closely connected to the motif of famine is the concept of hunger. Primarily, the narrative emphasizes physical hunger. Ironically, Elimelech and his family leave Bethlehem (*bêt leḥem,* 'house of bread') because they are starving. Naomi and Ruth return to Bethlehem hungry, compelling Ruth to seek food in the fields. In God's providence, he provides abundantly through Boaz. Ruth is satiated in Boaz's field, but also returns to Naomi with gleanings and roasted grain to relieve her mother-in-law's hunger (2:18). As interpreters of Ruth have noted, Boaz's down payment of barley points to a longer-lasting and more significant satiation for Naomi and her family (3:17; cf. 4:13–22).[29] The seed of Boaz would bring fullness and blessing not only to one destitute Israelite family but for all Israel, then for all peoples of the earth (cf. Matt. 1:1–17).

Along with physical hunger, a spiritual hunger can be detected in the book of Ruth. Although named *'ĕlîmelek,* 'My God is King', his departure from the Promised Land reflects a lack of recognition of God's sovereignty, of trust in God: a spiritual emptiness.[30] A father's practical apostasy has physical outcomes – barrenness in both his sons' marriages, and three deaths. In this light, Naomi's return is not only physical but also spiritual. The fact that the Hebrew word for 'return' (*šûb*) is also the word for 'repentance' opens the possibility of a deeper meaning than just a physical return. The author draws attention to

---

[28] Our thanks to Lindsay Wilson for these suggestions; personal correspondence, 24 June 2014.

[29] The gift of grain from Boaz not only provides food but also symbolizes future progeny. See Green 1982: 63–64; Sakenfeld 1999a: 66; Stone 2013b: 196–199.

[30] For a discussion of the irony of Elimelech's name and his actions, see Saxegaard 2010: 61–65.

this motif in chapter 1 by using the word twelve times (1:6, 7, 8, 10, 11, 12, 15 [x2], 16, 21, 22 [x2]).[31] The use of the word at the beginning and end of the chapter forms an *inclusio*, completing the journey motif, but not only in a geographical sense.

We are not told how much input Naomi had in the decision to leave the Promised Land. As the family departs, Elimelech is the subject of the verbs, with the rest of the family's participation secondary. At the end of the chapter, however, when Naomi returns she states, '*I* went away' (1:21), not '*We* went away'. Here Naomi claims some initiative and responsibility for the decision to leave Israel.[32] It seems that the family's departure was not purely a unilateral decision on Elimelech's part.[33]

Naomi's situation improves markedly when she decides to return to Israel. Upon hearing that Yahweh has broken the famine, she returns to Bethlehem. This sets in train a series of events that leads to her being blessed again. The upturn in her fortunes could be viewed as coincidental; but, from a biblical-theological viewpoint, departure from and return to the land is often more than just a physical departure. When Moses foresees Israel's disobedience leading to their expulsion, he also foresees their restoration, but only after the people of Israel return to God or repent (*šûb*; Deut. 30:1–5).[34] 'Return' is also regularly used by the Prophets for repentance. Amos's indictments particularly resonate with the Ruth narrative. The prophet indicts Israel for not repenting (*šûb*), despite God having sent famine, pestilence and the sword (Amos 4:6–11). Amos specifically states that God deliberately withheld rain in Israelite towns to induce Israel to repent, but they did not (4:7–8). These biblical texts, one from the Law and one from the Prophets, suggest that Naomi's return is not only physical; it is also a repentance from sin, a turning back to, and an acknowledgment of trust in, God. Hers was a return to God's sphere of blessing.

Indeed, this is consistent with the Old Testament focus on the relational, rather than the material, component of blessing. 'Blessing' is the central element of God's foundational promise to Abraham,

---

[31] The word *šûb* is used only three times in the rest of the book (2:6; 4:3, 15).

[32] Cf. Webb 2000: 42; Zakovitch 1999: 103.

[33] Other biblical texts support a wife's influence in decision-making. Many examples can be adduced, including Eve (Gen. 3:6), Rebekah (Gen. 27:46 – 28:5), Samson's wife (Judg. 14:15–20), Bathsheba (1 Kgs 1:11–31) and Job's wife (Job 2:9–10).

[34] The initiative, however, lies with the LORD, who enables repentance through a circumcision of the heart (Deut. 30:6); see Barker 2004: 163–168.

stated five times in two verses (Gen. 12:2–3). God's blessing includes a material component, land and offspring (12:2–3, 7).[35] Yet the fulfilment of God's promises to Abraham is the result of him obeying God, living rightly before God. Material abundance is a sign of God's blessing but this flows from a right relationship with God.[36] That living in right relationship with God is the highest blessing is reiterated elsewhere in the Old Testament. For instance, among the blessings listed for obeying God we find this description: 'I will make my dwelling among you, and my soul shall not abhor you. And I will walk among you and will be your God, and you shall be my people' (Lev. 26:11–12). In other words, living in sweet fellowship with God is the ultimate blessing.

If we hold this understanding of blessing, it makes some sense of Ruth's 'return' (*šûb*) to Bethlehem. The narrator states that Naomi returned, but he/she also specifies that Ruth 'returned from the country of Moab' (1:22). In a physical sense, it makes no sense for Ruth to 'return' to Israel. Yet in a spiritual sense, it is only when Ruth repents – that is, turns to trust in Yahweh (1:16–17) – that she begins to be blessed and becomes a blessing to others.[37] For it is through Ruth (and Boaz) that Naomi's emptiness/hunger (1:21) is satiated by the end of the Ruth narrative (4:14–17). Thus, Naomi's fullness can also be understood not only in physical terms, but also spiritual – a return to right relationship with Yahweh, and the blessings that flow from that relationship.

Further biblical-theological trajectories of famine

So far in this chapter we have outlined a theological understanding of famine in the Old Testament and read the famine in the book of Ruth in light of this. In this section we will trace the famine motif and the related idea of hunger through to the New Testament. As we touch on application for Christians today, we will see that Jesus and the gospel bring in elements of continuity and discontinuity with the Old Testament.

---

[35] A little further on in the narrative, Abraham is described as 'very rich in livestock, in silver, and in gold' (Gen. 13:2).

[36] Cf. Wenham (1987: 275): 'The importance of the theme of blessing lies in its significance as an indicator of a person's relationship with God'; see also McKeown 2008: 220.

[37] Holmstedt (2010: 100–101) suggests that Ruth's 'returning' is simply the way the narrator 'draws Ruth into the spotlight as a primary agent' with Naomi. On a narrative level this is true but it misses the deeper significance.

A famine in New Testament times highlights a Christian response to famine as well as the motivation for the response. A general famine is predicted by Agabus (Acts 11:28) during the time of the Roman emperor Claudius (ruled AD 41–54). It probably occurred between AD 45 and AD 48 and is well attested in extrabiblical sources (e.g. Tacitus, *Ann.* 12.43). The scarcity of food affected Judea and prompted Christians in the region to send material aid to the Christians in Jerusalem through Barnabas and Saul (11:27–30).[38] Just as the Jerusalem church had previously distributed 'to each as any had need' (2:45; 4:35), so now the believers in Antioch gave, 'everyone according to his ability' (cf. 2 Cor. 8:3). The principle of Christians sharing with those in times of need, including during times of famine, is reflected in the 'act of grace' performed by the more affluent churches in Macedonia and Achaia, who contributed to the needs of the churches in Judea (2 Cor. 8 – 9). For Paul, it was emblematic of Gentile–Jewish unity in Christ, in that 'if the Gentiles have come to share in [the Jews'] spiritual blessings, they ought also to be of service to [the Jews] in material blessings' (Rom. 15:27). Yet the primary motivation for their giving is rooted in the gospel: the incarnation, death and resurrection of the Lord Jesus Christ (2 Cor. 8:9). Jesus became 'poor' for the sake of all humanity (Phil. 2:6–11) so that we might become 'rich'. This 'grace of Christ' is to be the example of 'genuine love' for all who follow him (2 Cor. 8:8–9), with generosity shown to those suffering in times of famine as one expression of this love.

A metaphorical element to famine and hunger can be detected in the Old Testament and is further developed in the New Testament. Through the prophet Amos God declares that a time will come when there will be a famine, although not of food. It will be a famine of hearing the words of God (Amos 8:11; cf. 1 Sam. 3:1), and it will come as a judgment on the sins of Israel, especially injustice and oppression of the poor (Amos 8:4–7). They have refused to hear and obey the word of God (cf. Ezek. 33:30–33) and so now God withholds his word as judgment, most likely by not sending prophets to deliver his word.[39] The severity of the deprivation is illustrated by the extensiveness of the people's search for God's word: although they search throughout the land, they will not find it (8:12). In the New Testament, the importance of God's word is reinforced by Jesus. When he was hungry after

---

[38] Paul's famine-relief visit may be the same as that mentioned in Gal. 2:10, or the visit mentioned in Gal. 2:10 may correspond to that in Acts 15. See the discussion in Bruce 1982: 105–128.

[39] Andersen and Freedman 1989: 697.

a forty-day fast, the devil tempted him to produce bread from stone, but Jesus' response is telling: 'Man shall not live by bread alone, but by every word that comes from the mouth of God' (Matt. 4:4; Luke 4:4). The quote is from Deuteronomy 8:3, where Moses explains that God subjected Israel to hunger to test them and to see if they would obey God's word. Israel's failure and Jesus' example show that obedience to and dependence on God's word should take the highest priority.

Physical famine is present in many countries today, but in most countries the greater problem is a famine of God's word. As Christians, we seek to alleviate hunger, both physical and spiritual. Physically, we aid both fellow Christians (e.g. Matt. 25:35, 40) and our enemies (e.g. Prov. 25:21; Rom. 12:20). Paul often reminds Christians to give to those in need,[40] including those lacking food.[41] As mentioned previously, through Christ's poverty we have become 'rich' in salvation and its blessings (2 Cor. 8:9), so in response many of us can give out of our surplus to the millions in our world suffering from hunger (8:14–15). Spiritually, we call people to turn to God to fill their emptiness and to experience the ultimate blessing of relationship with God. Indeed, Jesus says that those who truly hunger and thirst for righteousness will be filled with righteousness (Matt. 5:6). He also says that he is 'the bread of life' and those who come to him 'shall not hunger' (John 6:35; cf. vv. 48, 51). His flesh is the true bread from heaven that gives life to those who partake of it (6:48–58). In the Old Testament, Israel in the wilderness ate the manna from heaven but eventually died; those who 'feed' on the body and blood of Christ (those who believe in Jesus; 6:35, 47) will live for ever. It is only in obedience to Jesus' word that we can find true satisfaction.

Nonetheless, those who are 'in Christ' and follow in his footsteps may still experience both physical and spiritual hunger. Just as Jesus suffered hunger, Paul also describes going 'without food' as a regular occurrence during his ministry (2 Cor. 11:27; cf. 1 Cor. 4:11; 2 Cor. 6:5; Phil. 4:12).[42] God promises to provide his people with the necessities for life (including food, drink and clothing; Matt. 6:25–33). Indeed, Jesus asks us to pray that God would provide us with our

---

[40] E.g. Rom. 12:13; 2 Cor. 9:8; Gal. 6:6–10; Eph. 4:28; 2 Thess. 3:13. This is consistent with OT teaching, e.g. Deut. 15:11; Prov. 19:17; Isa. 58:7; Ezek. 18:7, 16.

[41] For a biblical theology of material possessions and Christian stewardship, see Blomberg 1999.

[42] Some interpret going 'without food' (*nēsteia*) as fasting but the immediate context suggests that 'the fasts were forced upon him by his poverty'; so Garland 1999: 501.

daily bread (Matt. 6:11; Luke 11:3).[43] Nonetheless, some who continue the ministry of Jesus and Paul may experience hunger as they suffer for righteousness' sake, and some may even be martyred by starvation.[44]

As mentioned above, in the Old Testament a spiritual famine was caused by God withholding his word (Amos 8:11–14), but he has now spoken finally and definitively through the Word, his Son (John 1:1; Heb. 1:1–4). No further word is needed, but as we await Jesus' return our appetites are only partially satiated. We find this longing in the words of Paul, who says he wants to 'know [Christ] and the power of his resurrection, and [to] share his sufferings' (Phil. 3:10). Paul already knows Christ but he wants to know him fully, to experience 'a deeper personal relationship' with Jesus.[45] As Paul says elsewhere, in this life we know only in part and we see only in part (1 Cor. 13:9–12), so we look forward to the day when our spiritual hunger will be fully satisfied.

Jesus predicts that famine will be part of the eschatological woes. In the Gospels he says that famines will occur along with wars, earthquakes and pestilence as signs of the last days (Matt. 24:7; Mark 13:8; Luke 21:11). This idea is taken up in the book of Revelation, where famine is one of the disasters that will bring devastation, along with the sword, pestilence, and wild beasts (Rev. 6:8).[46] These destructive events are unleashed when Christ opens the fourth seal and the pale horse goes out (6:7–8). Although not mentioned specifically, the opening of the third seal and the dispatch of the third rider also bring famine, as depicted by the scales the rider carries (6:5–6).[47] Because these events occur after Christ is described as seated on the throne (5:1), some of them began 'immediately after his ascension'.[48] The reassurance for Christians, however, is that nothing can separate us from the love of Christ Jesus, not even famine (Rom. 8:35–39).

Finally, freedom from famine conditions was to be a mark of the new age. Hannah rejoices in God's salvation by anticipating a cessation of hunger (1 Sam. 2:5), which is echoed by Mary in her hymn of

---

[43] This petition reflects our dependence upon God because the request is for bread for the coming day. If the prayer is uttered in the morning, it is for that day; if uttered at night, it is for the next day. See France 2007: 247–249.

[44] Carson 1999: 100.

[45] O'Brien 1991: 383.

[46] Cf. Ezek. 14:12–13 and Zech. 6:5–8.

[47] The rider of the black horse carries a pair of scales for rationing food during a time of famine (cf. Ezek. 4:9–10; Lev. 26:26). See Beale 1998: 380–382.

[48] Beale 1998: 371.

praise: 'he has filled the hungry with good things' (Luke 1:53). The prophets also included satiation as part of their imagery for God's redemption. Isaiah describes those returning from exile as not experiencing hunger (Isa. 49:10), and Ezekiel depicts a restored Israel as God's sheep, 'human sheep of [his] pasture', who 'shall no more be consumed with hunger in the land' (Ezek. 34:29). Indeed, on that day it will be more than just a lack of hunger pangs: it will be a time of plenty and of feasting on 'rich food' for the people of God (e.g. Isa. 25:6; Ezek. 36:29–30; Amos 9:13–15). Jesus' miraculous feedings in the Gospels symbolize the breaking in of the new age, but the final fulfilment awaits the return of Jesus, when there will be no more yearning or suffering for those who are God's people (Rev. 21:2–4). Indeed, for those who persevere, one reward will be that they will 'hunger no more, neither thirst any more' (Rev. 7:16). Then we will know and enjoy God fully.

Conclusion

In this chapter we considered the question of whether it was right for Elimelech to leave the Promised Land during a time of famine to sojourn in Moab. Using a biblical-theological approach, we proposed that he and his family should have remained in Israel. Today, the issue of leaving one country for another is still a vexed question for many Christians, especially since we live in 'the age of migration'.[49] 'Famine' or adversity – social, economic, political or spiritual – may cause some people to consider voluntary migration.[50] Space does not permit a comprehensive treatment of this topic, so we will end this chapter with a few brief reflections on the question of migration from a biblical-theological perspective.

Regarding the decision to migrate from one country to another, there is limited wisdom to be garnered from Elimelech's sojourn because both 'land' and 'covenant' have been transformed with the coming of Christ. The land of Israel was a physical place promised by God to Abraham in the covenant, but since the people of God are

[49] Castles, de Haas and Miller 2014.

[50] Castles, de Haas and Miller (2014: 25) note that the volume of migration increases with development within a country, since development increases 'people's *aspirations* and *capabilities* to migrate' (emphasis original). We leave aside the issue of 'forced migration' or 'forced displacement' because in these movements of people the scope for decision-making is often limited or non-existent. The main causes of forced migration are conflict, development policies and projects, and disasters. For further discussion, see Fiddian-Qasmiyeh et al. 2014.

now all who are 'in Christ' there is no physical equivalent to the Promised Land today.[51] In the Old Testament, Israel was a geopolitical nation but now the 'Israel of God' (Gal. 6:16) is dispersed throughout the world (1 Pet. 1:1). Christians are no longer under the old covenant, with its rules and regulations, blessings and curses; instead, we are under the new covenant instituted by Christ (Matt. 26:28; Luke 22:19–20; Heb. 8:8–13; 9:15–28). The New Testament tells us that we are essentially stateless, since we are 'sojourners and exiles' in this world, looking forward to our eternal dwelling (1 Pet. 1:4; 2:11; 2 Pet. 3:13).[52] This was true for Old Testament believers also: although Abraham and the other exemplars of faith lived in Canaan, they still looked forward to a better, heavenly country (Heb. 11:8–16).

Thus, if we have the opportunity and means to emigrate to another country, the decision about whether to emigrate or not, and which country we might choose, is a matter of judgment and wisdom, not a matter of right and wrong.[53] Whichever decision we make or whichever country we might be living in, we can treat it as our home and seek its welfare (Jer. 29:4–7) as we live out the tension of the 'now' and the 'not yet'. We can also rest in God's providence: he has placed each person in his or her respective country, and so, even if we do emigrate, he is still with us (Acts 17:26–28).[54] Irrespective of which country we are in, our underlying attitude is the crucial factor: we must seek first the kingdom of God and his righteousness (Matt. 6:33), and when we suffer 'famine' conditions we must remain firm in our faith in Christ as we look forward to our 'heavenly country' (Heb. 11:16; cf. Rev. 21 – 22). Nonetheless, the outcome of Elimelech's sojourn might at least give us pause to consider whether the grass is always greener on the other side.[55]

---

[51] For recent biblical-theological treatments of the theme of land, see Isaac 2015 and Martin 2015.

[52] In this sense, Naomi's exile in Moab is closer to our current experience as Christians than her return to the Promised Land.

[53] For a helpful classification of decisions in life, see Jensen and Payne 1997.

[54] God is involved in the movements of all peoples (cf. Amos 9:7).

[55] For a Christian treatment of immigration, see Carroll R. 2013.

Chapter Seven

God's hiddenness and human agency

Many commentators observe that in the book of Ruth God's presence is hidden: his actions are 'in the shadows',[1] he works 'behind the seen'[2] or 'scenes',[3] his face is hidden.[4] This chapter will compare and contrast God's hiddenness in the Ruth narrative with two other Old Testament accounts, in Judges and Esther. First of all, we will start with the Bethlehem sojourn narratives in the epilogue of the book of Judges (17 – 21) because they are the immediate canonical context for Ruth. We will then discuss the book of Esther since it is the narrative par excellence of God's hiddenness. We will read these narratives from Judges and Esther alongside Ruth to see what light they shed on God's hiddenness and human agency in the book of Ruth. In the final section of this chapter we will set our consideration of this biblical-theological theme of God's hiddenness and human agency within parts of the Old Testament and New Testament.

To begin with, a clarification of the use of the terms 'agency' and 'hiddenness' in the subsequent discussion is required. 'Agency' in relation to humans has two meanings: the capacity of a person to act, and the means of acting or instrumentality. Both of these aspects will be explored in our discussion of Judges, Ruth and Esther. Regarding God's hiddenness, a few things must be borne in mind. First, in the Bible God is described as present everywhere and at all times in his creation (e.g. 1 Kgs 8:27; Job 38 – 41; Ps. 139; Jer. 23:23–24; Amos 9:2–6), so it is not consistent with Scripture to speak of God's absence. Humans may feel that he is absent, as his presence in person or word or action might be concealed or hidden for a time, but he is never completely absent. Thus, when we describe God's presence as

---

[1] Campbell 1975: 28.
[2] Luter and Davis 1995.
[3] Darr 1991: 59. Cf. Bush (1996a: 47): God's control over events in his world is 'behind the scenes and in the shadows'.
[4] Eskenazi and Frymer-Kensky 2011: lii–liii. For God's hiddenness in Ruth, see, seminally, Hals 1969.

withdrawn or removed, it is a relative, not absolute, withdrawal. Second, God's presence is closely connected to God's blessing, so that when he withdraws his presence his favour is also removed to some extent. In effect, this is the opposite of God making his face to shine upon his people, which is linked to God's blessings of protection, deliverance and *šālôm* – 'well-being, health, prosperity and salvation' (Num. 6:24–26).[5] Third, when we speak of God 'hiding his face' and the like, these are anthropomorphic idioms, describing God in human terms, so that we can begin to understand something of God's person, actions and motivations. It may not be the case that God literally hides his face. Fourth, we will make a distinction between, on the one hand, the hiddenness of God's presence as manifest in person, action and word; and, on the other hand, God's hiddenness as a concealment of his purposes. There are complicated philosophical discussions surrounding both these aspects of God's hiddenness, but since our biblical-theological method focuses on, and primarily draws out, ideas and themes from the biblical text, we will bracket out these philosophical concerns.[6]

The hiddenness of God and human agency in the book of Judges

Following Michael Moore (2001: 27–41), we will adopt a 'canonical-historical' approach to reading Ruth against Judges 17 – 21.[7] He filtered Ruth's theological message through three lenses: wandering–restoration, religion–ethics, and chaos–kindness. The following discussion will be filtered through another lens: the hiddenness–agency lens. In Judges God slowly recedes into the background of the narrative as the story progresses, and his retreat is in parallel with the increase in sin and wickedness within Israelite society. God is present in word and action in the prologue (1:1 – 3:6) and the central narrative section (3:7 – 16:31) of Judges but recedes into the background in the

---

[5] Wenham 1981: 90.

[6] Ideally, an examination of God's hiddenness would be understood alongside the theme of God's presence. For a recent treatment of the theme of God's presence from a biblical-theological perspective, see Lister 2015. He divides God's presence into two categories: relational and redemptive. For other treatments of God's hiddenness, see Terrien 1978; Balentine 1983; Fretheim 1984; Burnett 2010. For recent introductory treatments of divine hiddenness from a philosophical perspective, see Schellenberg 2010; Murray and Taylor 2012.

[7] Merrill (1985: 131–133) calls these three narratives (Judg. 17 – 18; 19 – 21; Ruth 1 – 4) the 'Bethlehem trilogy'.

epilogue (17:1 – 21:25).[8] In the five chapters of the epilogue, God speaks only in reply to the Israelite tribes' enquiries and acts only to strike down Benjamin. The following discussion will thus explore the relation between God's increasing hiddenness and human agency.

The epilogue is constituted of two sojourns, both connected to Bethlehem (17 – 18; 19 – 21). In the first sojourn God is hidden, not acting directly in the narrative, but he is invoked by the characters. These mentions of God may be understood as him intervening through human agents, but the actions of the characters render this interpretation very unlikely. The first time God is mentioned sets the scene for the rest of the first sojourn narrative. As the narrative begins, we are introduced to a man name Micah,[9] whose actions and those of his mother illustrate the moral and religious chaos of the time. When Micah confesses to stealing 1,100 pieces of silver, it elicits an inexplicable double response from his mother. First, she invokes a blessing from Yahweh upon her son (17:2). Second, she dedicates the returned silver pieces to Yahweh 'to make a carved image and a metal image' (17:3). At best, we can view Micah's mother as sincere in her devotion to Yahweh. Nevertheless, this episode illustrates that by this time Israel had moved so far away from God and his expectations that there was no way that God could bless his people, no matter how sincerely religious they were. This scene closes with a disturbing tableau: three generations ensconced in idolatry at their household shrine (lit. 'the house of God/gods'; *bêt 'ĕlōhîm* [17:5]) – Micah, his mother, and his son, who had been ordained as a priest by Micah. The narrator closes with a clear evaluation: 'Everyone did what was right in his own eyes' (17:6).

As the first sojourn narrative continues, God remains hidden but again he is spoken of by the characters. The sojourn proper begins when a young Levite leaves Bethlehem seeking a place to stay (17:8). He happens to arrive in the hill country of Ephraim and at the house

---

[8] God is stirred to anger by Israel's apostasy (Judg. 2:12, 14, 20; 3:8; 10:7); he gives over or sells his people into the hand of their enemies (Judg. 2:14; 3:8; 4:2; 10:7); he is moved to pity by his people's groans (2:18); he sends angels/messengers to rebuke (2:1–3), commission (6:11–14) and instruct (13:3–5, 13–14, 18); he sends a prophet to reprimand (6:8–10); he sends an evil spirit to incite enmity (9:23); he raises up and empowers judges (2:16, 18; 3:9, 15), and grants them victory (e.g. 3:10; 4:23; 11:32–33); he blesses (13:24); and he performs a miracle (15:19). For a list of references to God, see Butler (2009: lxxx–lxxxiii), who notes that 'Yahweh' is used 175 times in 137 verses, in addition to references to 'God' (*'ĕlōhîm*).

[9] Micah means 'Who is like the LORD?', which is ironic since God does not appear in this narrative.

of Micah, who promptly offers him the position of personal priest (17:9–10). The Levite immediately accepts the position, which leads to Micah saying,[10] 'Now I know that the LORD will prosper me, because I have a Levite as priest' (17:11–13). Micah thinks that the presence of a Levite priest will ensure God's ongoing blessing. The priest essentially functions as a good-luck charm.

God is also mentioned on the lips of the priest as well as on those of the Danites. When the Danite spies ask the young Levite to enquire of God about the outcome of their journey, he replies that their journey will be successful because it is 'under the eye of [nōkaḥ] the LORD' (18:6).[11] Yet it is doubtful whether the Levite enquired of God at all because he responds as soon as he is asked. There is no description of him enquiring of God as would be expected of a priest; he does not even adjourn to his master's shrine to do so. Whether God would have answered him or not through this aberrant worship site is another matter, but the point is that the priest is confident to present his word with the same authority as God's. The priest's speech about God cannot be accepted as reliable because of his actions and the nature of his priesthood.

The last time God is on the lips of the characters is when the Danite spies return to present their reconnaissance report. They report that the land is 'very good' and encourage the rest of their tribe to migrate north to conquer the land, 'for God has given it into your hands' (18:10). Yet this is a pathetic parody of the initial reconnaissance and conquest of the Promised Land by Israel.[12] As such, it is highly unlikely that this migration was authorized by God, as claimed by the Danite spies (18:10). So again we wonder: how likely is it that God would bless the work of those involved in syncretism, and who worship God at false worship sites? For the first sojourn narrative ends

---

[10] The Hebrew is literally 'saying' but it could be either a soliloquy or what Micah is 'thinking'.

[11] The meaning of the Levite's utterance is ambiguous because nōkaḥ can mean either 'in front of' or 'opposite to' (BDB, 647). Hence, it could mean that the Danite mission has God's approval or is under God's scrutiny; see Block 1999: 498.

[12] There are many contrasts between this migration and Israel's initial conquest, including: (1) in the initial entry to the Promised Land, it is described as 'holy war'; in this account it is not; (2) Israel entered Canaan to claim their promised inheritance; the Danites were seeking an inheritance (18:1) because the Danites had failed in their initial conquest (1:34); (3) The cities of the Canaanites were heavily fortified; the people of Laish 'lived in security', were 'quiet and unsuspecting', and were 'far from the Sidonians' who might have defended them (18:7, 10, 28); (4) God is explicitly mentioned as giving Israel the victory; here the narrator is silent about God's actions. See Webb 2012: 452–453.

with Danites worshipping Micah's carved image with their self-installed priest, rather than worshipping at 'the house of God' (*bêt 'ĕlōhîm*; 18:31) in Shiloh, which was the authorized worship site at the time.[13]

Thus, in this first Bethlehem sojourn narrative, God is hidden. One effect of God's hiddenness is to highlight the initiative and actions of the human characters. At times, the characters seek God's will through their shrine and the associated paraphernalia, and through their priest; at other times, they confidently pronounce God's will without consulting God at all. God is on the lips of the characters but most of the time they are only paying him lip service. As a result of the syncretism of the Israelites and their outright disobedience, the sovereignty of God as expressed in his guidance is undermined by the people and presented ironically by the narrator. For it seems his people seek and confidently pronounce his guidance, but is it likely that God would respond positively to people who do only what is right in their own eyes? Of course God may choose to do so, but is he likely to bless a people who have such a twisted understanding of him that it is hard for anyone to recognize if they seek the true and living God at all? God's person and actions are hidden in this narrative; moreover, his purposes are hidden from the characters as well.

In the second Bethlehem sojourn narrative God again remains in the background, with only one place where he is mentioned and two places where his activity is described. There is no mention of God as a Levite takes for himself a concubine from Bethlehem. After she absconds, the Levite takes her back from her father's house. As they travel north from her father's house they seek solace for the night in Gibeah, but they soon find out that this is an ill-advised choice, as Gibeah turns out to be a modern-day Sodom and Gomorrah.[14] What happens that night is repugnant and horrifying, replete with homosexual lust, cowardice and rape, and the concubine is left for dead. The people of Gibeah have forsaken God and it seems he has responded in kind. The Levite's callous disregard for the woman under his care shows that he is no better than the men of Gibeah. The Levite does, however, mention God when he ostensibly says that he is on the

---

[13] Shiloh was destroyed at the end of the period of the judges (Ps. 78:60; Jer. 7:12, 14; 26:6). There is no mention of Shiloh after the time of Eli and Samuel.

[14] This is deeply ironic, since Gibeah was within the Israelite territory of Benjamin. They could have chosen to lodge in the foreign city of Jebus instead, as indeed the Levite's servant advised (19:11). In their hospitality, Gibeah of Benjamin has degenerated to worse than the surrounding nations.

way to 'the house of the Lord' (*bêt yhwh*; 19:18).[15] Since the context of his statement is that he is seeking accommodation from a potential host, his mention of 'the house of the Lord' presents himself as both pious and innocuous. He does not point out that he is a Levite, but his mention of his pilgrimage to worship God portrays the idea that he is of no threat to a potential host. In other words, the Levite mentions God for his own selfish, self-protective ends.[16] God's name again is on the lips of a character, although the words on those lips are not necessarily reliable or trustworthy.

In the aftermath of the Gibean atrocities the characters again seek God's counsel; this time God is present through speech, but again his *purposes* are hidden, or at least obscured. Eleven tribes of Israel finally manage to congregate 'as one man' to God at Mizpah (20:1–2), but, ironically, their unity is for the purpose of making war among themselves, not against their Canaanite enemies (cf. 1:1).[17] A civil war is incited by the Levite (20:3–11) and, consistent with their widespread failure to obey God's law, the eleven tribes fail to ascertain the facts of the case from more than one witness (e.g. Num. 35:30; Deut. 17:6). Instead, they make a rash vow to take vengeance upon those of Gibeah without consulting God (20:8–10).[18] It seems that their prejudiced mindset leads them to ask God the wrong questions and even misinterpret God's answers. Note their enquiry of God: it is not 'Should we go to fight against the tribe of Benjamin?' but 'Who shall go up first?' (20:18). The troops had already been mustered and now the allied tribes were champing at the bit to make war (20:17). God responds in the same way as he did the first time Israel asked the question (1:1), and Judah heads off first to battle against its kinsmen.[19] In a sense, God gave them the right answer to the wrong question. So from that perspective it is no great surprise that the united tribes are heavily defeated (20:21). Indeed, God did not guarantee victory (cf. 20:28).

---

[15] So MT, which is followed by ESV, NIV, HCSB. The LXX reads 'my house', which is followed by NASB, NRSV and NJPS.

[16] The pronouns in the central portion of the Levite's speech betray his concern only for himself, not for the rest of his travelling party: '. . . but no one has taken *me* into his house'. Cf. Butler 2009: 423.

[17] Elsewhere in Judges Deborah rebukes tribes who fail to join the war (Judg. 5); Ephraimites do not join Gideon (ch. 8) or Jephthah (ch. 12); Danites do not support Samson (chs 14–16); and the Judahites want to maintain the status quo with the Philistines (15:11).

[18] Satterthwaite 1992: 81.

[19] Cf. Webb (2012: 482), who notes that the selection of Judah is also appropriate because the concubine is from Judah.

With weeping, the united tribes again enquire of God, but this time they entertain the possibility of not going to battle against their 'brothers' (20:23). Their description of Benjamin as 'brothers' may reveal a softening of their resolve towards the enemy,[20] but it also betrays the internal inconsistency in their request, for who goes to war against kin? God again says, 'Go up against them', but ominously there is again no assurance of victory. Once again, the united tribes experience military futility (20:24–25). It is only after their third and final enquiry of God that he guarantees them victory, and so the united tribes finally defeat Benjamin (20:27–48).

When we examine this narrative closely, we find that God is largely hidden in this sojourn narrative, too. He stays on the sidelines and leaves his people to their own devices. In a way, it is what they want, since they have abandoned God and his authority, each man doing what is right in his own eyes. Not acknowledging God as king, each man is effectively his own king, and so they face the consequences of their decisions made without God. In this second sojourn narrative, God intervenes only episodically, and answers only curtly to enquiries. The difficult part for the Israelite enquirers, and for us as readers, is that God's purposes are not clear. Why does Israel twice suffer defeat even after God has told them to fight against Benjamin? No explanation is given in the narrative, so whatever reasons we come up with will be tentative.[21] Perhaps it is best to view God's answers as his means of punishment upon his people, who are left to face the dire consequences of their chosen course of action. They are determined to wage war against their own brethren, so God allows them to face the full consequences of where that determination will lead them.[22] In this reading, God judges not only Benjamin (21:15) but also the other eleven tribes (cf. 2:15).[23]

---

[20] Matthews 2004: 195.

[21] The fact of differing views among commentators attests to the obscurity of God's purposes. For example, Butler (2009: 449–450) suggests that in their first two enquiries Israel did not ask with priestly involvement and ritual preparation, and Davis (2000: 217) suggests that it may be a case of knowing 'divine will . . . and yet finding that path marked more by trouble than success'.

[22] At the very least, we can confirm that this theological principle is consistent with what he reveals elsewhere about similarly rebellious behaviour (esp. Rom. 1).

[23] Webb (2012: 503): 'Clearly the narrative as a whole is about retribution, but it is not simply about eleven of Israel's tribes punishing one. It is also about Yahweh punishing them all.' Cf. Davis (2000: 217), who raises the possibility that Israel were repentant only after their first two defeats, which implies that those defeats were judgment from God.

Nonetheless, even in his judgment we find glimmers of God's grace. For, after their defeats, united Israel zealously and desperately turns back to God with weeping and fasting, with burnt offerings and peace offerings (20:26; 21:2–4).[24] There is at least some degree of restoration of the relationship between God and Israel. However, the extreme ends that God uses reflect the degree of estrangement between God and Israel because of their recalcitrant idolatry and profound disobedience. Another glimmer of hope can be found in God's preservation of Benjamin. This breach in the tribes of Israel is judgment from God's hand (21:15), but Benjamin is not wiped out completely. There is still hope for this tribe, although Israel's solution to revive the decimated tribe is almost worse than the original crime that triggered the whole dire episode. So what we find is that God again has stepped back from the spotlight of the narrative, and one can only imagine him shaking his head in disapproval. That the crimes against the daughters of Shiloh (21:16–24) come so quickly after Israel's 'return' to God (20:26; 21:2–4) only shows the shallowness of their repentance, how entrenched they were in their rebellion, as well as the distance they had moved away from God and his word. Indeed, 'everyone did what was right in his own eyes', not in the eyes of God (21:25). Adherence to God's word had been jettisoned, and the outcome was disastrous.

Thus, in the two Bethlehem sojourn narratives God is either hidden or distant. He intervenes twice in the second sojourn narrative, in response to the Israelites' enquiry and to bring judgment. Even when he does speak to Israel, his purposes for them are obscured, both to the characters and to us, the readers. In part, the hiddenness of God's purposes is because we are his creatures, and cannot know the full scope of his plans. Even if we could view the entirety of God's plans, in our finiteness we could not fully comprehend God's specific purposes in those plans. Nonetheless, in the sojourn narratives God's hiddenness seems to be due primarily to Israel's rebellion against him, and reflects the degree of estrangement

---

[24] Weeping, fasting, sitting before God, and offering peace and fellowship offerings (20:26) would indicate a desire to restore the relationship with God; cf. Wong 2006: 68 n. 96; Block 1999: 560. Yet Israel's words to God, in trying to lay the blame on him for their predicament (21:3), may be evidence that their sacrifices are intended to coerce God into helping them find a solution, not evidence of true repentance; cf. Webb 2012: 496–497. Further evidence of their insincerity may be found in the narrator's description of Israel coming before God (*'ĕlōhîm*), not Yahweh (*yhwh*) (21:2); see Block 1999: 570; Butler 2009: 455–456. Hoyt (2012: 143–158) argues that it is questionable whether Israel genuinely repents at all in Judges.

between God and Israel.[25] The glimpses of God's grace amidst his judgment show that, although he has hidden his face from his people, he has not abandoned them completely.

The hiddenness of God and human agency in Esther

The book of Esther has the distinction of being the only book in the Old Testament in which God does not feature.[26] What are we to make of a biblical book wherein God is completely hidden? Is this omission an embarrassment to the pious reader? There is a temptation to explain away this awkward phenomenon, but our argument is that the omission of any mention of God is deliberate and must be viewed as an authorial strategy. In other words, the failure to refer to God is intentional and serves a function in the narrative.[27] A number of narratival features show that God could easily have been brought into the story of Esther, but these opportunities were not taken up by the biblical writer. These include what are routinely religious practices, the coincidences that regularly punctuate the story, the strong emphasis on Jewish ethnicity, and the inner-biblical allusions and parallels that can be discerned by the biblically literate reader.

What elsewhere in the Bible are religious practices (e.g. fasting, lot-casting), in the book of Esther have no overt religious reference.[28] In Esther 4, when Esther is faced with the prospect of death as the penalty for entering unsummoned into the king's presence, she calls for fasting 'on [her] behalf' (4:16), though it is not immediately clear how her fast (and the fast enjoined on others) can be to her advantage, for no mention is made of its usual accompaniment, prayer (cf. Neh. 1:4; Dan. 9:3) – namely prayer offered for her safety. Nor is there any link with the usual purpose of fasting, whether implied (2 Sam. 12:16, 21–23; Ps. 35:13–14) or stated (Jer. 14:12; 36:9; Ezra 8:23) – namely to move God to compassion so that he answers prayers for assistance or forgiveness (e.g. Judg. 20:26; 1 Sam. 7:6; Jon. 3:5–9). This makes the absence in Esther of any connection to prayer highly visible. The

---

[25] Cf. Satterthwaite 1993: 83.

[26] This assumes that Song 8:6 uses *Yah* in reference to God (Yahweh) and is to be translated 'the flame of *Yah*'. See the discussion provided by Exum 2005: 253–254.

[27] In a canonical story of deliverance, we expect God to be there, and, as noted by Fox (2001b: 235), '[s]uch a violation of expectations is surely no accident'. For fuller argumentation, see Goswell 2010.

[28] Cf. Loader (1978: 418): 'Motifs that certainly suggest a religious quality are introduced, but they are made to function in such a way that any theological significance is immediately veiled again.'

same applies to the reference to the fasting and lamentation of the Jews when the edict allowing their destruction is published (Esth. 4:3).

In Esther, God's ordering of events may be *assumed*, but it is not the lesson illustrated by any event in the book. The distinction that we have just drawn is important to observe. Scholars regularly provide a listing of the striking series of 'coincidences' reported in Esther. For example: the removal of Vashti as queen creates a vacancy at the top that Esther can fill; Mordecai chances to overhear the plot to assassinate the king; Esther is queen at a time of crisis (as remarked upon in 4:14b); Ahasuerus has insomnia and reads the report in the royal chronicles that describes Mordecai's service to the crown; Haman enters the court at the moment when the king is pondering the question of how to reward Mordecai; the king re-enters from the garden just as Haman falls upon the couch of Esther. As stated by Berg, 'These "coincidences" fall within the realm of possibility but nevertheless strain the laws of probability', for they all favour the Jews.[29] No one is that lucky! We suspect that the dice are loaded! The string of coincidences gives credibility to Mordecai's confidence that assistance will be forthcoming (4:14), but it does so without any positive assertion of God's providential ordering of events. This is also the implied explanation of Esther finding favour with the king and his officials, and even of her beauty and charm (2:9, 15, 17; 5:2, 8; 7:3; 8:5; 9:1, 25), for elsewhere in Scripture these can be signs of being chosen by God (e.g. 1 Sam. 16:12, 18). The narrator is not interested in *demonstrating* to his audience God's control of history, as, for instance, the author of Daniel clearly aims to do, through explicit references to God (e.g. Dan. 2:47; 4:2–3) and the element of the miraculous (e.g. Dan. 3:28–29; 6:22). The narrator remains tight-lipped about God's control of events, nor does any character allude to his possible involvement (cf. Ruth 1:20–21; 2:20). The story of Esther is not a subtle communication of the message that God is at work behind the scenes, though many well-meaning commentators have tried to turn it into that.

In the absence of explicit religious differentiation, Jewish ethnicity comes to the fore in the narrative, most notably in the theme of the inviolability of the Jewish people. The clearest statement of the theme is 6:13, where Haman's wife and advisers say that Haman cannot succeed against Mordecai, because he is 'of the Jewish people' (literally: 'of the seed of the Jews'), and the implication of the book

---

[29] Berg 1979: 104.

as a whole is that the Jews will survive the captivity (2:5, 6). The gentilic adjective 'Jewish', used as a substantive for 'Jew/Jews' (e.g. 2:5; 3:4, 6, 10, 13; 4:3, 7, 13, 14, 16), reaches a tally of fifty-two occurrences and far outstrips its nearest rival, the ten occurrences in Ezra–Nehemiah. What is important about Mordecai is his race: he is 'Mordecai the Jew' (5:13; 6:10; 8:7; 9:29, 31; 10:3). The Jews are called 'the people of Mordecai' (3:6 [x2]) and 'his [Mordecai's] people' (10:3 [x2]). It is because of Mordecai's ethnicity that Haman decides to destroy the Jews (3:6), and Haman is repeatedly styled 'the enemy of [all] the Jews' (3:10; 8:1; 9:10, 24). The Jews, though acknowledged to be special and different (3:8), are never said to be God's chosen people. Their identity and separateness is an expression of nationalism, which, however, in the Ancient Near East is never secular, for each nation has its own patron god(s), though nothing is said in the book about Jewish religious particularism. Moral peccadillos and uncertainties remain (e.g. Mordecai counsels Esther to conceal her nationality [2:10, 20]; she marries a pagan king [2:17]; Mordecai disobeys the king's command to bow to Haman [3:2]),[30] but it is plain that neither character deserves the life-threatening situation in which they find themselves. Nothing in the book says or implies that God's absence or hiddenness is a judgment on his people such that they are left to fend for themselves as best they can.

Mordecai confidently states that if Esther will not intercede with the king, help will surely come 'from another *quarter* [or place]' (4:14, annotation ours). This term, in context, is *not* a veiled reference to God, though it is regularly viewed as a circumlocution for God by commentators, ancient (e.g. Josephus, *Ant.* 11.227, 279–282), rabbinic (critiqued by Ibn Ezra) and modern.[31] Rather, it makes a spatial contrast with 'in the king's palace' (4:13). Mordecai's argument is that if help is not forthcoming from *inside* the palace (through Esther), then it will come from *outside* the palace (through some other agent, presumably human). The passage does not explain the reason for Mordecai's confidence, but it is certainly not given a theological basis.[32] This statement, therefore, is another example in the book of Esther of almost speaking about God but failing to do so.

Just below the surface of the narrative run a number of subtexts. For example, the deliverance depicted in the book of Esther is another

---

[30] Harvey 2003.

[31] E.g. Levenson 1997: 81; Moore 1971: 50.

[32] As noted by Fox (2001b: 244), 'Such confidence usually derives from and expresses a belief in God's covenantal care of Israel.' Cf. Bush 1996a: 396.

exodus, for this crisis in a foreign land replicates in certain ways the genocidal threat described in Exodus 1 – 2. The evil edict was written 'on the thirteenth day of the first month [Nisan]' (3:12), which is the eve of the Passover, with the planned slaughter of the Jews to take place eleven months later, on 'the thirteenth day of the twelfth month, which is the month of Adar' (3:13). The coincidence in time implies that an exodus-style deliverance may be anticipated.

Another example of inner-biblical allusion is the mention of the 'fear of the Jews' (8:17; cf. 9:2) and 'the fear of Mordecai' (9:3) that fell upon the general population and also incapacitated the enemies of the Jews. Elsewhere in Scripture such a reaction is attributed to divinely induced dread in a situation of holy war (e.g. Deut. 2:25; 11:25; Josh. 2:9, 24), but no such religious explanation is offered in the story of Esther.

The deadly competition between Mordecai and Haman is given an added dimension due to their respective lines of descent: Mordecai from Kish (father of Saul), and 'Haman the Agagite', from Agag, the king of Amalek,[33] with their pedigrees mentioned when both men are first introduced to the reader (2:5; 3:1). This is the intertextual undercurrent of the hostility between the two courtiers, recalling Saul's slaughter of the Amalekites and his sparing of Agag (1 Sam. 15). The antipathy between the two men reflects and replays the ancient quarrel of Israel and Amalek (Exod. 17:8–16),[34] upon whom God pronounced total destruction, and Mordecai's role, like that of his ancestor, is to destroy the Amalekites.

There are also the biblical parallels with other Jews who, despite mishaps and opposition, serve God's people and prosper in the service of foreign kings. Esther and Mordecai, like Joseph, Daniel, Ezra and Nehemiah, are examples for diaspora Jews to emulate. As noted by Beal, such examples of inner-canonical dialogue in the book of Esther 'only makes its lack of reference to divine presence or Jewish religious practice all the more striking'.[35]

The fact of the matter is that God is completely hidden in the book of Esther and the narrator does not wish him to be brought back into the story. The author has made a concerted effort to keep God out of the story told in the book of Esther. What could be the motivation for such an unusual (for the Bible) strategy? The answer appears to

---

[33] For Haman's Agagite/Amalekite connection, see LaCocque 1987; Miller 2014: 62–65.
[34] Bickerman 1967: 196–199.
[35] Beal 1997: 117.

be that this was done with the aim of focusing attention upon the human initiative and daring of the Jewish protagonists, especially as modelled by Esther.[36] God's control of events, while assumed, is not stated, precisely so that the roles of Mordecai, Esther and the other Jews might take centre stage.

Despite the literary absence of God, the fact that the book of Esther has found a home in the biblical canon shows that it has always been viewed as a religious text, so that it should not be labelled as 'secular'.[37] This is confirmed when notice is taken of the alternative canonical placements of the book.[38] In the Hebrew canon, it is one of the five scrolls called the *Megillot*. This is a liturgical grouping which classifies Esther as a festal scroll, in line with the various banquets described in the narrative and with the fact that it is read at the feast of Purim. The book begins with two successive banquets set in Ahasuerus' third regnal year (1:3–9), and it ends with two others set in his twelfth year (9:17–18), held by the Jews to celebrate their victory over their enemies. The correspondence between the banquet pairs at the beginning and end of the book is one of a number of indications that the Purim connection is not incidental to the story.[39] From the beginning, the book anticipates its conclusion in the two-day Jewish festival.

In the Greek canon, Esther is found in a quite different setting among the 'Histories' (as also in the English Bible). The divine super-intendence of events is an explicit feature of preceding books (Kings, Chronicles and Ezra–Nehemiah) and implies God's providential ordering of the events in Esther as well. This is a far cry, however, from meaning that the book of Esther is to be read as an illustration of God's providence. Like the figures of Zerubbabel, Ezra and Nehemiah, the Jewish hero and heroine of the book of Esther serve as models of energetic effort and risk-taking for the sake of the welfare of the Jewish people.

Can there be a 'theology' of a book that does not mention God at all? If theology is defined broadly to include ethics (as it should be), then we can speak of a theology of Esther. God's noticeable absence in the book of Esther is a deliberate authorial strategy, and the story is not to be rehabilitated for pious use by reinserting God into the

---

[36] See Berg 1979. Likewise, Freedman correlates the absence of any reference to divine assistance with the assertive character of Queen Esther (2005: 117).

[37] See Anderson 1950.

[38] For a brief discussion of the possible effects of the positioning of the book of Esther, see Dunne 2014: 121–125.

[39] See the cogent argument of Berg 1979: 31–47.

story. The canonical book moves in a different direction. Depicting a challenging situation faced by diaspora Jews, the author's prescription for Jewish survival is that Jewish men and women act with the kind of energy and daring exemplified by Esther and Mordecai. Put in Christian terms, the book parades and applauds the faithful and heroic efforts of believers in a situation of crisis. It encourages God's people to live out their faith in a hostile environment with intelligence, resourcefulness and courage.

The hiddenness of God and human agency in Ruth

In Judges God is present in word and action, in Esther God is not described as saying or doing anything, while in Ruth God's intervention lies somewhere between these two books. In Ruth God does not speak directly; he does not communicate through a messenger; he does not intervene in spectacular ways. God is mostly hidden but evidence for his presence can be found from at least two sources: the narrator and the main characters.

The narrator mentions God twice. The first time the narrator mentions God is in regards to breaking the famine. Strictly speaking, this is hearsay, because the narrator reports that Naomi 'heard in the fields of Moab that the LORD had visited his people and given them food' (1:6). The narrator does not say explicitly that God broke the famine. That may be what we, as readers, are to understand, and probably what took place in reality. Yet we told that it is what Naomi *heard*. In contrast, the second mention of God's action is unequivocal: 'And the LORD *gave* [*wayyittēn*] her [Ruth] conception, and she bore a son' (4:13). There is an especially marked emphasis on God's direct intervention in this verse, because the normal phrasing for a pregnancy elsewhere in the Old Testament is, 'She conceived . . . and bore' (e.g. Gen. 29:34–35; 30:19; 38:4) or '[God] opened her womb' (e.g. Gen. 29:31; 30:22). There is a hint of the miraculous because she had been unable to become pregnant in her ten-year marriage to Mahlon.[40] The throng at the town gate had wished that God would make (*yittēn*) Ruth fertile like the matriarchs (4:11), and here God responds to their prayer. Thus, God's direct action in Ruth's pregnancy is strongly emphasized at this point to make sure it is not missed. God's two acts of giving fertility (1:6; 4:13) function as bookends, pointing to God's providential care over all activities in the narrative.

[40] Cf. Block 1999: 726.

In addition to these two actions of God, there is perhaps a more subtle intervention in chapter 2. The beginning of the chapter sets up Boaz as a potential benefactor, and then Ruth 'just happened to end up [*wayyiqer miqrehā*] in the portion of field belonging to Boaz' (2:3, our translation). From Ruth's perspective this event might have seemed coincidental, and this is the surface idea portrayed to a reader. However, the event's juxtaposition with the earlier narratorial introduction of Boaz (2:1) is suggestive of God's hand in this apparent serendipity. As Phyllis Trible (1978: 176) observes: 'Within human luck is divine intentionality.' This understanding is reinforced by two intertexts. The same combination of *miqre* ('chance/fate') and *qārâ* ('happen/befall') occurs in Ecclesiastes 2:14, where it is stated that 'fate' is beyond the control of humanity. The second intertext is the narrative of Abraham sending his servant to find a wife for Isaac (Gen. 24:12–27), in which the servant prays that God would grant him success (*qārâ*; 24:12) in his task. As the servant thanks God for fulfilling his request afterwards, the clear understanding is that God has superintended the outcome (24:26–27). When these two episodes are placed next to the Ruth narrative, God can be seen to work behind the scenes for readers attuned to inner-biblical allusions.

God's presence in action might be scanty in the narrative, but we are constantly reminded of him through the speech of the main characters. In chapter 1 Naomi laments that the hand of Yahweh has gone out against her (1:13) and that he has brought her back empty and brought calamity upon her (1:21). That these two complaints are addressed, respectively, to her daughters-in-law and the women of the town instead of to God shows her sense of abandonment by God and perhaps also her lack of faith.[41] These laments show that Naomi cannot understand the purposes of God in her life, but also that she feels that God's *presence* is hidden. She has experienced major personal tragedies, so much so that she feels 'empty' (1:21). Primarily, her sense of emptiness is because she has lost her husband and two sons, but this emptiness is accentuated because she feels that it is evidence that God has abandoned her. Commentators point out the irony here: she is not empty because her loyal daughter-in-law is standing beside her. Yet she is also not empty because God is still with her. While she was in Moab she heard that God's presence and blessing had been manifest in Israel by him breaking the famine and giving his people food. Now that she has returned to Bethlehem, she has also returned

---

[41] Cf. McKeown 2015: 115; Saxegaard 2010: 104.

to the sphere of God's blessing. As the narrator points out, Naomi and Ruth return right 'at the beginning of barley harvest' (1:22). God has not abandoned her. He is not only with her people but also with Naomi, with the provision of food as one tangible indication. God's hand might have previously gone out against her but it is now extended towards her in blessing.

Before these mentions of God's actions in her life, Naomi prays that God might provide husbands for her widowed daughters-in-law (1:8–9). Indeed, as Gow (2000: 176) points out, prayers on the lips of the characters play an important role in the book's theology:[42] Boaz prays that God might reward Ruth for her loyalty to Naomi (2:11–12); Naomi prays for God's blessing on Boaz (2:20); Boaz asks for God's blessing on Ruth for seeking him as a redeemer (3:10); the throng at the town gate pray for fertility and prosperity for Ruth and Boaz (4:11–12); the women of the town bless God for providing a redeemer and pray that Obed's name be perpetuated (4:14–15). These prayers culminate in the marriage of Boaz and Ruth, and in God's provision of Obed. The cumulative effect of these prayers is to point to God's behind-the-scenes control of the whole narrative. His direct action is mentioned only at the beginning and end of the narrative but, through the prayers of the characters, we, the readers, are not allowed to forget about the potential presence and action of God. That his plans and purposes are accomplished by the end of the narrative reinforces the fact that he was acting all the way through. We suggest that when Naomi looked back on her life she could discern God's hand, even when he seemed to be absent.

God's actions in the Ruth narrative are minimal and understated. Yet, unlike the sojourn narratives at the end of Judges, this does not indicate God's disapproval of his people's actions. In Judges God's hiddenness was in response to his people's rebellion and a sign of his judgment. In Esther, by contrast, there is no indication that God's hiddenness is a judgment on his people. The Jews are under potential threat due to the evil machinations of an enemy, Haman. The book of Ruth may be placed somewhere in between. At the beginning of the narrative Elimelech and Naomi take their family out of the Promised Land and terrible tragedies befall them. God is not

---

[42] The following expressions of thanksgiving and blessing mention God in the third person, as though they are primarily meant for the ears of other characters in the narrative. Although the speeches, unlike most biblical prayers, do not address God directly in the second person, they can be considered prayers since God would be understood to overhear them. Cf. Sakenfeld 2003: 141.

mentioned in the section (1:1–5), and his hiddenness may reflect a lack of mindfulness of God, a lack of dependence upon him in action or prayer, by Elimelech and his family. Whatever the case, in the outcome of the sojourn to Moab, it is clear that Naomi felt abandoned by God. Yet God remained present and active. In the Ruth narrative God's mode of action is quiet and continuous: he is working in and through the seemingly mundane day-to-day agency of people who lived according to his will to achieve his purposes.

Human agency is prominent in the book of Ruth. It is seen most clearly in Ruth's two main acts of *ḥesed*, which entail initiative and risk. Boaz pinpoints the two acts as he speaks to Ruth on the threshing floor: 'You have made this last kindness greater than the first' (3:10). The kindness that Ruth showed earlier was to Naomi, when she gave up the security of her land, people and gods for those of her mother-in-law. In contrast to Orpah, Ruth took the initiative to ignore Naomi's urgings to remain in Moab, to commit herself to her, and to follow her back to Bethlehem.[43] As a foreigner, the risk was that she would not be able to find a husband in Israel.

The second act of kindness that Boaz mentions is Ruth choosing him instead of other, more eligible bachelors. The pertinent factor is that Boaz describes the other potential husbands as 'young men', in contrast to his more mature status. Boaz's age cannot be ascertained for certain but his style of language and the way he addresses Ruth would indicate that he is at least of Naomi's generation or above.[44] Yet Ruth takes the initiative to choose him, which he identifies as an act of kindness because in doing so she raises the possibility of Elimelech's land being restored to the family and of Elimelech's name being 'raised up' along with the property. A husband who was not from Elimelech's clan would not be able to function as a kinsman-redeemer. One risk she takes in choosing the more elderly Boaz may be that her chance of conceiving is reduced.[45] At the very least, a younger husband would have a longer time frame in which to provide

---

[43] Ruth also shows initiative in asking to glean in the fields outside Bethlehem and in her conversation with Boaz in his field. See Lau 2011: 102–103.

[44] Both Naomi (2:2, 22; 3:1, 16, 18) and Boaz (2:8; 3:10–11) call Ruth 'my daughter'. Holmstedt (2010: 46–49) presents evidence that the author of Ruth used 'style shifts' in the Hebrew language spoken by the main characters to mark out Ruth's foreign status, and to show that Naomi and Boaz are from an older generation. The line of Jewish interpretation suggesting that Boaz is eighty years old may exaggerate his age (*Ruth Rabbah* 6.2). After all, he is still able to protect his pile of grain on the threshing floor at night.

[45] Cf. Duguid 2005: 173.

for her. In short, in selecting Boaz Ruth put her loyalty to Naomi and her family above her own best interests.

The importance of human agency can be seen further in Ruth's initiative on the threshing floor. After Naomi outlines her threshing floor plan, Ruth assures her that she will do all that she has said (3:5). The narrator proleptically confirms that Ruth does 'just as' her mother-in-law commanded (3:6) – but does she? For it seems that she goes against her mother-in-law's plan by telling Boaz what to do instead of waiting for him to tell her. However, it is best to understand this sequence of events as Ruth seizing the opportunity when Boaz enquired, 'Who are you?' (3:9). Naomi's plan sketched the steps Ruth was to take only up to the point of the conversation with Boaz, not the words she was to speak. One can imagine Ruth anxiously lying in wait for hours, then, when the time finally comes, blurting out all that is on her heart: 'I am Ruth. Spread your wings over your servant, for you are a redeemer' (3:9). Ruth's intent is consistent with her mother-in-law's plan: to find security through a husband (3:1; cf. 1:9).[46] In this way, Ruth's ability to use circumstances as they are presented to her to achieve her aims highlights the role of human action.

The other aspect of human agency, God acting through people, can also be seen in the interactions between Ruth and Boaz. In her proposal to Boaz on the threshing floor, Ruth uses the word 'wing' (*kānāp*), which is the same word that Boaz used previously in his prayer: 'The LORD repay you for what you have done, and a full reward be given you by the LORD . . . under whose wings [*kĕnāpāyw*] you have come to take refuge' (2:12). By reusing the same word Ruth is effectively asking Boaz to be the agent through whom Yahweh will answer his prayer. In Boaz's dealings with the nearer kinsman in the legal proceedings at the town gate, we find human initiative coming to the fore again. He orders proceedings so that they are within legal bounds but he sets things up to maximize his chances of gaining Ruth as his wife. The ultimate success of Ruth's proposal through the determination and careful planning of Boaz throws the spotlight on human initiative; nonetheless, both aspects of human agency are intimately intertwined.

This intertwining is also evidenced in Naomi's benediction, proclaimed as Ruth returns from her first day of gleaning (2:20) – but to

---

[46] Halton (2012: 30–43) argues that Naomi's plan is 'an attempt at sexual entrapment'. This would be similar to Tamar's manipulation of Judah (Gen. 38). If this is the case, Ruth shows initiative by deviating from Naomi's plan and *not* taking advantage of Boaz, but instead requesting marriage.

whom is Naomi referring? She exclaims either, 'May he be blessed by the LORD, who has not abandoned his kindness [*ḥesed*] to the living and the dead' (e.g. NRSV, NASB, ESV) or 'May he be blessed by the LORD because he [i.e. Boaz] has not abandoned his kindness to the living and the dead' (e.g. NIV, NLT, CEV).[47] Is it Yahweh or Boaz showing unceasing kindness? The immediate context would suggest Yahweh but a comparison with 2 Samuel 2:5, which provides a structural parallel, would point to Boaz as the one who shows unceasing kindness.[48] Not unexpectedly, scholars are divided on this issue, as reflected in the different Bible translations. It may be best to view this as a case of deliberate ambiguity on the part of the author: that is, it refers to both Yahweh and Boaz. As such, it brings out both aspects of human agency: God is the ultimate source of kindness, not ceasing to act in blessing towards the living and the dead; specifically, God will show kindness through the initiative and actions of Boaz. Stated another way, it will be through Boaz's acts of kindness that Ruth will eventually find rest, which a reader already knows is God's provision (1:9).

Care needs to be taken to maintain a balanced view of human agency. On the one hand, we do not want to overemphasize God's use of human agents to fulfil his purposes to the detriment of the importance of human initiative and action. On the other hand, an overemphasis on human action can also negate God's foreknowledge, sovereignty and providence. For instance, Eskenazi and Frymer-Kensky (2011: li–lii, 88) suggest that God intercedes only 'after the human protagonists have done their best', and it is the words and actions of God-centred human beings that 'bring God's presence into the world' and 'prompt God to show up, as it were'. Similarly, Hawk (2015: 42) asserts: 'By foregrounding human agency, Ruth portrays God at work *in response to* rather than *as the cause of* human acts of blessing and *ḥesed*, played out against the frame of his role as the author of life and provision.' These commentators are correct to point out the prominence of human initiative in Ruth but they end up overstating their case. Hawk's position is more balanced but still throws too much weight on human initiative and action. In the book of Ruth the narrator may explicitly attribute only one action to God at the end of the narrative, but, as discussed above, God is also mentioned

---

[47] Lit. 'May he be blessed by the LORD who ['*ăšer*] has not forsaken his kindness [*ḥasdô*] for the living and the dead.' The debate surrounds the referent for 'who' (*ăšer*) and the pronominal suffix 'his' in *ḥasdô* ('his kindness').

[48] Cf. Rebera 1985: 317–327.

indirectly, especially in guiding Ruth into Boaz's field (2:1–3).[49] Additionally, every prayer throughout the narrative is answered by the end (1:8–9; 2:12, 19–20; 3:10; 4:11–12, 14). God's guidance of the events in Ruth may be unexpressed but can still be detected.[50] As such, it is not that the actions and words of the characters 'bring God's presence into the world' so much as remind us of his continuous providence. It is not that God has an open plan, waiting to see the effects of human actions, but that he has a plan which he fleshes out through the words and actions of people.

To summarize, the Ruth narrative shows that although God's direct actions can be sparse and mostly hidden, he works consistently and effectively *through* the godly actions of his people. Certainly, God accomplishes his purposes through all the actions of all people, both good and bad. The sojourn narratives in Judges show that even the disobedience of God's people cannot derail the trajectory of God's covenant promises with Israel. The disobedience of and the evil choices made by God's people may not be what God desires but they do not thwart his overall plans. Similarly, the book of Esther shows that God can use selected individuals to stop the evil intentions of the enemies of his people, even if the motives of those individuals might at times be mixed or their actions compromised. Again, the evil intentions of humans, in this case those who are not of the people of God, cannot thwart his plans. The Ruth narrative shows that God can accomplish his purposes even with only a few faithful people within a predominantly disobedient or anarchic nation.[51] He even effects his plan through the ordinary motivations and actions of his people.[52] However, perhaps from the Ruth narrative we can conclude that God works most effectively through the agency of a faithful people, instead of or in spite of a disobedient people. For it is through the initiative, motivated by kindness, of the seemingly insignificant characters in the book of Ruth that God would bring forth the most feted king of Israel, who himself would become an ancestor of the greatest king of all.

---

[49] Hals (1969: 12): 'Even the "accidental" is directed by God.'

[50] As Hals (1969: 12) observes, 'The tenor of the whole story makes it clear that the narrator sees God's hand throughout.'

[51] Hints of the anarchy described in Judg. 17 – 21 can be found in the book of Ruth, especially in the danger for Ruth as she gleans in the field (Ruth 2:9, 22). See Shepherd 2001: 444–463.

[52] These ordinary hopes, intentions and actions include 'a young girl's accidental steps and an old woman's risky plan'; see Hals 1976: 759.

The hiddenness of God and human agency in the Old Testament

Space constraints do not permit a comprehensive examination of these intertwined themes in all of the Old Testament, so in the following discussion we provide selected examples that impact on our understanding of Ruth. We draw on passages from the Pentateuch, wisdom literature, the Psalter and the Prophets.

The Pentateuch

We will consider only two examples of God's hiddenness in the Pentateuch: an instance where God's hiddenness is not a manifestation of his judgment, and a passage where it is.[53] God would have seemed hidden to the Israelites as they suffered in Egypt. A new king arose in Egypt who forgot how Joseph had preserved Egypt in time of famine, and in their bitter enslavement the Israelites could be forgiven for thinking that God had forgotten them (Exod. 1:1–14). God's promise of offspring is fulfilled many times over (1:7; 12:38), but they are not a nation in their own land. After four hundred years of slavery they cry out to God, who responds to their cry for rescue based on the covenant he had made with their forefathers (2:23–25; 3:7–8). The irony in the narrative is that it seems Pharaoh is in control but in reality God is working behind the scenes. Both aspects of human agency are in view as Pharaoh opposes God but ends up as an instrument of divine purposes.[54] Unlike in Judges and just like in Esther, God's people are not suffering because of any specific sin. God had told Abraham that Israel would be strangers in a foreign land and would be mistreated for four hundred years (Gen. 15:13). Similar to the narratives of Esther and Ruth, through the actions of some seemingly insignificant people who feared him and risked their lives in obedience to him (the Hebrew midwives), God made sure his promise to Abraham would be kept and his people would keep multiplying (Exod. 1:15–22). Through the birth of a special child (2:1–10), God was quietly pursuing his plan of rescue even before Israel cried out to him (2:23–25).

---

[53] In the Pentateuch the classic verse describing God's hiddenness and human agency is Gen. 50:20, where Joseph proclaims to his brothers: 'As for you, you meant evil against me, but God meant it for good, to bring it about that many people should be kept alive, as they are today.'

[54] This tension is manifest in passages that speak of Pharaoh hardening his heart (8:15, 32; 9:34), other passages that describe God hardening Pharaoh's heart (4:21; 7:3; 9:12; 10:1, 20, 27; 11:10; 14:4, 8, 17) and others only stating that Pharaoh's heart was hardened (7:13, 14, 23; 8:19; 9:7, 35). See Enns 2000: 130–131; Beale 1984: 129–154.

Elsewhere in the Pentateuch the withdrawal of God's presence leads to the withdrawal of deliverance for his people. In Deuteronomy, God's abandonment of his people will occur because of their disobedience, especially idolatry:

> Then my anger will be kindled against them in that day, and I will forsake them and hide my face from them, and they will be devoured. And many evils and troubles will come upon them, so that they will say in that day, 'Have not these evils come upon us because our God is not among us?' And I will surely hide my face in that day because of all the evil that they have done, because they have turned to other gods. (Deut. 31:17–18)

As a consequence of Israel's sin, God foresees that he will remove his provision and protection from them.[55] As we will see below, this is indeed what unfolds in Israel's history.

Wisdom literature

The book of Job is the prime example of God's hiddenness in the wisdom corpus.[56] In his suffering, Job felt that God had withdrawn his presence from him (Job 23:8–9). Perhaps more disconcerting for Job was that God had withdrawn his word from him. What Job yearned for was a word of explanation for his suffering from God. Job called for an audience with God because he was confident of his innocence (23:3–7, 10–12); yet at the same time he was terrified at the thought of God's presence (23:15). Throughout his suffering, Job asked many questions, but God chose to remain silent and not provide Job with answers. In Job's situation, both God's person and purposes are hidden. Similar to Esther and the book of Exodus, Job is suffering not because of any specific sin; so God's hiddenness is not an expression of his judgment, unlike what we saw in Judges. A similarity between Job and the book of Ruth is that laments are found on the lips of Job and Naomi, who both suffer under the hand of 'the Almighty' (šadday).[57] Job protests his innocence but Naomi's culpability is ambiguous

---

[55] Cf. the detailed curses for covenant disobedience (Deut. 28:15–68).

[56] It is noteworthy that most of the thought experiments of Qohelet in the book of Ecclesiastes are conducted as though God were absent.

[57] This divine name is found in Ruth 1:20–21 and thirty-one times in Job, especially clustered in chs. 22 and 27. 'Bitterness' (Ruth 1:20; Job 27:2), a speech of complaint to others and the broad movement of loss, complaint and restoration also connect the books of Job and Ruth; see Nielsen 1997: 51.

at best; in any case, for both sufferers there is a strong sense of the inexplicability of God's purposes because God has no word for their situation. Naomi primarily complains to her daughters-in-law and the women of the town, whereas Job primarily presents his complaint to God.[58] Naomi's faith in God may not be as robust as Job's, but both characters point to a correct response when God seems hidden.[59]

The Psalter

The Psalms are littered with questions raised by the problem of God's hiddenness. Naomi voices her inability to discern the person and purposes of God, and so do the psalmists. These questions asked of God are particularly found in the so-called 'lament' psalms, and include:

- 'Why, O LORD, do you stand far away? Why do you hide yourself in times of trouble?' (Ps. 10:1)
- 'How long, O LORD? Will you forget me for ever? How long will you hide your face from me?' (13:1)
- 'Awake! Why are you sleeping, O LORD? Rouse yourself! Do not reject us for ever! Why do you hide your face? Why do you forget our affliction and oppression?' (44:23–24)
- 'I say to God, my rock: "Why have you forgotten me? Why do I go mourning because of the oppression of the enemy?"' (42:9)
- 'How long, O LORD? Will you hide yourself for ever? How long will your wrath burn like fire?' (89:46)

Common to these laments is a sense of a withering of life. If the shining forth of God's face brings blessing (Num. 6:25; Pss 31:16; 67:1; 80:3, 7, 19; 104:15; 119:135; Dan. 9:17), here we find the opposite when his face is hidden. For the psalmists, the hiddenness of God is associated with a lack of deliverance: he does not hear; he does not answer; he forgets. Often in the Psalms, God's hiddenness is not associated with specific iniquity.[60] At other times, God's hiddenness is a

---

[58] Naomi's complaint to the women of the town can be understood as also addressed to God at some level; see Sakenfeld 2003: 141.

[59] Fox (2013: 22) asserts that Job's professions of faith 'stand uneasily alongside his accusations of God and his expressions of despair'. This is only partly true because heartfelt articulations to God of the pain triggered by his hiddenness can be an expression of faith. They may also be a means of coping with the anguish, setting the suffering person on the path to healing. In his honesty before God, Job stands alongside the likes of Jeremiah, the author of Lamentations, Habakkuk, the psalmists and Jesus.

[60] In fact, in the Psalms the 'hiding of God's face' is linked only once to God's anger (27:9) and twice to sin (51:11); so Balentine 1980: 152.

consequence of sin. Sin and God's presence are both found in David's penitential psalm (Ps. 51), which is a response to his crimes committed against Bathsheba and her husband Uriah (cf. 2 Sam. 11:1 – 12:15). Paradoxically, David both asks God to hide his face from his sin and then pleads with God not to remove his presence, his Holy Spirit, from him (51:9, 11). In between these supplications is the reason why David asks God to avert his face: he pleads for cleansing and renewing (51:10). Thus, in the Psalms God's hiddenness may be, but is often not, a manifestation of his judgment; rather, more commonly it is that God's purposes are obscured from the psalmists' vision. This is consistent with our findings in Exodus and Job, and to a certain extent in Ruth. As we find in Job and Ruth, the psalmists often find God's hiddenness inexplicable.[61] Put another way, God's hiddenness is expressed in his silence, or his not answering the psalmists' questions.[62]

The Prophets

The link between God's hiddenness and Israel's judgment is made clear in the Prophets. In Ezekiel, the destruction of the temple and the exile of the house of Israel led to a crisis of faith because it seemed that God had abandoned them. John Kutsko (2000: 4, 154) summarizes the core issues as: 'theodicy (Why is Israel in exile?), theophany (Where is God in exile?), and theonomy (What power does God have in exile?)'. God may have seemed absent to Israel but Ezekiel's message is that God is present and active in all the events that have befallen them: Israel is in exile because it is God's judgment for their sin; God is still present with them despite the absence of a temple; God is powerful over nations and their 'gods', and he will act to restore his people to their land.

The first temple vision (Ezek. 8 – 11) showcases the sins Israel were committing and connects these sins to God's hiddenness. Idolatry was the prime sin, and in their corrupt worship they had incorporated the syncretistic worship of foreign idols with the worship of Yahweh (8:1–18). All these abominations were taking place in the very location of God's representative presence with his people – the temple. It is because of these iniquities that God is driven from his sanctuary (8:6).[63]

---

[61] Cf. Balentine 1983: 166.

[62] Our thanks to Ong Meng Chai for this insight. For God's silence in the OT understood within the context of the ANE, see Korpel and de Moor 2011.

[63] Along with these 'religious' sins, 'social' sins are also mentioned (8:17; 9:9; cf. 7:11, 23). For a discussion of God's abandonment of the temple as developed in interaction with similar Mesopotamian accounts, see Block 2000: 15–42.

When God's glory leaves the temple (10:1–22; 11:22–25), so does God's protection, leaving his people open to invasion by foreign military forces.[64] It is not that God has been defeated by Israel's enemies and their deities, for the vision makes it clear that the destruction of Jerusalem and the temple comes from God himself (9:1–8; 11:1–13).[65] Or, as God confirms in retrospect, '[T]he house of Israel went into captivity for their iniquity, because they dealt so treacherously with me that I hid my face from them and gave them into the hand of their adversaries' (39:23).[66] That God 'hides his face' is not to be understood as God's absence in the judgment of his people; rather, instead of acting towards his people in blessing, he now acts towards them in punishment. This is reflected in the anthropomorphic idiom used elsewhere in Ezekiel, that God will 'set his face against' a person in judgment (e.g. 14:8; 15:7). In short, there is an indisputable action and consequence here: Israel forsakes God and his commands, which leads to God withdrawing his presence (hiding his face) from Israel as a manifestation of his wrath and judgment.[67]

Yet, as is consistent with God's character throughout the Bible, amidst judgment we find grace. In relation to God's hiddenness, he may seem absent in exile but the visions of the glory of God (1:4–28; 10:1–21) reveal that God is present everywhere, even in Babylon.[68] Four cherubim form God's mobile throne-chariot, with wheels that transport God in all directions (1:5–21; 10:9–22).[69] God indeed is everywhere, even outside the borders of the Promised Land, with his people in Babylon. Moreover, his presence is described more specifically: God abandons his sanctuary (*miqdāš*; 8:6) and his glory departs to the mountain on the east side of Jerusalem, the Mount of

---

[64] The halting nature of the departure of God's glory may indicate his reticence to leave his house and his people. But as a holy God, he must bring judgment against his recalcitrant, rebellious people. God's glory would return to the temple some twenty years later (40:1).

[65] God predicted the siege of Jerusalem in the sign-act that Ezekiel enacted (4:1–3). In this sign-act an iron pan symbolizes the barrier between Israel and God: he cuts himself off from Israel; he is implacable and will not listen to their cries (cf. 8:18; for God not listening to Israel's cries in the other prophets, see Isa. 1:15; Jer. 11:11; Mic. 3:4; Zech. 7:13). The iron pan and Ezekiel's attitude of 'turning his face toward' Jerusalem 'communicate God's abandonment of the city'; see Duguid 1999: 88.

[66] God forsaking his people because they have failed to maintain the requirements of the covenant is found in other prophets also, e.g. Jer. 7:28–29; 12:1, 7.

[67] Cf. 2 Esdras 1:25: 'Because you have forsaken me, I also will forsake you.'

[68] Further description of God's grace is found later in this vision (11:17–20), which anticipates the restoration oracles in Ezek. 36 – 37; 39:25–29.

[69] The multitude of eyes in the rims of the wheels (1:18; 10:12) indicates that God is able to see everything everywhere.

Olives (11:23). It does not stop there; it continues to be a sanctuary (*miqdāš*) with his people in exile, wherever they may be scattered (11:16). He has abandoned his temple but he has not abandoned his people. The surprising and unique use of the word 'sanctuary' indicates that God is personally present with his people in exile, and that they will be able to worship him even in an unclean land.[70] This use of sanctuary opens the way for its use in the New Testament, where the place of worship is personalized in Jesus (e.g. John 2:19–22). It is to him we now turn.

The hiddenness of God and human agency in the New Testament

We will now trace the trajectory of God's hiddenness through the New Testament. Due to the constraints of space, we will focus in particular on Jesus' abandonment by God.

Perhaps the best-known example of God's hiddenness in the New Testament is Jesus' cry of dereliction on the cross. The passion narratives lay stress on the abandonment of Jesus not just by God, but also by all of Jesus' followers and God's own people.[71] Jesus is crucified with just two thieves next to him, but even they recede to the background of the narrative so that the spotlight is just on Jesus and God.[72] Yet at the hour of death, Jesus, quoting from Psalm 22:1, cries 'My God, my God, why have you forsaken me?' (Matt. 27:46; Mark 15:34). As in the psalm, so now with Jesus: God remains silent (Ps. 22:2).[73] At the point of death Jesus is completely alone; even God has abandoned him. How are we to understand this cry of forsakenness?

There are some explanations that can be rejected. First is the idea that Jesus felt abandoned by God but, in reality, he was not. In this view, the words of Jesus refer to his feeling of desolation. Yet it would be better to take Jesus' words at face value: if he says God has forsaken

---

[70] Block 1997: 349. Nonetheless, the full phrase is 'a sanctuary *mě'aṭ*' ('in small measure' [NJPS] or 'for a little while' [ESV, NIV]), which reveals that God's presence in exile will not be to the same degree or length of time that it had been previously.

[71] For example, in Matthew Jesus is abandoned by his disciples (26:56) and Peter (26:69–75), and is then effectively rejected by the Jews (27:39–40) and Jewish leaders (27:41–43).

[72] The two criminals also revile Jesus, just as the Roman soldiers (27:27–31) and the Jews had.

[73] The turning point of the psalm is when God 'answers' the psalmist (Ps. 22:21). The motif of God answering forms an *inclusio* in this psalm; see Stuhlmueller 1982.

him, we should take that as indicating what really happened. Second, in quoting the beginning of Psalm 22, Jesus refers to the whole psalm, which ends with a note of trust and reassurance. Jesus' cry is thus one of faith, and looks beyond suffering to triumph.[74] There is some truth to this, for Jesus remained firm in his faith; but the strong and clear note of Jesus' cry is one of agony, not victory. Only the beginning of the psalm is quoted by Jesus, and the verse indicates that he was cut off from his Father.

It is best to interpret Jesus' cry as a witness to some form of withdrawal of God's presence from Jesus. For one who had experienced a perfect relationship with the Father from eternity past, this rupture would have caused a degree of pain and anguish that we, as finite creatures, cannot grasp. God the Father was somehow separated from God the Son, as indicated by the cosmic darkness (Matt. 27:45; Mark 15:33; cf. Amos 8:9–10).[75] Old Testament prophets assert that God cannot bear to look upon evil (Hab. 1:13) and that sin separates people from God (Isa. 59:2). Jesus, who bore the weight of the world's sins, is at this point separated from God's presence for our sake, and he thus experienced the full force of God's judgment.[76]

There are a few points of significance for our discussion of God's hiddenness. God usually 'hides his face' from and manifests his judgment against a person or people because of their sin. As noted above, in the case of Jesus, he withdraws his presence because of the sins of the world: Jesus is unique in the Bible in suffering judgment he did not deserve. Although characters in Scripture felt that human support had failed and/or that God was absent or had forsaken them (e.g. Job and Naomi), it was only Jesus who was truly forsaken by everyone he knew. Unlike others in the Bible, at no point was God's plan obscure to Jesus; yet he was willing to carry it out to completion, fully trusting in God (e.g. Matt. 26:39, 42). Ironically, for those who conspired and acted against Jesus, God's plan was hidden, yet their personal motivations and volition did not derail God's purposes.

Indeed, God was working despite the evil intentions of those who crucified Jesus. As the apostle Peter states: 'This Jesus, delivered up

---

[74] E.g. Trudinger 1974: 235–238. In relation to Mark 15:34, see Donahue and Harrington 2002: 451.

[75] Carson 2010: 646.

[76] It is not for us to speculate how the Father and Son are separated; cf. Carson (2010: 647): 'If we ask in what ontological sense the Father and Son are here divided, the answer must be that we do not know because we are not told.' See also Morris 1965b: 48–49.

according to the definite plan and foreknowledge of God, you crucified and killed by the hands of lawless men' (Acts 2:23). It seemed that the Jewish leaders and the Romans had the upper hand as they conspired to kill Jesus, but in reality what they did was fulfilling God's plan to use Jesus' death to save many. Both aspects of human agency are once again apparent. God hid his face from Jesus and he was handed over to his adversaries, but through these human agents God accomplished his salvation purposes.

Conclusion

This chapter explored God's hiddenness, which is the concealment of his person or activity in the biblical text and/or the obscurity of his purposes. To different degrees, both aspects of God's hiddenness were found in the three narratives we discussed: Judges, Esther and Ruth. One effect of God's hiddenness is to highlight the initiative of the human characters. In Judges it foregrounds human initiative in a negative way, and in Esther and in Ruth human initiative is portrayed as mostly positive. Whether human initiative is positive or negative, God still accomplishes his purposes and fulfils his plans. This principle remained true as we traced the intertwined themes of God's hiddenness and human agency through the Old Testament and the New Testament.

The different responses to God's hiddenness in the three narratives point to some appropriate initiatives for Christians today. Often in times of difficulty or suffering it seems as though God is hidden or distant. At other times he may seem present but we cannot understand God's purposes in our pain. If, as in Judges and perhaps at the beginning of Ruth, God withdraws as an expression of judgment because of sin, then the correct response is to examine our lives, to repent of sin and to seek God's forgiveness. As the apostle John assures us: 'If we confess our sins, he is faithful and just to forgive us our sins and to cleanse us from all unrighteousness' (1 John 1:9). If, as in Esther, we suffer simply because we are God's people, the correct response is to keep trusting him, to keep praying and to keep doing good (cf. Isa. 8:17; 1 Pet. 4:19). As we keep doing these things in faith, as we see the characters in Ruth doing, we can gain assurance from the apostle Peter's words: 'And after you have suffered for a little while, the God of all grace, who has called you to his eternal glory in Christ, will himself restore, confirm, strengthen, and establish you' (1 Pet. 5:10).

Chapter Eight

Redemption in Ruth

Redemption is a central theme that courses through the Bible, and hence an important theme in biblical theology. In common Christian parlance, 'redemption' simply means 'salvation'. We will examine the biblical evidence to determine if the word has a more specific meaning. Since redemption has been dealt with elsewhere,[1] in this chapter we will focus on the aspects of redemption relevant to the Ruth narrative. This chapter will consider the redeemers in the book of Ruth within the narrative itself, and then consider the contribution of Ruth to the biblical-theological theme. The final section of this chapter will consider if Boaz is a type of Christ or not.[2]

Redeemers in Ruth

In the Ruth narrative Boaz is the kinsman-redeemer who immediately springs to mind but two others are actually named.[3] Mr So-and-So is a kinsman-redeemer more closely related to Naomi than Boaz. Naomi is aware of this, since she refers to Boaz as 'one of our redeemers' (*miggō'ălēnû*; 2:20). She also refers to him as 'our relative' (*mōda'tānû*) instead of 'our kinsman-redeemer' (*gō'ălēnû*) when she outlines her threshing floor scheme to Ruth (3:2). In turn, Ruth in her initiative makes it clear to Boaz that she wants him to act as her kinsman-redeemer (3:9). However, she says 'a redeemer' (*gō'ēl*) not 'the redeemer' (*haggō'ēl*; cf. 4:1, 3, 6, 8), reflecting her awareness of another, nearer kinsman-redeemer. Boaz's response to Ruth confirms this, and the stage is set for this nearer kinsman to respond to his obligation (3:12–13). At first he accepts the role of kinsman-redeemer for Naomi and the field belonging to Elimelech (4:4), but when Ruth

---

[1] See especially Morris 1965a: 11–64 and Stott 1986: 175–182. Stott discusses redemption as one of the images of salvation, along with propitiation, justification and reconciliation.

[2] Material in this chapter has been adapted with permission from Lau 2012–2016b.

[3] Although she is not named as such in the narrative, Ruth's central and indispensable role in Obed's birth means that she, in a sense, is also a 'redeemer' for Naomi. Through Ruth's actions Naomi's life is restored: from empty and bitter to fulfilled and satisfied (cf. 1:3–5, 21 with 4:15–17).

is included as part of the deal, he reneges (4:6). This nearer kinsman functions as a foil for the one who will accept the responsibility: Boaz.

The second kinsman-redeemer apart from Boaz is Obed. The first sentence of the blessing given by the women of the town might lead to the understanding that they are referring to Boaz as the redeemer (4:14), but the second sentence of their blessing makes it clear that they are referring to Boaz's son, Obed (4:15). It is surprising that Obed is identified as a kinsman-redeemer, since elsewhere in the Old Testament a redeemer is always an adult. How does Obed function in this role? When Obed grows up, he will protect and provide for Naomi in her old age (4:15), a role usually given to biological sons. Even as a child he 'redeems' Naomi from her bitterness and emptiness (1:20–21), for now 'a son' has been born to her (4:17). Although they can never be fully replaced, the sons (*yelādîm*; 1:5) she lost have been replaced by this son (*yeled*; 4:17).[4] Of course, Obed is not literally Naomi's son; indeed, the baby is not even related to her by blood, since his parents are Naomi's daughter-in-law and a relative of her deceased husband's. However, through the working of the levirate law, the son is in Elimelech's line and so is legally hers. Thus, consistent with the meaning of his name, 'servant', Obed serves Naomi both at his birth and when he is fully grown.

Obed is involved in redemption in another way. His birth signals the continuation of Elimelech's family line. As Boaz says, taking Ruth as his wife means that it is possible to perpetuate the name of the dead (Elimelech and Mahlon in particular) in his inheritance (Ruth 4:10; cf. v. 5). Obed's birth signifies the restoration of what was lost, the 'raising up' of descendants for the deceased. As Boaz describes it, Elimelech and Mahlon were each 'cut off from among his brothers and from his native place' (4:10). Without an heir to continue the family line, it 'teeters perilously on the brink of annihilation'.[5] In this sense, Obed lives up to his name by 'serving' Elimelech and Mahlon by redeeming their honour, reputation and posthumous existence.[6]

Finally, reading Obed as kinsman-redeemer within the storyline of the Old Testament may anticipate another redeemer.[7] In the historical

---

[4] This is the only place in the OT where *yelādîm* is used of adult men. It is also translated as 'lads', 'children' or 'youth'; see BDB, 409. Conspicuously, elsewhere in Ruth 1 the regular word for sons (*bnym*) is used (1:1, 2, 3, 11, 12).

[5] Hubbard 1991: 15. In ancient Israel, when a family died out it ceased to exist metaphysically.

[6] Cf. Block 1999: 720.

[7] Our thanks to T. D. Alexander for suggesting some of the ideas in this paragraph (personal communication, 14 November 2011).

period in which the book of Ruth was set, the nation of Israel was in desperate straits. The heart of Israel's problem was moral and religious anarchy (Judg. 17 – 21).[8] By the end of the book of Judges, it seems as if Israel's situation was almost irredeemable. Yet there is a strand of royal hope running from Genesis to Ruth and beyond.[9] In particular, there will be a future king from the tribe of Judah (Gen. 49:8–12). Indeed, the faint glimmer of hope at the end of the book of Judges rests in a future king (17:6; 18:1; 19:1; 21:25). Understood within this trajectory, it may be not only that Obed will redeem Naomi in the present time of the narrative and the immediate future, but that a future descendant of Obed will redeem Israel in a future generation. There is a hint of a type anticipating a future event within the Old Testament:[10] Boaz transforms Naomi's future as her kinsman-redeemer; Obed redeems a father's house within Israel; and Boaz's great-grandson, David, will redeem the nation of Israel.[11] To rephrase it in terms of his name and role: Obed the 'servant' became the forebear of one whom God called 'my servant David' and by whose hand God would 'save [his] people Israel' (2 Sam. 3:18). An even greater servant king would come from David's house (Luke 1:69).

The third and most prominent kinsman-redeemer in the book of Ruth is Boaz. He is named as such by Naomi and Ruth (2:20; 3:9), and he himself confirms this designation (3:12; 4:4). Boaz's characteristics and actions will be discussed in the next section.

The contribution of Ruth to redemption

The Ruth narrative provides a concrete, particular example of redemption. The redemption in Ruth adds a colourful thread to the rich tapestry of this biblical-theological theme. We will consider what the Ruth narrative highlights about the redeemed, the cost, the redeemer, and the kinship connection.

---

[8] Note especially the refrain, 'Everyone did what was right in his own eyes' (17:6; 21:25).

[9] See Alexander 1998b: esp. chs. 3–6.

[10] For further discussion about what constitutes a type, see later in this chapter. Typological links can be found not just between the Testaments but also within the OT. Osborne (2001: 930) mentions the exodus in Isa. 57:7–12 and the wilderness in Ps. 95:7–12. For other OT examples, see Beale 2012: 16, 20 22; Baker 2010: 171–172.

[11] Samson, the last judge in the book of Judges, is said to 'begin to save Israel from the hand of the Philistines' (Judg. 13:5). He only begins the process that will be completed by King David (2 Sam. 5:17–25; 8:1). David does not eradicate the Philistines but they are not a serious threat to Israel after his time (cf. 1 Kgs 4:21; 2 Kgs 18:8).

The redeemed

The story of Ruth provides a vivid illustration of the desperate state of those who need redemption. For a modern reader, the immediate and most pressing need that comes into view is Naomi and Ruth's material poverty. Naomi returns to Bethlehem because she hears that God has broken the famine in Israel (1:6). However, bereft of male support and without mention of any ancestral land, the widows don't have bread on their table. The destitute widows are left to the mercy of landowners who might or might not allow a foreign woman to glean in their fields (2:2). Through the resourcefulness of Ruth and the generosity of Boaz, their hunger pangs are assuaged – at least for the duration of the barley and wheat harvests (2:23). The end of the harvest seasons is the trigger for Naomi's threshing floor scheme, which is aimed at securing marriage for Ruth, along with a ticket out of destitution for both widows (3:1). At this point in the narrative a more desperate need requiring redemption comes into focus.

In the broader context, the greater need requiring redemption is the threat of extinction of an Israelite family line. This would have been an acute concern for an ancient Israelite because ongoing existence was thought to continue through the family name on a landed inheritance. The problem of the extinction of the family line is already raised in the introduction of the Ruth narrative, when all the males in Elimelech's line die out (1:5). Part of Boaz's exuberant response to Ruth on the threshing floor stems from his realization that Ruth's marriage request contains the potential for Elimelech's line to be continued (3:10). Boaz makes this clear at the town gate, when he explains the reason for the inclusion of marriage to Ruth with the land purchase: 'to raise up [*lĕhāqîm*] the name of the deceased on his inheritance' (4:5, our translation). 'Raise up' has been translated as 'maintain' (NIV) or 'perpetuate' (ESV), but in this instance 'raise up' is to be preferred because it brings out the idea that, at that point in time, Elimelech's legacy was dead. He had no heir to continue his name, to perpetuate his existence; his legacy needed to be resurrected. If a son were not born to continue Elimelech's family line on his property, he would be cut off from his clan and from representation at the assembly at the town gate (4:10). A family line is about to be snuffed out, and in this case the one who needs help is dead – so he certainly can't help himself!

In the Old Testament, this powerlessness is a key condition of those requiring redemption. Those redeemed were formerly held under the authority or control of another, and in that state were not able to gain release under their own power. As a people, Israel suffered under the ruthless oppression of Pharaoh, and cried out to God because they could not break their bondage (Exod. 2:23). As a nation, Israel would again be under the authority of a foreign power in Babylon. Again, they would need God to intervene in their weakness to redeem them. For instance, the prophet Jeremiah envisions the restoration of both Israel and Judah, who will be ransomed and redeemed by God 'from hands too strong' for them (Jer. 31:11). In the end, Zion will be saved, and it is no surprise that its people will be called 'the Redeemed of the LORD' (Isa. 62:12).

Weakness is also a condition of individuals who require redemption in the Old Testament, not just of Israel as a nation. In the Psalms, God's redemption of Israel as a nation is present, but the majority of uses of *g'l* (redeem) and *pdh* (redeem/ransom) refer to God's action towards individuals.[12] God rescues individuals from different forms of danger, but in all instances he redeems those who cannot help themselves –the weak, the poor and the needy (e.g. Ps. 72:12–14). God is also presented as advocating on behalf of those who are powerless under the law and those who do not have legal representation, such as the fatherless (Prov. 23:11).

In the law, God also makes provision for the redemption of those too weak to secure release themselves. Primarily, this is the role of the kinsman-redeemer, which is outlined in Leviticus 25. This chapter is all to do with freedom and release from bondage: laws in relation to the Sabbath year (vv. 1–7), the jubilee (vv. 8–22), redemption of land and houses (vv. 25–34), redemption of the poor and maintaining freedom (vv. 35–46), and redemption from indentured service. Redemption of property and slaves by a kinsman-redeemer (*go'el*) was the most common form of redemption in the Old Testament. This redeemer was a close male relative from the same clan. The closer the familial relation, the greater the obligation to redeem on behalf of the family member in need (Lev. 25:25). It is not restricted to immediate family (e.g. brother, father), since the law also includes uncles and cousins in the potential list of kinsman-redeemers (Lev. 25:49). Beyond this list, any blood relative from his clan can redeem

---

[12] The verses referring to God redeeming (using root *g'l*) individuals are: Pss 72:14; 103:4; 119:154; and redeeming the nation: Pss 74:2; 77:15; 106:10; 107:2. The verses referring to God redeeming (using root *pdh*) individuals are: Pss 26:11; 31:5; 34:22; 49:15; 55:18; 71:23; 119:134; and redeeming the nation: Pss 25:22; 44:26; 78:42; 130:8. Psalm 69:18 uses both verbs in parallel in reference to redemption of an individual.

(Lev. 25:49). In short, whoever can redeem a relative should do so, with the greater responsibility falling to nearer kin. If the Israelite did not have a kinsman-redeemer but acquired sufficient means, he could redeem his land or himself.

Land was an inheritance from God, with Israelites simply tenants on his land (Lev. 25:23–24). Therefore, land could not be permanently sold outside the family, and at the jubilee the land reverted to the original tenant or his heirs (Lev. 25:8–23).[13] If an Israelite became impoverished, he could sell the usufruct of his land. At this point, a kinsman-redeemer could redeem the property and restore it to the family. The amount paid for redemption was determined by the number of years it was held by the buyer (Lev. 25:27).

A kinsman-redeemer was also obliged to redeem relatives sold into slavery (Lev. 25:47–53).[14] If an Israelite became destitute and sold himself to a resident alien, the Israelite held the same rights of redemption as regards the land. That is, a relative could redeem him or, if he gained the means, he could redeem himself. The amount to be paid was calculated in light of the years to the next jubilee. Similarly to the land, if the Israelite was not redeemed, he was to be released at the year of jubilee (25:54–55).

In all these circumstances (redeeming property and slavery on the behalf of a relative), the kinsman-redeemer intervenes on behalf of another who is not only in need, but unable to redeem himself.

Ruth and Naomi's economic and social bondage points to the spiritual bondage of all humanity. We might or might not be enslaved to material poverty but the New Testament makes it clear that we are all slaves to sin, which leads to death (e.g. Rom. 5:12; 6:16–20, 23). As Christians, we are redeemed from the curse of the law (Gal. 3:13), and released from slavery to the law and the power of sin (4:5). Rescue is from God's judgment of our trespasses. Just like Ruth and Naomi and the family line of Elimelech, we need someone to intervene to redeem us. In fact, Paul says that in our natural, sinful state, we are 'dead in our trespasses' (Eph. 2:5; Col. 2:13) – we cannot save ourselves.

The cost

The issue of the costly nature of redemption is raised by the nearer kinsman-redeemer. When it becomes clear that the redemption would

[13] Cf. Levine 1989: 174.
[14] For the proposal that Lev. 25:25–55 represents three stages of destitution, see Milgrom 2000: 2191–2193.

trigger a levirate marriage with Ruth, the nearer kinsman reneges on the deal. His stated reason is that it would ruin his inheritance (4:6). The initial cost of redeeming the property isn't the issue: the nearer kinsman was willing to pay that price (4:4). One problem was the ongoing cost of feeding Naomi and Ruth, and any children through Ruth. The vicissitudes of subsistence agriculture meant this increased burden would increase the risk to himself and his family. The downward spiral into poverty and then bond-service highlights the dreaded possible outcome (Lev. 25:23–55). Moreover, the initial and ongoing cost would have no ultimate benefit for the nearer kinsman, since the property would be inherited only by any son he would produce with Ruth: it would not be divided among the nearer kinsman's other sons. And when the property was transferred to the heir who would continue Elimelech's family line, any benefit of the produce of the land would be lost. The nearer kinsman's response, by contrast, highlights the cost that Boaz was willing to bear.

Out of kindness Boaz is willing to redeem Elimelech's property and marry Ruth. Boaz's response on the threshing floor reveals that he found Ruth attractive, especially her virtuous character (3:10–11). Even so, Boaz's decision still entailed significant risk, as voiced by Boaz's foil, Mr So-and-So (4:6). If Boaz did not have children already, there was also the risk that Ruth was infertile and so could not produce an heir to continue his line. The risk came with a high cost, as discussed above. Despite knowing the risk and the cost, Boaz followed through on his commitment.[15]

Sometimes the costly nature of redemption is downplayed. For instance, Robert Hubbard (2000b: 716) defines redemption as 'The release of people, animals or property from bondage through outside help'. Hubbard mentions 'outside help' but does not specify the nature of this assistance. Leon Morris (1965a: 61), however, demonstrates that the payment of a price is a 'necessary component' of redemption. This is clear in relation to two words linked to the concept of redemption in the Old Testament: *pādâ* ('ransom' or 'redeem') and *kōper* ('ransom').[16]

---

[15] For further discussion of the motivations of Mr So-and-So and Boaz in regard to redeeming the land and marrying Ruth, see Lau 2011: 74–83. Additionally, if Rahab was an ancestress of Boaz (Matt. 1:5), this might have predisposed him to act in kindness towards foreigners, including Ruth. Most scholars accept that the Rahab listed in the Matthean genealogy is the Rahab in the Joshua narrative (Josh. 2; 6:17, 23–25). See especially Brown 1982.

[16] The biblical-theological approach focuses not only on words and word studies but also on concepts and themes in the Bible's storyline; so e.g. Rosner 2000: 6–8.

However, it is not as clear as Morris suggests that 'redemption' (*go'el*) always includes a price.

There are at least three instances in the Old Testament where redemption is used more generally. First, redemption is commonly used in the Psalms for God's rescue of individuals from enemies (e.g. Pss 31:4–5; 69:18), Sheol and death (49:15), oppression and violence (72:14). At times, God may deliver individuals through intermediaries, such as kings, as they act in a God-like way (e.g. 72:12–14).[17] The psalmists' prayers are an expression of their confidence in a God who can deliver: he redeemed Israel from Egypt, so he can redeem again for the psalmist.[18] This usage is also found in Job, in the sense of preserving or saving people from calamities such as war and famine (Job 5:19–22).[19] Second, the role of a 'redeemer of blood' was to redeem the life of a relative by killing the relative's murderer (Num. 35:16–29; Deut. 19:4–13; cf. Josh. 20:1–6; 2 Sam. 14:8–11). Third, God acts as redeemer by advocating on a person's behalf in legal cases (Prov. 23:11). Similarly, Job also famously affirms the presence of a redeemer who will take up his case and bring it before the court of heaven. He declares, 'My redeemer lives' but it is not clear who the redeemer is and when Job expects to be redeemed (Job 19:25–27). Nonetheless, by the end of the book it is God who has vindicated Job before his friends (42:7).[20] Thus, in these three instances the transactional element, with the payment of a price, is not clearly in view. Nonetheless, Morris' insistence that redemption is more specific than just 'deliverance' or 'salvation' is consistent with the most prominent uses of 'redeemer' in the Old Testament.

Overall, the biblical-theological picture places emphasis on redemption through a price or a cost.[21] Indeed, in the Old Testament,

[17] That the human king follows in the way of God, commissioned to care for the weak and the poor on God's behalf, can be seen in Ps. 72:1–2. God's justice and righteousness are granted to the king (72:1) so that he can maintain righteousness and justice (72:2). For further discussion, see e.g. Hossfeld and Zenger 2005: 213, 216.

[18] Cf. Craigie and Tate (2004: 260): '[T]he word "redeem" recalls the Exodus; as God had redeemed his people in the Exodus from Egyptian slavery (cf. Deut. 7:8), so too the psalmist prays for redemption.'

[19] See chapter 6.

[20] Note the repetition of the key words 'know' (19:25; cf. 42:2) and 'see' (19:26; cf. 42:5) in Job's response to God (42:1–6). Cf. Habel 1985: 309. For discussions of alternative interpretations of Job 19:25–27, see Clines 1989: 457–466; Hartley 1988: 292–297.

[21] Marshall (1974: 153–154 n. 4) clarifies 'price' and 'cost' in relation to redemption: 'It would be more precise to use the term "price" for those cases where some *payment* or exchange is *received* by the person from whom the captive is delivered, and to use the term "cost" for whatever *expenditure* of money, life and effort is *demanded* on the part of the redeemer' (emphasis original).

redemption often involves a commercial transaction. The redemption of property and slaves performed by a kinsman-redeemer occurred through the payment of a price (Lev. 25:25–33, 48–51), which was calculated according to the number of years until the jubilee (Lev. 25:48–52). A redemption price for all firstborn was also due to Yahweh. In commemoration of Israel's redemption from Egypt and the tenth plague, every firstborn male was to be consecrated to God (Exod. 13:2).[22] When firstborn Israelite sons were one month old, they were to be redeemed by paying five shekels to the priests (Exod. 13:13–15; Num. 3:47–48). Also, a redemption price could be paid for those who made a vow of persons, either themselves or a child (Lev. 27:2–8). Objects 'vowed to the LORD' also could be redeemed at a price, calculated as their value plus 20 % (Lev. 27:13, 15, 19). All these cases of personal redemption required the payment of a price.

National redemption also involved a cost. Israel's redemption from Egypt required not the payment of money but the expenditure of God's power. By the strength of his outstretched arm and mighty hand God overcame the power of Pharaoh with 'great acts of judgment' (Exod. 6:6; Deut. 7:8). That God expended great power to ensure his people's redemption is underlined elsewhere in the Old Testament (e.g. Neh. 1:10; Ps. 77:14, 15). As Morris (1965a: 22) argues, 'This stress on Yahweh's effort seems to be the reason for applying the redemption terminology to his dealings, for it is regarded as the "price" which gives point to the metaphor.' The concept of an inherent cost associated with redemption is also argued by Brad Embry (2013: 263), who observes that the terms 'redeem' (gā'al) and 'acquire' (qānâ) are used in combination in Moses' song (Exod. 15:13–16). He argues that Yahweh's act of redemption of Israel in the exodus is also 'an act of acquisition . . . [I]t is Yahweh's "payment" for Israel.'

God's redemption in the exodus is effected by the blood of the Passover lamb; the exodus and the Passover are presented as inseparable events (Exod. 12). There is no consensus about the significance of the blood of the lamb smeared on the doorposts.[23] However, at least three factors point to the blood as symbolizing more than just protection:

---

[22] However, a firstborn donkey could be redeemed by a sheep (Exod. 13:13; 34:20). This redemption may have been for practical, not cultic, reasons; see Durham 1987: 179.

[23] Most commentators agree that the blood is protective, but many baulk at any further significance. For an exception, see Motyer 2005: 132–137.

1. Blood as the essence of life is already known by this time in the storyline of the Bible (Gen. 9:4).[24]
2. The blood of the lamb preserves the life of the Israelite firstborn; the contrast is with the Egyptian firstborn who are not spared since they aren't protected by the daubed blood of a slaughtered lamb (Exod. 12:29–30).
3. The idea of an animal life laid down for a human life is also found in the following chapter, where the firstborn Israelite son can be redeemed by the sacrifice of an animal (Exod. 13:1–2, 11–16).

Thus, not only the exodus but also the Passover contained an element of cost. The Passover lamb anticipated the idea of substitutionary atonement,[25] which is expanded upon elsewhere in the Pentateuch.[26] In the Old Testament, the concept of God paying a ransom price (*kōper*) in exchange for his people is also found in Isaiah 43:3–4. In these verses, nations (Egypt, Cush, Seba) are paid as the price for exchange, either metaphorically or literally, as an extended empire for Cyrus.[27]

The New Testament authors develop this idea of the costliness of redemption. They especially apply the concept of the price that must be paid to redeem people from slavery, as well as that of God's national redemption. Jesus' death is the ransom paid for the deaths of many (Matt. 20:28; Mark 10:45). The apostle Paul makes it clear that Christians have been 'bought with a price' (1 Cor. 6:20; 7:23); we have redemption through Jesus' blood (Eph. 1:7). The apostle Peter also speaks of redemption by the payment of a ransom: not the payment of silver or gold (such as Boaz paid), but the priceless blood of Christ. Believers have been ransomed from their futile way of life through the sacrifice of Christ, the lamb without blemish (1 Pet. 1:18–19). In Revelation, the Lamb is worthy of praise because he ransomed people from all over the earth by his blood (Rev. 5:9). This imagery is reminiscent of the Passover lamb, whose blood delivered the Israelite firstborn (Exod. 12).

[24] Blood as life essence is found elsewhere in the Pentateuch: Lev. 17:11, 14; Deut. 12:23.

[25] Cf. Fretheim (1991: 138): 'It is the *life given* that provides life for Israel' (emphasis original).

[26] Wenham (1979: 94) suggests that all the animal sacrifices included an element of substitutionary atonement. See especially Lev. 16, the Day of Atonement.

[27] For the former suggestion, see Oswalt 1998: 140; and for the latter, see Webb 1996: 175.

Consistent through both the Old Testament and the New Testament, the redeemed are freed to serve God, who places ethical demands on them. In the Old Testament, Israelites are redeemed from oppressive bondage under Pharaoh to become slaves of God (Lev. 25:42, 55). In response, Israelites were to act generously and with compassion towards sojourners (e.g. Deut. 10:19), hired servants (e.g. Deut. 15:13–15), and the marginalized and underprivileged (e.g. Deut. 24:17–21). God's redeemed people were not to repeat the oppression and cruelty of their former masters (e.g. Deut. 24:18, 22). In the New Testament, Zechariah, John the Baptist's father, highlights the fact that redemption leads to serving God without fear (Luke 1:68–75). The sacrifice of Jesus means that Christians have been 'bought with a price' and are now slaves to Christ (1 Cor. 6:19–20; 7:22). We have been bought with a price to do God's will. This includes glorifying God with our bodies (1 Cor. 6:20) and not seeking to be enslaved to human opinion and wisdom (1 Cor. 7:23).[28] Ultimately, our redemption is to result in the praise of God's glory (Eph. 1:14).

The redeemer

The Ruth narrative highlights the essential character, motivation and ability of a redeemer. In buying the field and marrying Ruth, Boaz acts with an element of selflessness; he acts for the benefit of others who are in need. To be sure, Boaz possibly had mixed motives: his attraction to Ruth's noble character, and the possible lack of an heir himself. Nonetheless, his actions in redemption were not without risk. This risk is raised by the nearer-kinsman, who is concerned that he will ruin his own inheritance (4:6). If Boaz himself lacked an heir, there was a risk associated with marrying Ruth, since she had been barren for up to ten years of marriage (1:4–5). This points to the selfless element of redemption, for Boaz had to risk his immediate security in having to provide for Naomi and Ruth, and he also risked his future legacy by marrying Ruth, who might have remained infertile. As he states, he is acting for the sake of his fellow clansman, to raise up Mahlon's name and ongoing existence (4:10).

Indeed, Boaz's actions can be understood as being characterized by *ḥesed*. There is some debate about whether Naomi is extolling Yahweh's or Boaz's *ḥesed* in 2:20.[29] It may be that the referent is left deliberately ambiguous. Nevertheless, whether Boaz is explicitly

---

[28] Cf. Fee 1987: 320.
[29] See the discussion in chapter 7.

described as doing *ḥesed* or not in the Ruth narrative, it is clear that this infuses much of his actions.[30] Acts of *ḥesed* are generous, often going beyond obligation or what is strictly required, for the benefit of someone who is not able to help him- or herself.[31] As discussed above, kindness is also expressed in acts of self-sacrifice that often contain inherent risk. Such is the character and motivation of a redeemer.

Yet these qualities of a redeemer are of no value unless that person is able to redeem. In the book of Ruth, Boaz is presented as 'a man of great worth' (*'îš gibbôr ḥayil*; Ruth 2:1 ['a worthy man', ESV]). The word translated 'worth' (*ḥayil*) has the basic meaning 'strength, power', and is used in military (of an army), physical (of a man), material (wealth of a person) and moral (virtue of a person) senses.[32] In the book of Ruth, the description of Boaz as 'a man of great worth' would encompass the last two senses, and 'great' (*gibbôr*) would imply that Boaz is a particularly fine example.[33] His moral worth has just been discussed but it is his material worth that provides the means for him to redeem: for Boaz is presented as a wealthy landowner (Ruth 2). He possesses fields, along with a foreman to supervise his male and female servants. Thus, not only is Boaz willing, but he is also able to redeem Ruth.

Expanding our view to the rest of the Old Testament, we find that God is the great Redeemer. God's redemption of Israel from slavery in Egypt is the original and foundational act of redemption (Exod. 6:6). The seminal nature of the exodus is evidenced in all sections of the Old Testament. In the Law the exodus is motivation for obeying the whole law (e.g. Exod. 20:2; Deut. 5:6), as well as individual laws (e.g. Exod. 13:1–16; Deut. 24:17–18). The Prophets draw on the exodus as the paradigm for Israel's redemption from Babylonian exile (e.g. Isa. 40:1–11; 43; Jer. 16:14–15; 23:7–8; Ezek. 20:33–34). In the Psalms the exodus is the foundational redemptive event (e.g. Ps. 106:8–10). Not surprisingly, then, 'Redeemer' (*go'el*) is a popular title for God – especially in Psalms (19:14; 78:35) and Isaiah (Isa. 41:14; 43:14; 44:6, 24; 47:4; 48:17; 49:7, 26; 54:5, 8; 59:20; 60:16; 63:16).

As Redeemer, kindness (*ḥesed*) is one of God's core characteristics. God underlined this characteristic by declaring it twice as he passed

[30] See chapter 7.
[31] Cf. the definitions by Clark 1993: 267; Sakenfeld 1978: 55; Andersen 1986: 44. In the OT, *ḥesed* has a strong element of benevolence over obligation; *pace* Sakenfeld.
[32] See BDB, 298; *HALOT* 1:311–312.
[33] See BDB, 1368; *HALOT* 1:172.

by Moses. His kindness is described as both abounding and enduring (Exod. 34:6, 7).[34] This characteristic is closely linked with Israel's redemption (*g'l*) from Egypt in the Old Testament (e.g. Exod. 15:13).[35] This characteristic of God also motivates his redemption of his people from spiritual bondage. This type of redemption is developed in the Prophets and Writings. The background to this development is the exile. Israel are languishing in a foreign land and need to be redeemed, just like in Egypt. However, unlike in Egypt, Israel are in exile because of their sin. Hence, this time round Israel need a double redemption – both physical and spiritual.[36] Thankfully, God is up to the task. For those who repent, forgiveness and a clean slate are available (Isa. 44:21–28, esp. v. 22). The urgency of repentance for redemption is also found elsewhere in Isaiah (59:20). In Psalm 130, usually dated to the post-exilic period, God is also declared as the one who will redeem his people from their iniquities and 'the evil situations set in motion by them' (Ps. 130:8).[37] Indeed, with Yahweh is kindness (*ḥesed*), and his redemption (*pdh*) is plentiful (Ps. 130:7). God not only redeems Israel from captivity but also deals with the underlying problem that led to their captivity – sin.

To summarize, in the Old Testament God is willing to act on behalf of another who is in need, to redeem from slavery or harm those who cannot help themselves. This bondage is revealed to be both physical and spiritual. Moreover, God is able to redeem. As Hubbard notes, God is the ideal and prime Redeemer in the Old Testament because 'he has overwhelmingly superior power, cosmic stature, and infinite wealth'.[38]

The role of the human kinsman-redeemer in the law echoes that of the great Redeemer. This is revealed in God's motive clauses in Leviticus 25: why he commands his people to be involved in releasing and redeeming. Because God has released them from bondage to slavery in Egypt, they are not to be enslaved to each other (Lev. 25:38,

---

[34] This declaration of God's character becomes central to understanding what he is like (e.g. Neh. 9:17, 31; Pss 86:15; 103:8; 136; Jer. 32:18; Dan. 9:4; Joel 2:13; Jon. 4:2).
[35] God's steadfast love is repeated as a refrain in every verse of Ps. 136. His works of creation (136:4–9), redemption (vv. 10–16, 23–24), inheritance (vv. 17–22) and provision (v. 25) are all evidence of his steadfast love.
[36] Cf. Stead and Davies (2013: 53), who discuss the mixing of atonement and redemption metaphors in Isa. 40 – 55, and point to the Servant as the one who will redeem Israel from their sins (Isa. 52:13 – 53:12).
[37] Hossfeld and Zenger 2011: 438. For arguments for a post-exilic date for this psalm, see Allen 2002: 255; Kraus 1989: 465–466; Hossfeld and Zenger 2011: 427.
[38] Hubbard 2000a: 197.

42, 55). They were redeemed from slavery in Egypt to be slaves of God. They can't be enslaved to anyone else again, including fellow Israelites. So, in a sense, the releases we find in Leviticus 25 are like mini-exoduses.[39] The Israelites are released from work every six years and every forty-nine years. Usufruct of land that is sold outside the clan is released to be returned to the original clan. People who are sold as indentured servants are released, freed from debt. Those who act as redeemers are, therefore, God-like in their actions. Just as God redeemed Israel from slavery in Egypt, kinsman-redeemers redeem land and people from bondage to debt. As such, kinsman-redeemers act on behalf of God. In their action of releasing relatives from slavery to debt, kinsman-redeemers also remind Israelites of God's great act of liberty for them: their redemption from slavery in Egypt in the exodus.

As we move to the New Testament, we find that God redeems people through his Son. God, who is rich in kindness, again demonstrates his 'kindness towards us in Christ Jesus' (Eph. 2:4–9; cf. Titus 3:4). Indeed, the role of redeemer is transferred to Jesus, who is both willing and able to redeem. In the Gospels, Jesus views his earthly mission as serving others and giving 'his life as a ransom [*lytron*] for many' (Mark 10:45; cf. Matt. 20:28). If, as seems likely, there is an allusion in this verse to the Suffering Servant in Isaiah, then this highlights Jesus' service to God as the Servant of Yahweh. The allusion to Isaiah also brings out the idea of Jesus' vicarious sacrifice to bring humanity release from sin (Isa. 53:10). The substitutionary aspect is already present in Mark 10:45, as evidenced in the use of the Greek preposition *anti* ('for', 'in place of'). In the context of the Gospel of Mark, Jesus asks, 'What can a man give in return for his life?' (Mark 8:37). Psalm 49:7–8 is the probable background for this question, which states that there is no life, indeed, no price, that can be paid to God to purchase an exemption from death.[40] Yet in Mark 10:45 Jesus pays with his life as a ransom to God. As James Edwards (2001: 328) notes: 'The death of the Son of Man on behalf of "the many" is a sacrifice of obedience to God's will, a full expression of his love, and a full satisfaction of God's justice.' Jesus willingly humbled himself to become a servant, to live a life of self-sacrifice on behalf of humanity because it was the will of God (cf. Phil. 2:6–8).

Moreover, by his sacrifice Jesus is able to redeem 'the many'. The single sacrifice of Jesus contrasts with the many lives of those for

[39] Cf. Hubbard 1991: 11.
[40] Cf. Marshall 1974: 167.

130

whom it is made. This contrast echoes Isaiah 53:11–12: the Suffering Servant bears the sin of 'the many', and through 'the righteous one', 'the many' are accounted righteous.[41] Jesus' death has 'infinite value because he dies . . . as the transcendent Son of Man'.[42] Hence, the scope of the redemption that Jesus brings is broadened compared to that in the Old Testament. Jesus is able to redeem not just relatives or even the nation of Israel, but an indeterminate 'many'. In fact, Jesus' death is a substitute for the deaths of all humanity.

The magnitude and scope of the redemption achieved by Jesus is expounded upon in the letter to the Hebrews. Drawing on the principles of the Old Testament sacrificial system and the Day of Atonement (Lev. 16), Jesus is presented as the ultimate high priest and sacrifice, whose own blood secures an 'eternal redemption' (Heb. 9:12). The previous sacrifices made under the old covenant at the sanctuary were temporary and external (9:1–10). By contrast, Jesus entered into the heavenly Holy Place and offered the perfect sacrifice of his own blood (9:1–14, 24). He is the mediator of a new covenant (9:15–22), and those 'who are called' can enjoy permanent forgiveness of sin (9:25–26). Again, Christ's self-sacrifice is described as effective in bearing 'the sins of many' (9:28); his death is a substitute for the lives of sinful humanity.[43] He is able to be the substitute for all humanity because he is an unblemished sacrifice, and because he is Christ, the Messiah, the Son of God.[44] His self-sacrifice is final for all time – past, present and future: 'once for all at the end of the ages' (9:26). Jesus willingly sacrificed himself, but that he 'was sacrificed' also points to his death being in accordance with the will and action of God.[45] In short, God redeems through his Son, who is both willing and able to save all humanity.

The kinship connection

The final contribution of the Ruth narrative to our understanding of redemption is the familial relationship between the redeemer and the redeemed. This relationship is emphasized by the use of kinship terms in the narrative. Even before Boaz arrives on the scene, the narrator

[41] Most commentators make the link to Isa. 53, e.g. France 2002: 421; Lane 1974: 383–385. But see the words of caution in Gundry 1993: 591.

[42] Lane 1974: 383.

[43] Christ died for all humanity but it is only those who are called by God who will enjoy an 'eternal inheritance' (Heb. 9:15; cf. 3:1).

[44] Cf. O'Brien (2010: 324): 'The dignity of his person guarantees the incalculable value of his sacrifice.'

[45] God's agency recalls Isa. 53:6, 12; cf. O'Brien 2010: 341.

points out that he is a 'relative' (*môda'*) of Naomi's deceased husband (2:1).[46] When Ruth reports Boaz's generosity in his harvest field, Naomi responds: 'The man is a close relative of ours [*qārôb lānû*; literally, 'near to us'], one of our redeemers' (*miggō'ălēnû*; 2:20). Again Naomi describes Boaz as 'our relative' (*môda'tānû*) when she presents her scheme to Ruth (3:2). Strictly speaking, this third mention of Boaz as a relative is superfluous, since the reader and Ruth already know this; but Naomi's question is rhetorical, providing motivation for Ruth to seek marriage with Boaz, as a close relative. Interestingly, although Naomi avoids using 'redeemer' (*gō'ēl*) in outlining her scheme to Ruth, it is this closer kinship term that Ruth uses in her conversation with Boaz (3:9). Since Ruth doesn't fall under any of the legal categories for redemption (slavery, blood or land), it is likely that she is using the term generally here, for Ruth knows that a redeemer has a greater responsibility to assist another member of his clan who is in need. Ruth's motive clause certainly has the desired effect on Boaz,[47] who is immediately spurred into plotting a course of action (3:11–13).

In the story of Ruth, we find that the closer the familial relation, the greater the obligation to redeem. Ruth asks Boaz to redeem her but he points out that there is a nearer kinsman who has the first right to redemption (3:12–13). Boaz reinforces what Naomi said before in reverse order: he is a kinsman redeemer (*gō'ēl*) but there is one who is closer (*qārôb*; 3:12; cf. 2:20). This principle of the priority of familial proximity is consistent with what we find in the law regarding redemption of land (Lev. 25:25).[48] The principle is spelt out in the section of the law about redeeming hired servants.[49] The obligation to redeem is not restricted to immediate family (e.g. brother or father), but includes uncles and cousins (Lev. 25:49). Beyond this list of kinsmen, any blood relative from the clan can redeem (Lev. 25:49). In short, whoever can redeem a relative should, with the greater responsibility falling on nearer kin.

The Hebrew word used for God's redemption of Israel from Egypt draws on this kinship connection. Instead of *pdh*, which has more

---

[46] This is reading the *qere* (cf. Prov. 7:4) instead of the *ketiv*. The *ketiv* (*myd'*) does not alter the understanding of the word significantly, since 'one who was known' is similar to 'relative'. In any case, Naomi later identifies Boaz as 'a relative of ours' (2:20).

[47] Ruth says to Boaz: 'Spread your wings over your servant, *for you are a kinsman-redeemer*' (3:9, our translation).

[48] The centrality of the clause 'his nearest redeemer' in Lev. 25:25 is emphasized by the verse's chiastic structure; see Milgrom 2000: 2194.

[49] An Israelite debtor could not become a 'slave' because God had redeemed his people from Egyptian slavery to be his slaves alone (Lev. 25:42, 55).

overt connotations of a transaction, *g'l* is used, which portrays Yahweh as a redeemer in kinship terms (Exod. 6:6; cf. 15:13). In the exodus, God intervenes to release his relatives from bondage and to restore family wholeness. Terence Fretheim (1991: 93) describes God acting in the exodus as a 'rescuing kinsman' who vindicates 'the rights of one wronged'.[50] The use of kinship terminology for the relationship between God and Israel is consistent with the level of intimacy between God and Israel in the book of Exodus. After redeeming Israel from bondage, God promises to take Israel as his special people (Exod. 6:7). They were his people in an exclusive way; no other peoples on earth were in covenant relationship with God. This covenant is fully ratified, and hence Israel is fully taken as God's own people, at Sinai.[51] Prior to God's promise to redeem Israel (Exod. 6:2–8) he has already revealed himself as Yahweh (3:13–15). In this self-identification, God reveals that he is a relational God who can be known personally by his people. Shortly after God's self-disclosure, he describes Israel as his son, his firstborn son (4:22–23). In the Old Testament the firstborn was favoured, received a double portion of inheritance and was specially devoted to God.[52] All these privileges of the firstborn reflect Israel's special kinship relation with God. Later in Exodus, Israel is described as God's unique possession (19:5), a people who enjoy the privilege of access to God, with God dwelling among them in the sanctuary (25:8).

This intimacy reflects the familial nature of the covenant relationship God had already established with Israel's ancestors. In Exodus 6 God acts as a kinsman based on a pre-existing covenant with the forefathers of Israel (Exod. 6:4). God calls himself the 'God of your fathers' (3:15–16; 4:5) and he redeems Israel because he 'remembered' his covenant with 'Abraham, Isaac and Jacob' (6:5, 8; cf. 2:24). As F. M. Cross (1998: 3–21) argues, the essence of covenant is kinship. Hence, Israel, as God's covenant people, were related to him as his own family by the covenant. Douglas Stuart (2006: 37 n. 54) applies this to Exodus: 'The purpose of God's covenant with his people in Exodus is just the start of the divine plan to redeem a family for himself.' Consistent with familial relationship is God's covenant promise to give Israel land as a possession by inheritance (Exod. 6:8; cf. Deut. 4:21, 38). The language of 'inheritance' is particularly

---

[50] Cf. Durham 1987: 72, 78.
[51] Cf. Stuart 2006: 172. In a sense, Israel was already God's people (Exod. 3:7, 10; 5:1; 7:4, etc.), but the relationship would be formalized with the covenant at Mt Sinai.
[52] Cf. Stuart 2006: 146.

relevant, for it draws from the realm of kinship: inheritance is given to an heir or a descendant.

The outcome of God redeeming his kinfolk based on the covenant with Abraham is an even closer relationship. The prophet Isaiah develops this idea of God as kinsman-redeemer with connotations of intimate kinship. He mixes his kinship metaphors: God is described as 'our Father, our Redeemer' (Isa. 63:16) and also as 'Maker', 'husband', 'Redeemer' (54:5). The latter reference to God in intimate relationship, as husband, finds particular resonance with the book of Ruth. James McKeown (2015: 125) draws parallels between God's redemption of Israel in the exodus and Boaz's redemption of Ruth. God redeems in the exodus based on a close relationship with his people, then confirms and deepens the relationship through the Sinai covenant;[53] after Ruth's redemption by Boaz, her relationship with him became closer through marriage. McKeown insightfully points out the increased intimacy in both cases.

The familial element of redemption is developed further in the New Testament. Since the price to redeem humanity from sin had to be paid by one of flesh and blood, Jesus condescended to us by becoming human (e.g. John 1:14; Rom. 8:3; Phil. 2:7). Incarnated as a member of humanity, Jesus could redeem us as our kinsman; an animal or an angel could not redeem us. He was born as a human so that he could conquer death, and deliver us from lifelong slavery to 'fear of death' (Heb. 2:14–15, 17).

Those who are now 'in Christ' are adopted into God's family as Jesus' brothers and sisters (e.g. Rom. 8:29; Heb. 2:11–13). The progression is detailed in Galatians 4:3–7. Formerly, we were all enslaved: either to the 'elementary principles of the world' (Gentiles) or to the law (Jews; 4:3–5).[54] Then God sent his Son to redeem us so that we might 'receive adoption as sons' (4:5). As Scott comments, 'Redemption is not an end in itself; the goal is rather redemption to a relationship with the Father established by "adoption".'[55] Although there is a vein of inclusivity in the Old Testament, it is in the New Testament that this theme is fully developed and available to all. This is evident in Galatians: both Jews and Gentiles can now be adopted into God's family (3:28–29; cf. Eph. 2:18). In sum, Jesus is our

[53] Cf. Williamson (2007: 75): 'Rather than establishing or framing . . . a divine–human relationship, a covenant seals or formalizes it.'

[54] For further discussion on the disputed phrase 'elementary principles/spirit' (*stoicheia*; Gal. 4:3), see Bruce 1982: 193–194.

[55] Scott 1992: 174.

kinsman-redeemer, bringing all peoples into God's 'household' (cf. Gal. 6:10).[56]

There are at least two significant benefits for Christians as members of God's family. The first benefit is inheritance. Now that we are no longer slaves to sin and the law, we are heirs through God (Gal. 4:7). The Old Testament people of God received a physical place – land – as their primary inheritance, and landed inheritance was a central concern in the book of Ruth. Christ is pre-eminent as the firstborn, but as co-heirs with Christ (Rom. 8:17) we also receive an inheritance from God. In fact, our inheritance is not just land in Canaan but the whole earth (Matt. 5:5; Rom. 4:13; cf. Eph. 6:3). Moreover, it may be that not only do we receive an inheritance *from* God, we also receive an inheritance *of* God: that is, 'heirs of God' (*klēronomoi theou*; Rom. 8:17) means that we inherit God himself.[57] What an incredible inheritance for God's children! Either way (or perhaps both), we partially enjoy this inheritance now, but we also look forward to the final inheritance that is stored up for us in heaven (e.g. 1 Pet. 1:4). We will only fully enjoy our inheritance as members of God's family when Christ returns again.

The second significant benefit we enjoy as members of God's family is that we are blessed with greater intimacy in our relationship with God. In the Old Testament God was present with his people, as symbolized in the sanctuary. Yet the Holy Place was not accessible to an Old Testament worshipper; the approach to God was barred. Now the way has been opened by means of the blood and flesh of Christ (Heb. 10:19–20).[58] Hence, in the new family of God there is a greater level of intimacy with God, as our Father. Since we are children of God, he sent into our hearts the Spirit of his Son, who cries out 'Abba, Father' (Gal. 4:6; cf. Rom. 8:15). The Spirit brings us a 'paternal awareness' that we have come 'home'.[59] Not only do we have the status of sonship, but the Spirit allows us to experience it.[60] We can even use the same term that Jesus uses in his intimate prayer to God. Indeed, Jesus asks us to pray to God as our 'Heavenly Father' (e.g. Matt. 6:9; Rom. 8:15).

---

[56] It is not necessary to reconcile the adoption and slavery metaphors, since they speak of different aspects of our salvation. The emphasis of adoption is belonging and all its benefits, while the emphasis of slavery is ownership and obedience.

[57] This is taking *klēronomoi theou* as an objective genitive. See Schreiner 1998: 427–428.

[58] The 'blood' and 'flesh' of Christ probably refers to Jesus' sacrificial death, which gained us access to the heavenly sanctuary; see e.g. O'Brien 2010.

[59] Burke 2006: 90.

[60] Stott 1968: 107.

For Christ has entered the Most Holy Place, opening the way for us to draw near to God 'in full assurance of faith' (Heb. 10:19–22).

Is Boaz a type of Christ?

There is no consensus about whether or not Boaz is a type of Christ. On the one hand, Younger (2002: 489), for example, insists: 'Instead of being a type with a clear antitype, Boaz is an agent – a human mirror – of the divine work.' On the other hand, scholars such as Hummel opine: '[T]here is legitimacy in the common evangelical practice of regarding Boaz in his capacity as a "redeemer" as a type of the Redeemer.'[61] Other commentators, such as Wilch (2006: 64), maintain the concept of typology but avoid the terminology of type and antitype because it 'requires explanation and delimitation'.[62] The best way forward may be to present a definition of 'type' and then consider if Boaz fits this definition.

A 'type' can be defined as a biblical person, place, institution, object or event that becomes a pattern by which later persons, places, institutions, objects or events are interpreted within the framework of God's redemptive history.[63] The essential elements of a type and its antitype (the later 'copy' that fulfils the former) include:

- Correspondence or resemblance: there is an obvious point of connection or commonality.
- Historicity: they are real and factual, not allegorical.
- Intensification or escalation: the antitype is greater than the type.[64]
- Theocentricity: both type and antitype are connected to God's actions in redemptive history.[65]

---

[61] Hummel 1979: 515. Cf. Rossow (1991: 17): 'Although Boaz's function in the narrative is not explicitly identified as typological, it would be imperceptive not to see some analogy between his redemptive activity . . . and the later redemptive activity of Christ.'

[62] Wilch prefers 'prophecy' and 'fulfillment' to 'type' and 'antitype'.

[63] Cf. Osborne 1979: 930. Some examples as listed by Osborne: persons (Adam, Melchizedek); places (Jerusalem, Zion); institutions (prophet, priest, king); objects (tabernacle, altar); events (flood, brazen serpent).

[64] Not all agree with this element; e.g. Baker (2010: 183): 'The essence of a type is that it is exemplary, and it is possible for something more advanced to be typical of something less advanced. Moreover it is possible for one thing to be a type of its opposite.' He gives the example of Adam (Rom. 5:14).

[65] Greidanus 1999: 219. France (1971: 39) notes that typology 'is thus essentially the tracing of the constant principles of God's working in history'. Baker (2010: 183) insightfully comments that the Bible contains other themes also, such as creation and the kingdom of God. We have subsumed these all under 'redemptive history', God's actions of redemption from creation to new creation.

Boaz fulfils these four elements.[66]

- The correspondences have been detailed in the previous section. There were commonalities in regards to the redeemer, the cost, the redeemed, and the kinship connection. God is the great Redeemer who redeems through Boaz in the book of Ruth, and redeems through Jesus in the New Testament.
- Both Boaz and Jesus are historical, not fictional, figures.
- Jesus, as antitype, fulfils the role of redeemer in a heightened and deeper way, especially the move from an emphasis on physical to spiritual redemption. He is the climactic redeemer.
- Jesus is clearly central to God's salvation in redemption history. Boaz is also connected to God's salvation but in a more indirect way. Obed, his son produced with Ruth, becomes the grandfather of David (Ruth 4:17–22), who is in the family line of Jesus (Matt. 1:1–16; Luke 3:23–38).

Before we definitely identify Boaz as a type of Christ, we must consider another criterion many interpreters use as a limiting factor. Some insist that the only legitimate types are those explicitly cited in the New Testament.[67] In this view, Boaz is not a type because he is not identified as such in the New Testament. His name is mentioned twice in genealogies as an ancestor of Jesus (Matt. 1:5; Luke 3:32), but he is not specifically mentioned as a type. The main concern of those who restrict types to New Testament affirmation is that implicit identification leaves typology open to misuse. It is true that fanciful and arbitrary connections can and have been extracted from Old Testament texts, with the result practically being allegory. These illegitimate readings may spring from examining the type without consideration of its meaning for its original hearers, or from searching for types in every small detail of an Old Testament text. Certainly, this twisting of Scripture is to be avoided. Nonetheless, there may be another way forward.

If some interpreters read too much into an Old Testament text, it may be that others read too little. Indeed, many interpreters argue

---

[66] Some scholars, e.g. Osborne (1979: 931), also add 'foreshadowing': that the type contains a prospective element. The OT author might not have recognized the 'typological force' in the original, but within God's plan the type anticipates a later reality. Other scholars deny this prospective element, maintaining that types are retrospective interpretation; e.g. Baker 2010: 181; France 1971: 39–40.

[67] Types explicitly mentioned in the NT include Adam, Abel, Melchizedek, Isaac, Moses, David, Solomon, Jonah, the tabernacle and the temple.

that accepting only explicit types is too restrictive. At least four reasons are given. First, the New Testament suggests that the Old Testament is fulfilled in more than explicit quotations in the New Testament (esp. Luke 24:25–27, 44–49; John 5:39–47). Second, it is an approach to interpretation that both Old Testament and New Testament authors used.[68] The corollary is that modern interpreters can follow the interpretive method of Jesus and the New Testament authors.[69] Third, the New Testament does not cite all of 'the instances of the OT's typological interpretation of itself'.[70] Fourth, a limitation to explicit types leads to a focus on some minor Old Testament characters (e.g. Jonah and Melchizedek), while other major characters (e.g. Joseph and Joshua) are omitted.[71] Beale (2012: 26) warns that the outcome of limiting typology to explicit mentions in the New Testament is that 'vast portions of the OT are lost to us'. For these reasons we would side with this category of interpreters. Moreover, the four elements of a type mentioned above help to safeguard against its misuse. Practically speaking, whenever the listed four elements of a type are found, it can be considered a type. Thus, we would suggest that Boaz is a type of Christ.[72]

Nonetheless, there are two caveats concerning Boaz as a type. First, we would focus on the redemptive element of Boaz as a type. As seen from our biblical-theological review of the 'redeemer' theme, God is the great Redeemer, both in the Old Testament and in the New Testament. When Boaz redeems Ruth, he is acting as an agent of Yahweh, and as such is a type of the greatest agent of Yahweh, Jesus. This focus on the redemptive element means that we bracket out other possible correspondences, such as the marriage of Boaz with Ruth anticipating the marriage of Christ with the

---

[68] Cf. Osborne (2001: 1223): 'It has been increasingly recognized that typology expresses the basic hermeneutic, indeed the attitude or perspective, by which both OT and NT writers understood themselves and their predecessors.' For OT, see Hummel 1964: 38–50. For NT, see Goppelt 1982: 198, who states that the typological method is predominant in the NT and 'characteristic of it'.

[69] See Beale 2012: 22–25.

[70] Hamilton 2012: 9. Cf. Baker (2010: 182): 'Typology is not only concerned with certain parts of the Old Testament but with the whole Bible, so there are an unlimited number of possible types.'

[71] So Murray 2013: 140. But see now Hamilton (2008: 52–77), who argues that Joseph is a type of Christ.

[72] Note the caution of Beale (2012: 24): '[T]he conclusions of all biblical interpretation are a matter of possibility and probability; the conclusions of typology must be viewed in the same way.'

church.[73] Second, identifying Boaz as a type does not mean that he is similar to Christ in every way.[74] Types and antitypes have similarities and differences,[75] which is what we demonstrated in our discussion concerning Boaz and Christ above.[76] Finally, this focus on the theme of redemption does not exhaust the biblical-theological connections to Jesus.[77]

Conclusion

In this chapter we highlighted the contribution of the book of Ruth to a biblical-theological understanding of redemption. The aim of our examination of this theme is a greater appreciation of God's redemption in Christ. For, as B. B. Warfield (1950: 325) comments:

> There is no one of the titles of Christ which is more precious to Christian hearts than 'Redeemer' . . . It gives expression not merely to our sense that we have received salvation from Him, but also to our appreciation of what it cost Him to procure this salvation for us . . . Whenever we pronounce it, the cross is placarded before our eyes and our hearts filled with loving remembrance not only that Christ has given us salvation, but that He paid a mighty price for it.

---

[73] *Pace* Rossow 1991: 17. Beale and Gladd (2014: 178–182) delineate the biblical-theological marriage trajectory: Gen. 2:24 is foundational for the Israelite conception of marriage; this type is applied to God's marriage to Israel (e.g. Isa. 54:5–6; 62:4b–5; Ezek. 16; 23; Hos. 1 – 3); in the NT Paul applies God's relationship with Israel to Christ's relationship with the church (Eph. 5:23–32). Thus, Adam and Eve's marriage foreshadows Christ's marriage to the church.

[74] Cf. France 1971: 41.

[75] E.g. Carson (2004: 407) notes that Paul appeals to various kinds of types, which are 'measured by the degree of likeness or unlikeness that subsists between type and antitype'.

[76] There are more similarities than differences, but there is not the strong contrast between type and antitype, such as with Adam and Christ (Rom. 5:12–21).

[77] E.g. Jesus' connection to the house of David was discussed in chapter 3.

Chapter Nine

Ruth and God's mission

Ruth is considered the prototypical convert in the Old Testament by many Christians and Jews.[1] She is a Moabite who makes the transition to Israelite, not only culturally but also religiously, by accepting Yahweh as her exclusive deity.[2] In this chapter we will consider the book of Ruth from the biblical-theological theme of the mission of God. We will especially focus on the tension between mission and law in the Ruth narrative. For Ruth to be finally incorporated into Israelite society seemed to require disobedience to two laws in Deuteronomy. How are we to understand this apparent discrepancy from a biblical-theological perspective? Then we will consider some missional implications of the interaction between law and narrative for God's people today, with an eye to a particular South-East Asian situation.[3]

Reading Ruth from a missional perspective

In this chapter we will use the term 'missional' to mean 'an adjective denoting something that is related to or characterised by mission'.[4] 'Mission' and '*missio Dei*' will refer to '[T]he sending activity of God with the purpose of reconciling to himself and bringing into his kingdom fallen men and women from every people, nation, and tongue'.[5] Missiologists have been developing a way of reading

---

[1] For a Christian perspective, see Wright 2004: 18; Hubbard 1988: 41. For a Jewish perspective, see *Midr. Ruth Rab.* 2:10 and Rashi's comment on Ruth 1:1, 3. For a discussion of Ruth's conversion in Targum Ruth, see Brady 2013: 133–146.

[2] Not all scholars view Ruth's vow as indicating her conversion. For references and further discussion, see Lau 2011: 92–95.

[3] Material in this chapter has been adapted with permission from Lau 2016.

[4] Wright 2006: 24. He eschews the use of the term 'missionary' because it conjures images of 'white, Western expatriates among "natives" in far off countries'.

[5] Ott, Strauss and Tennent 2010: xv, xvii. Similarly, Köstenberger and O'Brien (2001: 268–269) acknowledge that 'mission' is not a biblical word but conclude from their inductive biblical-theological study that it 'has to do with God's salvation reaching the ends of the earth . . . Clearly the notion of sending is central to any treatment of mission.' By contrast, we find Wright's (2006: 22–23) definition of mission too broad, especially the final phrase: 'our committed participation as God's people, at God's invitation and command, in God's own mission within the history of God's world *for the redemption of God's creation*' (emphasis added).

Scripture through the lens of the *missio Dei*. As yet, there is no consensus, although various emphases under the umbrella of this hermeneutic were summarized by George Hunsberger in 2008:[6]

1. the missional framework of biblical narrative;
2. the missional purpose of the text;
3. the missional locatedness of readers;
4. the missional engagement with cultures.[7]

This chapter will explore the first two elements separately and the final two elements together. So in our modification of the missional hermeneutic we will consider how the book of Ruth:

1. Witnesses to God's mission. The assumption is that the whole Bible presents us with the story of God's mission. Wright (2006: 29) is particularly strong on this point, suggesting that we think of 'a missional basis of the Bible' rather than a biblical basis for mission.
2. Functions as an instrument of God's mission. In this section we will consider how the book of Ruth shaped Israel for their involvement in God's mission. In particular we will focus on how the law was to be applied, and we will derive general principles instead of specific ways the book of Ruth was applied to a particular historical community.[8]
3. Shapes the church for participation in God's mission.[9] This section shifts the focus from the text to the people or community of God, and considers what it might mean for Christians to read the book of Ruth in light of a missional context.

The book of Ruth as witness to God's mission

The biblical-theological theme of the mission of God highlights the fact that the broad sweep of the Bible – from Genesis to Revelation –

[6] At the end of his article Hunsberger (2011: 319) mentions a fifth emphasis, related to the fourth, which has recently gained more prominence, viz reading the Bible together with the culturally and socially 'other'. The emphases detailed by Hunsberger have been applied to specific biblical books: Flemming 2011: 3–18; Flemming 2012: 161–178; Wright 2011: 112–129.

[7] The paper presented at the AAR and SBL Meetings, Fall 2008, is published as Hunsberger 2011: 309–321.

[8] For a discussion of how the book of Ruth could have shaped the community of God's people in the post-exilic period, see chapter 2.

[9] For a missiological reading of Ruth, see Thomas 2002: 155–170.

traces the story of God's mission in and for creation.[10] The storyline can be described as acts in a drama: creation, fall, Israel, Jesus the Messiah, church, and new creation.[11]

How does the book of Ruth fit into the metanarrative of God's mission? The Ruth narrative is set in the time of the judges, a time of spiritual and political anarchy (Judg. 21:25; cf. 17:6; 18:1; 19:1). Yet amidst Israel's unfaithfulness to God, God was still faithfully working to bring blessing to Israel, and through Israel to the whole world. Not only is Ruth the Moabite incorporated into Israel, but she becomes an ancestress of David, whose line ultimately leads to Jesus (Matt. 1:1–6). Also, Ruth as a foreigner links to the promise of blessing to 'all peoples' through Israel, as found in the Abrahamic covenant.[12] This theme of acceptance of outsiders into Israel will be expanded upon in the Prophets (esp. Isaiah), but its presence in the book of Ruth anticipates, ultimately, the multi-ethnic nature of the people of God (Rev. 5:9–10; 14:6).

Two texts in particular establish the missional identity and role of God's people in the Old Testament. The first is Genesis 12:1–3, the Abrahamic promise, which outlines God's redemptive plan.[13] God will make Abraham into a great nation, and through Abraham's seed bring blessing to all peoples of the earth.[14] Abraham is given two commands: to go (v. 1) and to be a blessing (v. 2). The fivefold use of 'bless' or 'blessing' in verses 2–3 emphasizes God's action to and through Abraham. God will bless whoever blesses Abraham, but the one who dishonours Abraham God will curse (v. 3a). Through Abraham all nations will be blessed (v. 3b).

There is debate about how to understand 'bless' (*nibrĕkû*; v. 3b). The main interpretive possibilities are passive ('will be blessed'; ESV,

---

[10] For more detail see, in particular, Wright 2006; Köstenberger and O'Brien 2001.

[11] Cf. the six acts in Bartholomew and Goheen (2004): (1) God establishes his kingdom: creation; (2) Rebellion in the kingdom: fall; (3) The king chooses Israel: redemption initiated; (4) The coming of the king: redemption accomplished; (5) Spreading the news of the king: the mission of the church; (6) The return of the king: redemption completed. Others outline a five-act drama, although with slightly different acts; e.g. Wright 1991: 7–29; Vanhoozer 2005.

[12] Ruth's designation as 'the Moabitess' is mentioned seven times in the book of Ruth (1:4, 22; 2:2, 6, 21; 4:5, 10), highlighting her outsider status. She also proclaims that she is a 'foreigner' (*nokriyyâ*; 2:10), even though in reality she is a 'resident alien' (*gēr*), one who has assimilated into Israelite society.

[13] For a detailed treatment of this text from a missional perspective, see Wright 2006: 191–221.

[14] In this passage Abraham is still called Abram, but we will refer to him by his later name for the sake of simplicity.

NIV) or reflexive ('will bless themselves'; RSV, NJPS). As Wenham notes (1987: 278), with either translation the sense is similar because the reflexive carries a passive reference.[15] Structurally, the passive is the best translation, as God's promises would proceed from the particular to the universal: a blessing to Abraham, a blessing (or curse) on those with whom he interacts, a blessing for all nations.[16] The accent is on the final clause: Abraham and his descendants will mediate God's blessing to all peoples of the world.

The reciprocal nature of blessing in the Abrahamic promise is found in the Ruth narrative. Indeed, as we trace the path of blessing, we find a virtuous cycle. Ruth blesses an Israelite, Naomi, by showing kindness to her. In turn, Boaz blesses Ruth.[17] Ruth then shows kindness to Boaz, who then shows further kindness to Ruth. In the end, God blesses Boaz and Ruth with conception (4:13). In this way Ruth builds up the house of Israel, raising the name of the dead upon his inheritance, and thus keeping alive the Abrahamic promise. For without offspring attached to the land, there is no continuation of the line of Perez and ultimately no blessing to the nations. Through Obed will come King David; God's promise to Abraham will continue through King David and his house; and so through David all families on earth are blessed (Matt. 1:1–6).

The second text, Exodus 19:4–6, provides detail about how God will bless the nations through Israel. God first reminds Israel that he redeemed them (v. 4), which serves as the grounds for the charge in 19:5–6. Israel are to respond to their salvation with obedience to the covenant that God had already established with Abraham (19:5; Gen. 12; 15; 17; 22).[18] There are three consequences of Israel's obedience: 'treasured possession', 'kingdom of priests' and 'holy nation' (19:5–6).[19]

[15] So also Waltke and Fredricks (2001: 206). Wenham suggests the less popular 'middle' sense, 'all peoples on earth will *find blessing*' in Abraham. See also the extended discussion in Wright (2006: 216–218). Some downplay the missional emphasis of this passage, e.g. Moberly (2009: 141–161).

[16] Sarna 1989: 89. For a recent presentation of the case for the passive sense of *nibrĕkû*, see Lee 2009: 471–472.

[17] This reciprocal blessing is similar to Rahab's situation: she showed kindness by concealing the Israelite spies; Yahweh shows kindness to Rahab through the Israelites (Josh. 2:12–14).

[18] Dumbrell 2013: 110–118. The Abrahamic covenant is best thought of as a single covenant instituted in four stages; cf. Gentry and Wellum 2012: 247–299, *pace* Williamson 2007.

[19] The interpretation of a reward conditional on loyalty follows, inter alios, Muilenburg 1959: 352–355. By contrast, Patrick (1977: 149) asserts that the three descriptors define the requirements of the covenant relationship: 'Being Yahweh's own possession, his holy nation and kingdom of priests, entails submitting to his will.' However, Davies

These phrases highlight Israel's special status, and their separateness from the world, for they are chosen from 'out of all nations' (v. 5).

At the same time, the three phrases define Israel's role as a nation *among* the nations of the world. 'For all the earth is mine' (v. 5) indicates that Yahweh's intention for Israel is that they become a blessing to the world, as promised to Abraham (Gen. 12:1–3).[20] Indeed, Dumbrell (2013: 117) suggests that the terms used to describe Israel provide 'a commentary on the way in which the promises of Genesis 12:1–3 will find their fulfilment'. As a 'kingdom of priests', Israel represented God before the nations, just as a priest did for the people.[21] Israel were to mediate God's presence to the nations and to help bring people closer to God. Being a 'holy nation' meant that they were a people set apart for God's service. This was to be reflected in their lifestyle, which was to be different from that of those around them. As such, as Durham (1987: 263) notes, they were 'a display-people, a showcase to the world of how being in covenant with Yahweh changes a people'. As Israel fulfilled this missional role, other nations would be drawn into covenant relationship with God.

The specific requirements of the covenant follow Israel's missional call (Exod. 20 – 23). The Torah provides instructions to help Israel live out their calling as a holy nation in all areas of life. As Ross Blackburn puts it, 'The means by which Israel carried out her missionary calling as a priestly nation was through keeping the law' (2012: 210). This leads us to the second dimension of a missional reading of the book of Ruth: how the narrative shapes and equips God's people to engage in the *missio Dei*.

The book of Ruth as an instrument of God's mission

The second element of the missional hermeneutic seeks to determine how the Ruth narrative functions as an instrument of the *missio Dei*. We will see that Boaz fulfils this missionary calling by keeping the law.

(2004: 46) notes that, ultimately, these readings are very similar if the reading of conditional reward is 'understood to be within the framework of an already established relationship'.

[20] Cf. Fretheim 1991: 212.

[21] Davies (2004: 238) points out that God's declaration (Exod. 19:6) primarily describes how Israel is related to God, rather than how the nation is to relate to the nations, 'though it is not denied that there may be implications for human relationships of what it means to be the chosen and treasured people of God'.

However, we also encounter a problem because it appears as though the law is actually broken to facilitate the incorporation of Ruth the Moabitess. So to determine how the book of Ruth functions as an instrument of the *missio Dei* requires an examination of how the law is applied in the narrative. Our assumption is that the Deuteronomic laws were well known by the time of the authorship of Ruth. This is consistent with the storyline of the Bible, where the law is given prior to the entrance to the Promised Land.[22] Even if we accept the historical-critical consensus of a late monarchic-era composition for Deuteronomy, it is likely that the laws were familiar to the author of Ruth, even if the laws had not reached their final Deuteronomic form.[23]

The book of Ruth's rhetorical aim

The promotion of kindness is primarily how the narrative functions to shape God's people as a missional community. Scholars debating the book of Ruth's rhetorical purpose fall into two broad camps which align with the two proposed historical periods in which the narrative arose: (1) as a pro-Davidic apology during the early monarchic period; (2) as a counter to the exclusionary application of the law in the restoration/Ezra–Nehemiah period.[24] Underlying both of these issues is Ruth's foreignness. How God's people were to treat Ruth as a foreigner is outlined in the law, but the way in which the law should be applied – according to the guiding principle of kindness – is the main rhetorical aim of the Ruth narrative.

The law and kindness

Boaz especially demonstrates how kindness guides application of the law. In the Old Testament kindness (*hesed*) has a strong element of graciousness and generosity.[25] Boaz's actions towards Ruth are generous beyond the requirements of three specific laws. First, in chapter 2 Boaz provides for Ruth in many ways beyond the specific requirements of the gleaning law (Lev. 19:9–10; 23:22; Deut. 24:19–21).

---

[22] Since our approach is biblical-theological, we will bracket out pro-inclusion texts that are found after Ruth in the storyline of the Bible (esp. Psalms, Isaiah), and focus on the laws in Deuteronomy.

[23] For a succinct survey of recent scholarship concerning the origins of Deuteronomy, see Block 2012: 27–33. Of course, there is no problem with a late monarchic date for Deuteronomy if, as some scholars propose, the book of Ruth was composed in the post-exilic period.

[24] For further discussion about the date of composition of the book of Ruth, see chapter 2.

[25] See Andersen 1986: 81.

The gleaning law requires the harvester to leave some of the harvest ungathered, but not only does Boaz ask for sheaves to be actively left behind, he gives special attention to Ruth by protecting her while she gleans in his field (Ruth 2:8–9, 10, 14, 15–16, 18). Second and third, Boaz was willing to redeem the field that belonged to Elimelech, along with marrying Ruth. Because of the unusual set of circumstances – the redemption of land without an heir to maintain the name of the dead on the property – the redemption law triggered the levirate law.[26] Boaz's willingness to redeem the field and marry Ruth is an act of kindness, as highlighted by the contrasting response of the nearer kinsman (4:6). Strictly speaking, there was minimal obligation on Boaz to redeem the field and perform the levirate duty because he was not the nearest kinsman, and he was not a brother-in-law (Lev. 25:23–25; Deut. 25:5–10).

This leaves the elephant in the room regarding the application of the law in the Ruth narrative: Boaz's intermarriage with a foreign woman. Does Boaz transgress the law? Two laws implore exploration: Deuteronomy 7:1–4 and 23:3–6. Deuteronomy 7 prohibits intermarriage with people living in the land of Canaan. The rationale is that 'they would turn away your sons from following me, to serve other gods' (Deut. 7:4). Yet the door for non-Israelites to be the beneficiaries of Yahweh's kindness is left ajar in 7:9, where the recipients are described in general terms: 'those who love him and keep his commandments'. Although Moabites are not included in the list of Canaanites (7:1), in principle this law would also apply to them if they too served 'other gods'.[27] Conversely, intermarriage with foreigners outside the land of Canaan is permitted under the law, presumably for those who transfer their allegiance (Deut. 21:10–14).[28] Thus, the reason for the proscription is religious, not ethnic. Ruth, however, had turned from her Moabite gods to devote herself exclusively to Yahweh (1:16–17; cf. 2:12).

There is a second law Boaz could have transgressed. Deuteronomy 23:3–6 (Heb. 4–7) prohibits Moabites from entering 'the assembly of the LORD'. Unlike the temporary prohibition for Edomites and Egyptians (23:8 [Heb. 9]), the ban on Moabites is 'even to the tenth generation' (23:3). The length of this exclusion from participating in

---

[26] See Lau 2011: 69–71.

[27] Cf. 1 Kgs 11:1–8; Neh. 13:23–27; Ezra 9:1; 10:10.

[28] Putting on new clothes and the regrowth of hair and nails indicate the female captive's new status. For external changes denoting a spiritual change see Gen. 35:2. Block (2012: 496) compares these actions to Ruth's vow of allegiance (Ruth 1:16).

corporate worship before Yahweh is 'for ever' (23:3, 6 [Heb. 4, 7]); that is, it is permanent.[29] So Ruth's marriage to Boaz, her acceptance by the Bethlehemite community, and her elevation to one of the matriarchs of Israel all seem to go against this ordinance. Moreover, King David should also have been excluded from the assembly of Yahweh since Ruth was his great-grandmother (Ruth 4:17–22). So how are we to understand the application of this law in the Ruth narrative? And how is it consistent with Israel living out their missional calling as a priestly nation by *obeying* the law?[30] We need to read the law within three contexts: (1) Deuteronomy 23:1–8 (Heb. 2–9); (2) the application of other laws in the book of Ruth; (3) Genesis 12:1–3.

We first need to understand the proscription within the context of Deuteronomy 23:1–8 (Heb. 2–9). Foreigners, namely Edomites and Egyptians, are not categorically banned from the assembly (23:8 [Heb. 9]). Conversely, it is possible for Israelites to be excluded from the assembly, such as those emasculated or those born of a forbidden union (23:1–2 [Heb. 2–3]).[31] Hence, God's people are 'ultimately a spiritual community'.[32] Egyptians, who showed hospitality to Israel, are accepted into the assembly. Hospitality was the cultural norm but in this instance it signifies more: it denotes those who promote God's purposes for his people. Moab did not provide for Israel as they journeyed to the Promised Land; Egypt hosted Israel during a precarious time in their existence.[33] Similarly, as direct descendants of Abraham through Isaac and Esau, Edomites are also closely linked to God's purposes. Presumably, these foreigners would devote themselves exclusively to Yahweh (e.g. Deut. 6:4–5).[34]

Second, we need to understand how other laws operate within the context of the Ruth narrative. As noted above, the gleaning, redemption and levirate laws are not applied restrictively, but generously according to the principle of kindness. Also as noted above, Ruth had accepted Yahweh as her exclusive deity. Hence, although she is of

[29] Cf. Tigay 1996: 211.

[30] Rabbinic sages suggested that Deut. 23:3–6 (Heb. 4–7) does not apply to Ruth because the law applies only to males (*Ruth Rabbah* 2:10). Against this reading is that the gentilic 'Moabite' functions as a collective noun for both males and females. Also, the law is applied to Moabite women in Neh. 13:1, 23.

[31] Those born of a 'forbidden union' include children born out of wedlock and those born as a result of incest (Lev. 18:6–20; 20:10–21) or other illicit sexual relationships (Deut. 22:13–29).

[32] McConville 2002: 353.

[33] Ironically, Egypt ends up enslaving Israel.

[34] The delay of three generations might allow time for 'demonstrable assimilation'; McConville 2002: 350.

Moabite ancestry, because of her faith in Yahweh she falls under the category of the covenant people of God. Moreover, as Georg Braulik (1999: 10–11) points out, the Ruth narrative inverts the behaviour of Moabites described in Deuteronomy 23:4–5 (Heb. 5–6):

- In Ruth 1 Moab grants hospitality to Elimelech and his family, Israelite famine refugees. The two sons marry Moabite women.
- In Ruth 2 a Moabite gleans in a field in Bethlehem to provide for her Israelite mother-in-law.
- In Ruth 3 Boaz prays that Yahweh might bless Ruth (3:10), one who has taken shelter under Yahweh's wings (2:12). This is in contrast to Moab, who hired Balaam to curse Israel (Num. 22:4–6).
- In Ruth 4 Naomi is blessed through her Moabite daughter-in-law (4:15), through the birth of a son 'to Naomi' (4:17).

In effect, the reproach of Deuteronomy 23:4–5 (Heb. 5–6) because of the historical actions of the Moabites is not valid for Ruth; the law can be applied flexibly. Furthermore, that she is characterized by kindness, a foundational aspect of Israelite identity, reinforces her place in the covenant community. Her abandonment of her homeland and family is identified as her first act of kindness (2:11), while her selection of Boaz is the second, greater act (3:10).[35] And Boaz describes her as a woman of 'noble character' (*'ēšet ḥayil*), the same description of the ideal Israelite wise woman (3:11; cf. Prov. 31:10–31).[36] Thus, she is a worthy member of God's covenant people.

Third, we need to understand the application of the law in the book of Ruth within the broader biblical-theological context. Gordon McConville (2002: 353) suggests that the admission of foreigners based on their treatment of Israel takes into account the Abrahamic promise; specifically, 'I will bless those who bless you, and him who dishonours you I will curse' (Gen. 12:1–3). As we have discussed, reciprocal blessing can be seen to take place in the book of Ruth.

However, perhaps more can be drawn from the Genesis link with the book of Ruth. Indeed, the Ruth narrative itself explicitly draws on Genesis narratives as intertexts:

---

[35] In selecting Boaz she displays kindness by choosing loyalty to Naomi and her family instead of personal gain. For, by selecting Boaz, a kinsman-redeemer, there is the chance that her father-in-law's field will be redeemed, and his family line will be perpetuated (3:12–13). See Lau 2011: 65–67.

[36] See chapter 4.

- Ruth is placed alongside the matriarchs Rachel and Leah (4:11; Gen. 29 – 30).
- Ruth is compared with Tamar (4:12; Gen. 38).
- Less conspicuously, although Ruth may be descended from Lot (Gen. 19:30–38), her behaviour on the threshing floor distinguishes her from Lot's eldest daughter.[37]
- Ruth's decision to leave Moab parallels Abram's journey (Gen. 12:1–9).[38]

This being the case, we have grounds to extend the Genesis allusion to the last part of 12:3: 'and in you all the families of the earth shall be blessed.' Deuteronomy 23:4–7 (Heb. 5–8) bases entry into the assembly of Yahweh on whether people promote, and do not hinder, God's purposes for his people, whereas Genesis 12:3 highlights the missional aspect of the people of God: to be a blessing to the peoples of the earth.

What we see in the Ruth narrative is this universal missional purpose being worked out in a specific situation.[39] Boaz fulfils Israel's missional calling by obeying the law, but his actions show that it may require more than just obeying the law's strict requirements. This is consistent with Gordon Wenham's (2000) proposal, that while the law outlines the baseline ethical requirement, narratives describe the ideal of godly behaviour.[40] He describes a 'gap between law and ethics' in the Old Testament, and observes that 'much more is expected of the righteous than merely keeping the letter of the law'.[41] His monograph focuses on two narrative books – Genesis and Judges – but his observations are applicable to the book of Ruth. Boaz's generous application of the law, culminating in him performing the levirate duty, leads to Ruth's eventual incorporation into the people of God. Although Ruth commits herself to Yahweh (1:16–17), she acknowledges that she is still on the margins of Israelite society (2:10). It is only after her marriage to Boaz that she is accepted by the Israelite community, as signalled by the blessing of the womenfolk of the town (4:11–12).

[37] Cf. Nielsen 1997: 68; Zakovitch 1999: 51.

[38] Some consider Ruth's journey as one of greater faith than that of the patriarch because Abram left his native land with a trust in God's promise, whereas Ruth left without any promise from God regarding her future; see LaCocque 2004: 53.

[39] For a discussion of the universal and the particular in mission, see Bauckham 2003.

[40] Wenham (1997: 17 n. 2) restricts 'the law' to 'the regulations and legal enactments contained in . . . the so-called law codes' (e.g. Exod. 21 – 23; Lev. 18 – 20; Deut. 12 – 25).

[41] Wenham 2000: 4.

Thus, Boaz's generous application of the law according to the principle of kindness highlights its importance for Israel in its missional role to bring blessing to all the peoples of the earth.

Reading the book of Ruth as missional communities

The third and final element of the missional hermeneutic considers how the Ruth narrative shapes and equips readers today for their witness as the people of God. In other words, how does the Ruth narrative shape the church for participation in God's mission? The New Testament makes it clear that the church continues the identity and role of God's chosen people, royal priesthood and holy nation (1 Pet. 2:9; cf. Rev. 1:6). So in the following we will briefly sketch some trajectories deriving from our reading of the Ruth narrative, with an eye to the local context of Malaysia. As one Malaysian theologian, Albert Walters (2007: 353), notes, 'The [Malaysian] churches have been preoccupied with their own existence and organisation, and correspondingly they have lagged behind in . . . concern for the social relevance and outreach of the gospel.' We will consider how the Ruth narrative shapes the Malaysian church to participate in God's mission in both these areas. However, we trust that the application is general enough to be applied to different global contexts.

Love and the law

Parallel to kindness as the guiding principle for applying the law, in the New Testament we find that love is the fulfilment of the law (Rom. 13:8–10; Gal. 5:14). Indeed, Jesus proclaims that the two greatest commandments are based on love: for God and for neighbour (Matt. 22:37–40; Mark 12:29–31). Since Christ fulfilled the law (Matt. 5:17), Christians are not required specifically to follow each of the laws in the Old Testament. Nonetheless, since God does not change, the principles underlying the laws are still valid for Christians and the church today. Three laws applied in the Ruth narrative have implications for us.

The gleaning law might not be literally applicable in developed countries, but the underlying principle to provide for the poor and marginalized in society still holds. As Malaysia journeys towards developed-nation status, there is a widening disparity between the wealthy and the poor. Yet there needs to be equal access to the country's God-given resources, and their more equitable distribution. The main responsibility for this lies with the government, but churches and Christian individuals can play a part. For instance, Christians can be involved in providing for 'invisible' asylum seekers from countries such as Myanmar.[42] Since Malaysia has not signed the 1951 UNHCR Refugee Convention or its 1967 Protocol, these refugees are not granted official status, so they do not have a right to work and the children do not have access to education. However, just as Israelites were motivated to follow the law because of God's kindness towards them, displayed primarily and foundationally in their redemption (e.g. Exod. 20:2; Lev. 25:38; Deut. 5:6; 24:18), so Christians are motivated to obey in response to God's kindness expressed in redemption in Christ (e.g. Eph. 2:4–7; 1 Pet. 1:18–19; Titus 2:14; 3:4–7). Assisting the marginalized in our society, such as refugees, is one way that we can be a conduit of God's kindness.

The redemption and levirate laws can also guide the church in caring for those in need. Just as the redemption law promoted assistance within the kinship group, the New Testament promotes doing good to all but especially to those in the family of God (Gal. 6:10). The specifics of the levirate law might not be relevant in most countries today,[43] but the principle of caring for widows is reinforced in the New Testament (e.g. Jas 1:27). The trajectory for the law regarding acceptance of foreigners into the assembly is traced through Christ, who has broken down the dividing wall of hostility. Now all have access to the Father in one Spirit (Eph. 2:11–18). Within a context of societal disunity, with divisions based on race and religion, the church in Malaysia can provide an especially strong witness to our unity in Christ.[44]

Outsiders

One aspect of the missional hermeneutic considers how an outsider might respond to reading biblical texts.[45] In this way, the text can directly function as an instrument of God's mission. In Malaysia, a Muslim friend who reads Ruth would identify with the God who is presented as sovereign (Ruth 1:20–21). However, he or she might also

[42] For example, by volunteering to provide education; see Young 2013. Of around 100,000 asylum seekers and refugees in Malaysia, 95.6% originate from Myanmar ('UNHCR Regional Office for South-East Asia Factsheet', September 2014, <http://www.unhcr.org/519f67fc9.pdf>, accessed 6 July 2016).

[43] There are still some societies in the world that practise a custom similar to this law, e.g. parts of Africa and South-East Asia. See e.g. Nu 2015: 57–72.

[44] See Rowan 2012.

[45] Hunsberger (2011: 314–316) focuses on the Christian community, but a non-Christian reader is mentioned in Russell 2010.

consider the Almighty to be great and unknowable. In Ruth, God is presented as a personal God, intimately caring for and providing for all of his creation, and directing all things for his purposes (e.g. 1:6, 22; 2:3; 4:13). Also, the gleaning, redemption and levirate laws foreshadow God's kindness in providing Jesus (Titus 3:4–7), who was more than a prophet. As God's Son, Jesus' blood has bought our redemption (e.g. Rom. 3:24–25; Eph. 1:7) and has solved the ultimate problem of humankind: spiritual destitution (e.g. Eph. 2:4–5). In Jesus we have hope that one day there will also be an end to physical pain and suffering (Rev. 21:4).

This sharing of the missional message of Ruth and its fulfilment in Christ points to the role of Christians today. In the Old Testament the people of God were to live out their priestly role and thus attract people to God. This so-called centripetal movement is seen in the Ruth narrative, as Ruth comes to Israel.[46] In the New Testament the attractional dimension of the church's witness remains (e.g. Matt. 5:14–16; 1 Pet. 2:9–12), but there is an added dimension, as Christ sends his people out to make disciples of all nations (Matt. 28:18–20). Recently, there has been a change in missional thinking due to the rise of Christianity in the Global South, the decline in Christianity in the West and the mass movement of people between countries. In some circles, the new mantra is 'mission on our doorsteps': that is, since the nations have come to us, the focus of our involvement in the *missio Dei* should be on those in our local communities or cities.[47] The book of Ruth contributes to our thinking about this missions strategy.

Since Ruth arrives on Bethlehem's 'doorstep' as an outsider, the ways Naomi and Boaz interact with her are instructive. Many commentators rightly comment on Naomi's imperfect faith in Yahweh and focus on Ruth's kindness in committing her loyalty to Naomi (1:16–17).[48] The sweep of the Old Testament attests to the disobedience of God's people and the outcome: Israel becomes a laughing stock among the nations, God's reputation is besmirched, and the nations' attraction to God is muted as a consequence (e.g. 1 Kgs 9:6–9; Ps. 34:13–14; Ezek. 5:14–15; 36:22–23). This disobedience and its outcome might be seen in microcosm in the voluntary exile of Naomi's family and the tragedies that follow.[49] Although Naomi's life was not a completely faithful witness to God, it did not discourage Ruth from

---

[46] *Pace* Kaiser (2012), who finds a centrifugal aspect to God's mission in the OT.
[47] See e.g. Payne 2012; Prill 2008.
[48] E.g. Block 1999: 639.
[49] See chapter 6.

following her, her people and her God. Perhaps God revealed something of himself to Ruth despite Naomi's blemished faith and tragic circumstances. Similarly, God still uses our imperfect faithfulness today to draw people to himself.

After Ruth arrived in Bethlehem, Boaz's life was a more reliable testimony to God's character. This was especially through Boaz's superabundant obedience to the law, as discussed above. Yet his whole life is presented as one of godliness and grace, in his actions and his speech (e.g. 'The LORD be with you'; 2:4). Speech was important for the people of God, for another aspect of their priestly role to the world was to proclaim the truth of God.[50] The teaching element of the priesthood is seen in different parts of the Old Testament (e.g. Lev. 10:10–11; Deut. 31:9–13; 2 Chr. 15:3; Mal. 2:6–7). The characters in the Ruth narrative do not formally teach the law, but in their day-to-day speech they testify to the truth of God to Ruth. In despair and then in elation, Naomi testifies to Yahweh's sovereignty and providence in all things (Ruth 1:8–9, 13; 2:20). Boaz's words to Ruth reinforce Naomi's theology (2:12; 3:10), as do the sentiments of the throng gathered at the town gate (4:11–12).[51] Thus, both the actions and the words of God's people are important in consolidating Ruth's faith in Yahweh and incorporating her into the people of God.[52]

In a similar way, Christians today can be an effective witness to outsiders who have come to 'our doorsteps'. The New Testament recapitulates our identity as priests to the world and our role of living as a royal priesthood and a holy nation (1 Pet. 2:9). As people who have received God's mercy, we are to respond by offering our lives as living sacrifices (1 Pet. 2:9–10; Rom. 12:1; cf. Heb. 13:15–16). Also, we are to proclaim God's excellencies or mighty acts so that God might be glorified (1 Pet. 2:9, 12). This is the same basic trajectory that we find in Exodus 19:4–6 and that we find fleshed out in the Ruth narrative. In short, as Christians we are saved by the gospel, we are to live out the gospel, and we are to proclaim the gospel to those whom God brings to our doorsteps. By God's grace, may he use us to draw outsiders to him through our priestly ministry.

---

[50] Cf. Stuart 2006: 423.

[51] Boaz also greets his harvesters with a blessing of God's presence. Although it is directed at his harvesters, Ruth could have overhead it, since Boaz then asks, 'Whose young woman is *this*?' (2:5). 'This' suggests that she was within earshot.

[52] For recent discussions of Ruth's immigration and assimilation, see Carroll R. 2013: 55–58; Southwood 2014: 102–131.

The risk of a missional life

The risk that Boaz takes in his interactions with Ruth the Moabite, culminating in his marriage to her, highlights the level of risk that might be involved in cross-cultural mission. Although the Ruth narrative carefully presents Boaz's intermarriage with a foreigner as not contravening the law in Ruth's particular circumstance, his decision still carried great personal risk. He risked his impeccable reputation (2:1) by marrying a foreigner. And as highlighted by the nearer kinsman's response to the offer of marrying Ruth, Boaz risked impairing his own inheritance (4:6). If Boaz was an heirless widower, as many scholars suggest,[53] his marriage to a previously barren Ruth carried even greater risk because he would not have an heir to maintain his family line on his landed inheritance.

Certainly, Boaz's involvement in cross-cultural missions did not require him to leave his home town. Nevertheless, the degree of risk involved in his missional life speaks to the situation for Christians in Malaysia in two ways. First, since proselytizing to people from the majority religion is illegal in most states, there is a fear and resultant reluctance to share the gospel of Jesus Christ.[54] Since there is a very real risk of punishment in these states, witnessing must be done in a discerning and discreet manner.[55] This may take the form of dialogue in a spirit of mutual respect and understanding,[56] or making friends with neighbours so that Christ can be shared naturally.[57] Second, in some Malaysian churches the promotion of cross-cultural mission does not extend beyond sending short-term mission teams from West to East Malaysia. Certainly, there is a great need in East Malaysia, where there is a colossal spiritual battle taking place between Islam and Christianity. However, a sole focus on missions within Malaysia may be to the detriment of global missions. It is important to be

---

[53] E.g. Davies 1981: 259; Morris 1968: 312; Rowley 1965: 192.

[54] Freedom of religion is enshrined in Article 11 of the Constitution of Malaysia, but proselytizing Muslims is prohibited in most states. For a list of the states where proselytizing is illegal, and fourteen other restrictions on the church in Malaysia, see Rowan 2012: 96–100.

[55] The punishment for infringing this law differs from state to state, but includes imprisonment for at least two years or corporal punishment.

[56] On dialogue between Christians and Muslims, see Chapman 1995: 172–225. On dialogue between Christians and Muslims in Malaysia, see Batumalai 1990: 113–142, 149; McAmis 2002: 115–117; Walters 2007: 322–350; Rowan 2012: 171–175.

[57] As reportedly said by a Muslim friend to Robert McAmis (2002: 109): 'If you do not share your faith with me and tell me what is nearest and dearest to your heart and life – your faith in Christ – I will consider it an insult.'

involved in local missions, but a global, centrifugal aspect also needs to be maintained. Everyone must be involved in God's mission, but some need to be sent to proclaim the gospel in foreign lands. This is the risk that some are called to take as they live out a missional life.

Conclusion

In this chapter we read Ruth within the biblical-theological theme of the mission of God, and we considered what the book might contribute to our understanding of mission. We situated the biblical text within the framework of the *missio Dei* and explored how the text functions as an instrument of God's ongoing mission in his world. Kevin Vanhoozer (2008: 21) comments: 'The way in which the church witnesses, through its language and life, is perhaps the most important form of theological interpretation of the Bible.' If this is the case, then a missional reading of biblical texts is eminently placed to shape and equip the church in its witness. At the very least, a dialogue between text, biblical theology and context enriches our appropriation of Scripture.

Chapter Ten

Conclusion

Our endeavour to provide a biblical theology of the book of Ruth is not aimed at competing with commentaries on Ruth and in no way do we attempt to render them superfluous. Commentaries give a detailed verse-by-verse explanation of the biblical text, whereas the present volume builds on such close studies of the text for the purpose of exploring its biblical-theological parameters in the context of Scripture as a whole. In the process, we believe that we have not only assisted the interpretation of the book of Ruth but also thrown light on the practice of biblical theology itself. In other words, this study of the story of Ruth has given attention to both content and method in biblical theology, and the conclusions we draw will refer to both these aspects. We have looked at the book of Ruth from a variety of angles and used a range of methodological tools to explore its biblical theology.

We explored the possible relevance of the book of Ruth to issues faced by the returnees in the early restoration period as depicted in Ezra–Nehemiah (chapter 2). The act of collecting sacred books in a 'canon' asserts their relevance to future generations as well as their compatibility one with the other. It is proper, therefore, that the books of Ruth and Ezra–Nehemiah enter into dialogue as constituent parts of the Old Testament canon, but they are not to be set at loggerheads as in the critical view that sees the author of the book of Ruth writing to oppose the exclusivist policies of Ezra and Nehemiah. Though seldom noticed, a hint of an inclusive outlook may be detected in the mention in Ezra–Nehemiah of the acceptance of foreigners (Ezra 6:21; Neh. 10:28; cf. Ezra 10:16–44), such that, even in Ezra–Nehemiah, exogenous marriages are only outlawed if foreign spouses fail to commit themselves to the God of Israel. The book of Ruth supports ethnic inclusiveness, the prime example being the acceptance of Ruth herself, and its focus would help to draw the reader's attention to these two passages in Ezra–Nehemiah. The reforms in Ezra–Nehemiah were not opposing marriage to foreign women like Ruth, namely women who had left their foreign gods behind and embraced the Israelite faith. In addition, there is no evidence that the book of Ruth contradicts or implicitly condemns the policy of breaking up foreign marriages. On the other hand, what is only alluded to in two places in Ezra–Nehemiah (the ready reception of proselytes) is the focus of attention in the book of Ruth. Put simply, Ruth and Ezra–Nehemiah are about different (but compatible) things. In terms of biblical theology, this is an example of how different canonical books supplement and balance each other, enabling a fuller presentation and application of God's many-sided truth.

The book of Ruth emphasizes that relationship with Yahweh is expressed in acts of kindness (*ḥesed*) and presents a generous application of the law. In line with this, Nehemiah's call for an immediate cancellation of debts and return of property does not follow strict legal stipulation but is certainly in accordance with the law's intention that Israelites should treat each other as 'brothers' (Neh. 5). Nehemiah's concern is the underlying morality of the creditors' behaviour rather than strict legal observance. The law is applied in accordance with its intentions rather than its specifics, and proper behaviour was marked by right motivation as well as right actions. In this regard, the behaviour of Boaz and the procedure and priorities of Nehemiah are only a short step from the love ethic of the New Testament as taught by Jesus (Matt. 22:37–40) and Paul (Rom. 13:8–10).

Minimal reference is made to the person of Ruth in the New Testament (only Matt. 1:5), but this is no barrier to linking the story of Ruth to the larger drama of salvation that includes the promise of a future messianic figure who will rule God's people (chapter 3). The book of Ruth is a story about David's ancestors, and the genealogy in Ruth 4:18–22 picks up the storyline from Genesis and *via Perez* connects David to the Abrahamic promise (Gen. 38:29; Ruth 4:12). The effect of the genealogy is to link Ruth's story to the Bible's 'main narrative' in Genesis to Kings (from creation to exile), in which God's provision of a king for his people is a major concern. The placement of the book of Ruth between the books Judges and Samuel in the Greek Old Testament canon (and subsequently the English Bible) is another factor that encourages a reading of the Ruth narrative in relation to the house of David. On this basis, one of its main points is the providential preservation of the family that produced King David. The book of Ruth shows that the workings of divine providence on behalf of David began during the lives of his ancestors, and what happened to Naomi and Ruth can be understood as giving hope for the future of the Davidic house. Despite the ancestors of David experiencing a time of extreme peril (the near-extermination of the family of Elimelech), God's kindness did not fail the family, and likewise (by implication) his kindness will not fail the dynasty of David. In other words, the exile must not be allowed to extinguish the hope of a coming king in David's line. The clear inference is that the Messiah will come. This is a hope taken up in the Prophets (e.g. Isa. 9; 11; 16) and the Psalter (e.g. Pss 2; 110). The New Testament, in turn, sees this expectation fulfilled in the birth of Jesus as 'king of the Jews' (Matt. 2:2). It proclaims that the risen Lord reigns as messianic King at the right hand of God (Acts 2:36; Rev. 5:5) and looks forward to the final universal reign of God (1 Cor. 15:20–28).

Reading the book of Ruth in the canonical context provided by the Hebrew canon, in which it is placed after Proverbs 31, encourages an appreciation of its heroine as an example of the wisdom ethic taught in the book of Proverbs (chapter 4). Proverbs 31 praises the character and deeds of 'a worthy woman' (*'ēšet ḥayil*), with this expression occurring in 31:10 (NRSV: 'A *capable wife* who can find?'), and the juxtaposed book of Ruth can be understood as going on to describe just such a woman. The thematic linkage between the books of Proverbs and Ruth is supported by the fact that in Ruth 3:11 Boaz calls Ruth 'a worthy woman' (*'ēšet ḥayil*). In this way, conjoining Proverbs and Ruth brings to the fore the ethical dimension of the actions of Boaz and especially of Ruth herself. In the person of Ruth is found a pattern of behaviour worthy of emulation by readers (e.g. an ethic of hard work and diligence [Ruth 2:7, 17; cf. Prov. 6:6–11), and the book of Ruth contains themes that find a place in Old Testament wisdom books (e.g. marriage to a suitable wife, theodicy, providence, the care of the poor and reward).

Consistent with an idealized woman as the epitome of true wisdom in Proverbs 31 and the interpretation of the heroine Ruth as a real-life example of the wisdom ethic of the book of Proverbs, in the Gospels, both by action and word, Jesus shows that he places a high value on women. In line with this evaluation, the Gospel writers depict women as exemplars of faith and of devoted service (e.g. Matt. 15:21–28; Luke 8:1–3). In addition, women were among the band of co-workers that made up Paul's mission team to the Gentile world. There is also a marked ethical focus in the Sermon on the Mount and the letter of James, but in neither is ethical teaching devoid of a theological foundation. In the case of the famous dominical sermon, what Jesus said and how he said it caused the crowds to recognize his unparalleled authority (Matt. 7:28–29; cf. 21:23–27), and the teaching of James has a Christological dimension to it (e.g. Jas 2:1; 5:7–8).[1] The letter of James, like the book of Ruth, can be read within a wisdom frame (NB Jas 1:5) and the letter contains typical wisdom themes (e.g. suffering, speech, rich and poor). Like the author of Ruth, the half-brother of Jesus makes use of Old Testament personages as moral examples (Abraham, Rahab, the prophets, Job and Elijah).

Ancient readers placed Ruth among historical books (between Judges and Samuel) in the Greek canonical tradition and put it alongside Proverbs 31 in the Hebrew canon. These alternate placements suggest the compatibility of the wisdom ideal (exemplified in the figure of Ruth) and the salvation-historical focus of the narrative book of Ruth (given the David linkage). Certainly, there is no evidence that these are incompatible or competing ways of interpreting the canonical book. This affirms the essential relation between ethics and biblical theology, and a biblical-theological approach does not need to deny or downplay the ethical implication of Old Testament narratives.

The conjoining of Ruth and the Psalter in the listing of Old Testament books in the Talmud (*Baba Bathra* 14b) helps to bring to light the thematic links between the two books that include the key terms 'refuge', 'wings' and 'kindness' (chapter 5). This way of ordering the books highlights the connection of Ruth with David as the chief psalmist. In addition, we found a transition from lament to praise in the structuring of both books, something that may not have been noticed if the books had not been neighbours in this way of ordering the canon. In the Psalter, David is shown to be one who 'takes refuge' in God just as did Ruth herself (2:12: 'under whose wings you have come to take refuge'), such that Ruth personifies the implied ethic of total reliance on God as taught in the Psalter. Just as Ruth embodies and experiences God's 'kindness' (*ḥesed*), so also in the Psalter David praises God as the one who 'shows kindness [*ḥesed*] to his anointed, to David and his offspring for ever' (Ps. 18:50). Such thematic links present Ruth as a model of the piety of the Psalter.

The canon of Scripture fosters the interaction of the texts within the bounds of the canon, and this dynamic was reinforced when later readers placed particular books side-by-side (e.g. Ruth and Psalms). Reading a biblical book in relationship with other biblical books both narrows its range of possible meanings and opens up new interpretive

---

[1] For the importance of theological images and themes in James, see Wall 1997: 27–34.

options as the contents of one canonical text throw light on another. We explored the significance for biblical theology of the relationship between narrative and poetry as affirmed by the placing of Ruth and Psalms next to each other, one aspect being the compatibility of history (the story of Ruth) and theology (expressed in the praise and prayer of the Psalter). The Ruth–Psalter collation implies that beliefs about God's character and his ways are not arbitrary but are valid conclusions drawn from Israel's historical experience of God's 'kindness' (e.g. as epitomized in the story of Ruth). Similarly, a rich theological reading of historical events is on display in the canticles put on the lips of Mary, Zechariah and Simeon in the Lukan birth narratives (Luke 1:46–55, 68–79; 2:29–32). In these songs the theology of Luke's Gospel is sounded, one prominent feature of which is its theme of salvation (1:47, 69, 71, 77; 2:30; cf. 2:11; 3:6; 19:9–10).[2]

The famine motif (chapter 6) is part of the larger themes of judgment and salvation, and this motif in the book of Ruth needs to be read in the context of the whole of the Bible. Biblical theology is interested in how various motifs run through Scripture, for they have a role in connecting earlier and later events in salvation history. What we find in the Bible are recurring typological patterns of analogous events and persons. Links to Genesis in the story of Ruth, especially in chapter 4 (via reference to Rachel, Leah, Perez and Tamar), suggest that what happens to the family of Elimelech should be read against the backdrop of the land theology of the patriarchal narratives (Gen. 12 – 50), where repeated famines raise the option of leaving the Promised Land (Gen. 12:10–20; 20:1–18; 26:1–17). The different responses of the patriarchs to the threat of famine (leaving/not leaving) assist in evaluating the action of Elimelech in moving to Moab. In addition, a scrutiny of wisdom literature helps to prevent the wrong kind of moralizing, for it is plain that famine is not always a divine punishment for the disobedience of God's people but may be a test, and, especially in books like Proverbs and Job, the nexus between sin and suffering is loosened, so that readers of Ruth are warned against rushing to judgment concerning the behaviour of Elimelech.

Understood as a test, famine becomes an opportunity for God to demonstrate that he can and will provide for his people, and the proper human response is trust in God to provide (and Elimelech may have failed in this regard). A biblical-theological approach incorporates

---

[2] See Marshall 1970: 77–102.

both 'theology' in the narrow sense of the word (what is said about God's character, ways and purposes) and the ethical implications of what is revealed about God (here a response of trust). In line with this, the use of the key Hebrew term *šûb* (meaning either 'return' or 'turn' [= repent]) in the story of Ruth and its wider use in Scripture suggest that departure from and return to the land are more than just physical movements but have a moral dimension. As a result, what we see happening in the book of Ruth is also a return to right relationship with God and the blessings that follow from that relationship. On this basis, the story of Ruth continues to speak to Christians who may still experience physical and spiritual hunger, and we learn that the experience of scarcity is not necessarily to be understood as a judgment of God. The tracing of the famine/hunger motifs into the New Testament leads to the consummation of God's purposes in the eschaton when hunger will be no more. This eschatological hope supports the response of trust and faithfulness by believers in the present.

Our exploration of God's hiddenness and human agency (chapter 7) is an example of the theological reading of the text of Scripture. The Bible tells us what it is important to know about God and how humans are to behave if God is who he is revealed to be. In other words, we read Scripture with the aim of understanding God's person, actions and motivations and what this means for who we are and how we should live. There is at present something of a renaissance in the appreciation of the theological dimension of Scripture, and this trend is something to be encouraged.[3] It can be understood as a return to older modes of reading the Bible that were mainstream until the rise of critical scholarship in the wake of the Enlightenment. By contrast, critical approaches to the Bible have often been 'theologically deaf' (a penetrating critique made by Brevard Childs).[4] We should not, however, attempt to force all the books of the Bible into exactly the same theological mould; it is to be expected that they will have disparate emphases and interests for they address different times and situations, though as component parts of the biblical canon their compatibility is assumed, even as their (measure of) variety is to be celebrated and exploited to speak to a variety of circumstances.

We offered a theological reading of the story of Ruth through the hiddenness–agency lens. In this story, God's purposes and actions

---

[3] This does not imply, however, a blanket endorsement of all that is done by practitioners of 'Theological Interpretation of Scripture'. For a thoughtful evaluation of the movement, see Carson 2011.

[4] Childs 1964.

remain largely hidden but God is spoken of by characters within the story. In other words, God's presence in action might be scanty in the narrative (1:6; 4:13), but the reader is constantly reminded of him through the speech of the main characters (e.g. 2:12, 20). We used the books of Judges and Esther as theological conversation partners and foils for Ruth, with the aim of sharpening our reading of Ruth as well as sampling something of the variety on show in Scripture. In Judges, God's hiddenness seems primarily to be a judgment on Israel's rebellion against him, and the actions of the human characters are almost always morally suspect. It is not clear that the same divine motivation lies behind the omission of any reference to God in the book of Esther, though there is moral ambiguity in a number of the actions of Mordecai and Esther (e.g. her marrying a pagan king). God is completely hidden in the book of Esther and we argued that the narrator does not wish him to be brought back into the story. The Jewish hero and heroine of the book of Esther serve as models of energetic effort and risk-taking for the sake of the welfare of the Jewish people. God's actions in the Ruth narrative are minimal, yet, unlike in the sojourn narratives at the end of Judges (chs. 17–21), this does not indicate God's disapproval of his people's actions. God works through the actions of Boaz and Ruth, who are models and agents of divine kindness (*hesed*) in restoring the family fortunes. The climax of the themes of God's hiddenness and human agency in the Bible is the experience of Jesus on the cross, when he was abandoned by God as he bore the penalty of human sin, even as God worked through the wicked actions of the human agents of Jesus' fate to accomplish our salvation.

The biblical-theological approach focuses not only on words but also on motifs and themes in the Bible's storyline, and redemption is a major theme in the history of salvation as outlined in the Bible (chapter 8). A 'motif' has the concrete sense of a recurrent image or object (e.g. famine), whereas 'theme' is broader and various related motifs may contribute to one theme. Our exploration of the theme of redemption in the story of Ruth was enriched by a wider survey of this theme in Scripture, and, in turn, what was discovered in Ruth provides an illustration and instance of redemption that prevents this rich theme degenerating into an abstract concept unconnected to real people and real-life situations. We found the following key features: the powerlessness of those needing to be redeemed; the cost to be paid by the one who redeems; God as the great Redeemer (who can, of course, make use of human agents); the scope of redemption covering the economic, social and the spiritual realms; and the familial relationship between the redeemer and the redeemed. More than one kinsman-redeemer is to be found in the book of Ruth: Mr So-and-So, Obed and, most prominent of all, Boaz. This study enabled a more careful definition of typology, and we gave a cautious estimation of Boaz as a 'type' of Christ – insofar as he was a divine agent for the redemption of the decimated family of Elimelech. The similarity of their persons was limited to this one feature. The exodus rescue is the Old Testament paradigm of redemption, but any reading of the story of Ruth would be incomplete without tracing the theme of redemption into the New Testament, wherein the role of redeemer is transferred to Jesus, the God-man, who was both willing and able to redeem. Jesus, as 'antitype', fulfils the role of redeemer at a higher and more profound level.

Ruth's incorporation into the people of Israel encourages a missional reading of her experience (chapter 9), interpreting the story of Ruth in the wider context of the biblical canon that describes the mission of God (*missio Dei*) to a lost and disordered world. This mission is rooted in the fact of creation and is announced in God's promises to Abraham to bless the world through his family (Gen. 12:1–3). It is reflected in the role of Israel as 'a display-people' who were meant to be a model of kingdom living (e.g. Deut. 4:5–8). In addition, what is described in the book of Ruth anticipates the formation of a multi-ethnic people through the gospel mission (Rev. 5:9–10; 14:6). The narrative of Ruth helps to equip God's people to engage in the *missio Dei* by promoting an ethic of kindness (*ḥesed*) as the guiding principle in the application of the law. Boaz's actions towards Ruth are generous and move beyond strict legal requirements, applying the anti-Moabite laws in Deuteronomy 7 and 23 with appropriate flexibility. Likewise, a narrow interpretation of the gleaning, redemption and levirate laws would not have compelled Boaz to go to the lengths that he did to help Ruth and Naomi. In the book of Ruth, therefore, we are not far from Jesus' summary of the Old Testament law in the form of the two love commandments (Matt. 22:37–40). Also relevant is the risk-taking of the apostle Paul in his law-free mission to Gentiles. Any attempt to write a comprehensive 'biblical theology of mission' would need to include consideration of the book of Ruth.

In summary, with the book of Ruth as our focus, we have sought to contribute to the ongoing exploration and refinement of both content and method in biblical theology. With regard to content, the book of Ruth contributes to key biblical themes and motifs (e.g. famine, redemption, kindness) and the elucidation of Ruth itself was enriched by a wider survey of the teaching of Scripture. Our missional reading interpreted the story of Ruth in the context of the biblical canon that describes the mission of God. We found that Ruth also assists in equipping God's people to engage in the *missio Dei* by promoting an ethic of kindness (*ḥesed*). Reading the book of Ruth between Judges and Samuel (as in the Greek OT canon) helped us to link the story of Ruth to the larger biblical drama of salvation, giving hope of the coming of a future messianic figure who will rule God's people (a hope fulfilled in Jesus). Conjoining Proverbs 31 and Ruth (as in the Hebrew canon) brought to the fore the ethical dimension of the actions of Ruth and Boaz as wisdom models and instruments of divine kindness. Placing Ruth next to the Psalter (as in the Talmudic listing of biblical books) affirmed the compatibility of history (the story of Ruth) and theology (expressed in the praise and prayer of the Psalter). We found no evidence to suggest that these are incompatible ways of interpreting the canonical book of Ruth.

In seeking to contribute to biblical-theological method, we demonstrated the importance of a broad understanding of what biblical theology is, namely that it should encompass history, theology, ethics, doxology and missional concerns. Biblical theology does not need to deny or downplay the ethical implications of Old Testament narratives. Who God is and how he acts (theology) has moral implications (ethics). The salvation-historical record of God's dealings with his people is to be celebrated and expressed in prayer and praise to God. The interpretation of Scripture must have at its forefront God's mission to a lost and fallen world and should equip God's people for involvement in that mission. Bringing Ruth into dialogue with Ezra–Nehemiah showed how different canonical books supplement and balance each other. The rich variety to be found in Scripture is not to be viewed as a problem to be solved so much as recognized as a resource for hearing God's truth in whatever time or situation we find ourselves.

Bibliography

Ackerman, S. (1998), *Warrior, Dancer, Seductress, Queen: Women in Judges and Biblical Israel*, The Anchor Bible Reference Library, New York: Doubleday.

Ackroyd, P. R. (1976), 'God and People in the Chronicler's Presentation of Ezra', in J. Coppens (ed.), *La Notion biblique de Dieu*, BETL 41, Leuven: Leuven University Press, 45–162.

Adams, S. L. (2014), *Social and Economic Life in Second Temple Judea*, Louisville: Westminster John Knox.

Alexander, T. D. (1997), 'Further Observations on the Term "Seed" in Genesis', *TynB* 48: 363–367.

——— (1998a), 'Royal Expectations in Genesis to Kings: Their Importance for Biblical Theology', *TynB* 49: 191–212.

——— (1998b), *The Servant King: The Bible's Portrait of the Messiah*, Leicester: Inter-Varsity Press.

Allen, L. C. (2002), *Psalms 101–150*, WBC 21, Nashville: Thomas Nelson.

Amit, Y. (1994), 'Literature in the Service of Politics: Studies in Judges 19–21', in H. G. Reventlow, Y. Hoffman and B. Uffenheimer (eds.), *Politics and Theopolitics in the Bible and Postbiblical Literature*, JSOTSup 171, Sheffield: Sheffield Academic Press, 28–40.

——— (2000), *Hidden Polemic in Biblical Literature*, tr. Jonathan Chipman, Biblical Interpretation Series 25, Leiden: Brill.

——— (2009), 'The Book of Judges: Dating and Meaning', in G. Galil, M. Geller and A. Millard (eds.), *Homeland and Exile: Biblical and Ancient Near Eastern Studies in Honour of Bustenay Oded*, VTSup 130, Leiden: Brill, 297–322.

Andersen, F. I. (1986), 'Yahweh, the Kind and Sensitive God', in P. T. O'Brien and D. G. Peterson (eds.), *God Who Is Rich in Mercy: Essays Presented to Dr. D. B. Knox*, Homebush West, NSW: Lancer Books, 41–88.

Andersen, F. I., and D. N. Freedman (1989), *Amos*, New York: Doubleday.

Anderson, B. W. (1950), 'The Place of the Book of Esther in the Christian Bible', *JR* 30: 32–43.

Bailey, K. E. (2008), *Jesus through Middle Eastern Eyes: Cultural Studies in the Gospels*, Downers Grove: IVP Academic.

Baker, D. L. (2010), *Two Testaments, One Bible: The Theological Relationship between the Old and New Testaments*, Nottingham: Apollos.

Balentine, S. E. (1980), 'A Description of the Semantic Field of Hebrew Words for "Hide"', *VT* 30: 137–153.

—— (1983), *The Hidden God: The Hiding of the Face of God in the Old Testament*, Oxford: Oxford University Press.

Bar-Efrat, S. (1980), 'Some Observations on the Analysis of Structure in Biblical Narrative', *VT* 30: 154–173.

Barker, P. A. (2004), *The Triumph of Grace in Deuteronomy: Faithless Israel, Faithful Yahweh in Deuteronomy*, Paternoster Biblical Monographs, Carlisle: Paternoster.

Bartholomew, C. G., and M. W. Goheen (2004), *The Drama of Scripture: Finding Our Place in the Biblical Story*, Grand Rapids: Baker Academic.

Barton, J. (2007), *Oracles of God: Perceptions of Ancient Prophecy in Israel after the Exile*, new edn, London: Darton, Longman & Todd.

Batumalai, S. (1990), *A Malaysian Theology of Muhibbah: A Theology for a Christian Witnessing in Malaysia*, Kuala Lumpur: Seminari Theoloji Malaysia.

Bauckham, R. (1997), 'The Book of Ruth and the Possibility of a Feminist Canonical Hermeneutic', *BibInt* 5: 29–45.

—— (2003), *Bible and Mission: Christian Witness in a Postmodern World*, Grand Rapids: Baker Academic.

Bauer, J. B. (1963), 'Das Buch Ruth in der jüdischen und christlichen Überlieferung', *Bibel und Kirche* 18: 116–119.

Baylis, C. P. (2004), 'Naomi in the Book of Ruth in Light of the Mosaic Covenant', *BibSac* 161: 413–431.

Beal, T. K. (1997), *The Book of Hiding: Gender, Ethnicity, Annihilation, and Esther*, London: Routledge.

Beale, G. K. (1984), 'An Exegetical and Theological Consideration of the Hardening of Pharaoh's Heart in Exodus 4–14 and Romans 9', *TrinJ* 5: 129–154.

—— (1998), *The Book of Revelation*, Grand Rapids: Eerdmans.

—— (2012), *Handbook on the New Testament Use of the Old Testament*, Grand Rapids: Baker Academic.

Beale, G. K., and B. L. Gladd (2014), *Hidden But Now Revealed: A Biblical Theology of Mystery*, Downers Grove: IVP Academic.

Beattie, D. R. G. (1977), *Jewish Exegesis of the Book of Ruth*, JSOTSup 2, Sheffield: JSOT Press.

—————— (1994), *The Targum of Ruth*, Aramaic Targums 19, Edinburgh: T&T Clark.

Beckwith, R. (1985), *The Old Testament Canon of the New Testament Church and Its Background in Early Judaism*, Grand Rapids: Eerdmans.

—————— (1991), 'A Modern Theory of the Old Testament Canon', *VT* 41: 385–395.

Beekman, J., J. Callow and M. Kopesec (1981), *The Semantic Structure of Written Communication*, 5th rev., Dallas: SIL.

Berg, S. B. (1979), *The Book of Esther: Motifs, Themes and Structure*, SBLDS 44, Missoula: Scholars Press.

Berger, Y. (2009), 'Ruth and Inner-Biblical Allusion: The Case of 1 Samuel 25', *JBL* 128: 253–272.

Berlin, A. (1983), *Poetics and Interpretation of Biblical Narrative*, Bible and Literature Series 9, Sheffield: Almond Press.

Berquist, J. L. (2008), 'Resistance and Accommodation in the Persian Empire', in R. A. Horsley (ed.), *In the Shadow of Empire: Reclaiming the Bible as a History of Faithful Resistance*, Louisville: Westminster John Knox, 41–58.

Bertman, S. (1965), 'Symmetrical Design in the Book of Ruth', *JBL* 84: 165–168.

Bickerman, E. (1967), *Four Strange Books of the Bible: Jonah, Daniel, Koheleth, Esther*, New York: Schocken Books.

Blackburn, W. R. (2012), *The God Who Makes Himself Known: The Missionary Heart of the Book of Exodus*, Downers Grove: InterVarsity Press

Blenkinsopp, J. (1988), *Ezra–Nehemiah: A Commentary*, OTL, Philadelphia: Westminster.

Blidstein, G. J. (1974), "*Atimia*: A Greek Parallel to Ezra x 8 and to Post-Biblical Exclusion from the Community', *VT* 24: 357–360.

Bliese, L. F. (1988), 'Chiastic Structures, Peaks and Cohesion in Nehemiah 9:6–37', *BT* 39: 208–215.

Block, D. I. (1997), *The Book of Ezekiel: Chapters 1–24*, NICOT, Grand Rapids: Eerdmans.

—————— (1999), *Judges, Ruth*, NAC 6, Nashville: Broadman & Holman.

—————— (2000), 'Divine Abandonment: Ezekiel's Adaptation of an Ancient Near Eastern Motif', in M. S. Odell and J. T. Strong (eds.), *The Book of Ezekiel: Theological and Anthropological Perspectives*, Atlanta: Scholars Press, 15–42.

—————— (2012), *Deuteronomy*, NIVAC, Grand Rapids: Zondervan.

Blomberg, C. L. (1999), *Neither Poverty Nor Riches: A Biblical Theology of Material Possessions*, Leicester: Apollos.

Bockmuehl, M. (2006), *Seeing the Word: Refocusing New Testament Study*, Studies in Theological Interpretation, Grand Rapids: Baker Academic.

Böstrom, L. (1990), *The God of the Sages: The Portrayal of God in the Book of Proverbs*, CB OT 29, Stockholm: Almqvist & Wiksell.

Botte, P., and P.-M. Bogaert (1996), 'Septante et versions grecques', in L. Pirot and A. Robert (eds.), *Supplément au Dictionnaire de la Bible*, Paris: Letouzey & Ané, 12:535–691.

Bovell, C. (2003), 'Symmetry, Ruth and Canon', *JSOT* 28: 175–191.

Brady, C. M. M. (2013), 'The Conversion of Ruth in Targum Ruth', *Review of Rabbinic Judaism* 16: 133–146.

Brandt, P. (2001), *Endgestalten des Kanons: Das Arrangement der Schriften Israels in der jüdischen und christlichen Bibel*, BBB 131, Berlin: Philo.

Braulik, G. (1999), 'The Book of Ruth as Intra-Biblical Critique of the Deuteronomic Law', *AcT* 19: 1–20.

Brenner, A. (1993a), 'Women Poets and Authors', in A. Brenner (ed.), *A Feminist Companion to the Song of Songs*, Sheffield: JSOT Press, 86–97.

——— (1993b), *A Feminist Companion to Ruth*, Sheffield: Sheffield Academic Press.

——— (1999), *Ruth and Esther: A Feminist Companion to the Bible*, Sheffield: Sheffield Academic Press.

Brettler, M. (1989), 'The Book of Judges: Literature as Politics', *JBL* 108: 395–418.

Brown, R. E. (1982), '*Rachab* in Mt 1,5 Probably Is Rahab of Jericho', *Bib* 63: 79–80.

Broyles, C. C. (2001), 'Traditions, Intertextuality, and Canon', in C. C. Broyles (ed.), *Interpreting the Old Testament*, Grand Rapids: Baker, 157–175.

Bruce, F. F. (1982), *The Epistle of Paul to the Galatians: A Commentary on the Greek Text*, NIGTC, Exeter: Paternoster.

Brueggemann, W. (1991), 'Bounded by Obedience and Praise: The Psalms as Canon', *JSOT* 50: 63–92.

——— (1997), *Theology of the Old Testament*, Minneapolis: Fortress.

Bullock, C. H. (2011), *Encountering the Book of Psalms: A Literary and Theological Introduction*, Encountering Biblical Studies, Grand Rapids: Baker Academic.

Burke, T. J. (2006), *Adopted into God's Family: Exploring a Pauline Metaphor*, NSBT 22, Nottingham: Apollos.

Burnett, J. S. (2010), *Where Is God? Divine Absence in the Hebrew Bible*, Minneapolis: Fortress.

Bush, F. W. (1996a), *Ruth, Esther*, WBC 9, Dallas: Word Books.

——— (1996b), 'Ruth 4:17: A Semantic Wordplay', in J. E. Coleson and V. H. Matthews (eds.), *'Go to the Land I Will Show You': Studies in Honor of Dwight W. Young*, Winona Lake: Eisenbrauns, 3–14.

Butler, T. C. (2009), *Judges*, WBC 8, Nashville: Thomas Nelson.

Camp, C. V. (1985), *Wisdom and the Feminine in the Book of Proverbs*, Bible and Literature Series 11, Sheffield: Almond.

Campbell Jr, E. F. (1975), *Ruth: A New Translation with Introduction, Notes, and Commentary*, AB 7, Garden City, NY: Doubleday.

Carr, D. M. (2011), *The Formation of the Hebrew Bible: A New Reconstruction*, Oxford: Oxford University Press.

Carroll R., M. D. (2013), *Christians at the Border: Immigration, the Church, and the Bible*, Grand Rapids: Brazos Press.

Carson, D. A. (1995), 'Current Issues in Biblical Theology: A New Testament Perspective', *BBR* 5: 17–41.

——— (1999), *Jesus' Sermon on the Mount and His Confrontation with the World: An Exposition of Matthew 5–10*, Grand Rapids: Baker.

——— (2004), 'Mystery and Fulfillment: Toward a More Comprehensive Paradigm of Paul's Understanding of the Old and New', in D. A. Carson, P. T. O'Brien and M. A. Seifrid (eds.), *Justification and Variegated Nomism*, Grand Rapids: Baker, 393–436.

——— (2010), 'Matthew', in T. Longman III and D. E. Garland (eds.), *The Expositor's Bible Commentary*, rev. edn, vol. 9, Grand Rapids: Zondervan, 23–670.

——— (2011), 'Theological Interpretation of Scripture: Yes, But . . .', in R. M. Allen (ed.), *Theological Commentary: Evangelical Perspectives*, London: T&T Clark, 187–207.

Cassuto, U. (1964), *A Commentary on the Book of Genesis, Part II: From Noah to Abraham, Genesis VI 9 – XI 32, with an Appendix: A Fragment of Part III*, Jerusalem: Magnes Press.

Castles, S., H. de Haas and M. J. Miller (2014), *The Age of Migration: International Population Movements in the Modern World*, 5th edn, New York: Guilford Press.

Chapman, C. (1995), *Cross and Crescent: Responding to the Challenge of Islam*, Leicester: Inter-Varsity Press.

Childs, B. S. (1964), 'Interpretation in Faith: The Theological Responsibility of an Old Testament Commentary', *Int* 18: 432–449.

——— (1979), *Introduction to the Old Testament as Scripture*, London: SCM.

Chisholm Jr, R. B. (2013), *A Commentary on Judges and Ruth*, Grand Rapids: Kregel Academic.

Ciampa, R. E. (2007), 'The History of Redemption', in S. J. Hafemann and P. R. House (eds.), *Central Themes in Biblical Theology: Mapping Unity in Diversity*, Nottingham: Apollos, 254–308.

Clark, G. R. (1993), *The Word Hesed in the Hebrew Bible*, JSOTSup 157, Sheffield: Sheffield Academic Press.

Clifford, R. J. (1999), *Proverbs: A Commentary*, OTL, Louisville: Westminster John Knox.

Clines, D. J. (1984), *Ezra, Nehemiah, Esther*, NCB, London: Marshall, Morgan & Scott.

——— (1989), *Job 1–20*, WBC 17, Waco: Word.

Cohen, M. (1997), '*Ḥesed*: Divine or Human? The Syntactic Ambiguity of Ruth 2:20', in Y. Elman and J. S. Gurock (eds.), *Hazon Nahum: Studies in Jewish Law, Thought, and History Presented to Dr. Norman Lamm on the Occasion of His Seventieth Birthday*, Hoboken: Ktav, 11–38.

Collins, C. J. (1997), 'A Syntactical Note [Genesis 3:15]: Is the Woman's Seed Singular or Plural?', *TynB* 48: 139–148.

Cooper, A. (1983), 'The Life and Times of King David According to the Book of Psalms', in R. E. Friedman (ed.), *The Poet and the Historian: Essays in Literary and Historical Biblical Criticism*, HSS 26, Chico: Scholars Press, 117–131.

Craigie, P. C., and M. E. Tate (2004), *Psalms 1–50*, WBC 19, 2nd edn, Nashville: Nelson.

Creach, J. F. D. (1996), *Yahweh as Refuge and the Editing of the Hebrew Psalter*, JSOTSup 217, Sheffield: Sheffield Academic Press.

Cross, F. M. (1973), *Canaanite Myth and Hebrew Epic: Essays in the History of the Religion of Israel*, Cambridge, MA: Harvard University Press.

——— (1998), 'Kinship and Covenant in Ancient Israel', in *From Epic to Canon: History and Literature in Ancient Israel*, Baltimore: Johns Hopkins University Press, 3–21.

Darr, K. P. (1991), *Far More Precious Than Jewels: Perspectives on Biblical Women*, Louisville: Westminster John Knox.

Daube, D. (1956), *The New Testament and Rabbinic Judaism*, London: The Athlone Press, University of London.

Davies, E. W. (1981), 'Inheritance Rights and the Hebrew Levirate Marriage: Part 2', *VT* 31: 257–268.

Davies, J. A. (2004), *A Royal Priesthood: Literary and Intertextual Perspectives on an Image of Israel in Exodus 19:6*, JSOTSup 395, London: T&T Clark International.

Davis, D. R. (2000), *Judges: Such a Great Salvation*, Fearn: Christian Focus.

Davis, E. F. (2006), 'Beginning with Ruth: An Essay on Translating', in P. S. Hawkins and L. Cushing Stahlberg (eds.), *Scrolls of Love: Ruth and the Song of Songs*, New York: Fordham University Press, 9–19.

Dell, K. J. (2006), *The Book of Proverbs in Social and Theological Context*, Cambridge: Cambridge University Press.

Dempster, S. (1997), 'An "Extraordinary Fact": *Torah and Temple* and the Contours of the Hebrew Canon', *TynB* 48: 23–56, 191–218.

––––––– (2003), *Dominion and Dynasty: A Biblical Theology of the Hebrew Bible*, NSBT 15, Downers Grove: InterVarsity Press.

––––––– (2015), 'A Wandering Moabite: Ruth – A Book in Search of a Canonical Home', in J. Steinberg and T. J. Stone with the assistance of R. M. Stone (eds.), *The Shape of the Writings*, Siphrut: Literature and Theology of the Hebrew Scriptures 16, Winona Lake: Eisenbrauns, 87–118.

Donahue, J. R., and D. J. Harrington (2002), *The Gospel of Mark*, Collegeville: Liturgical Press.

Donaldson, L. E. (1999), 'The Sign of Orpah: Reading Ruth through Native Eyes', in A. Brenner (ed.), *Ruth and Esther: A Feminist Companion to the Bible (Second Series)*, Sheffield: Sheffield Academic Press, 130–144.

Driver, S. R. (1913), *Notes on the Hebrew Text and the Topography of the Books of Samuel*, Oxford: Clarendon.

Duguid, I. M. (1999), *Ezekiel*, NIVAC, Grand Rapids: Zondervan.

––––––– (2005), *Esther and Ruth*, Phillipsburg: P&R.

Dukan, M. (2006), *La Bible hébraïque: Les codices copiés en Orient et dans la zone séfarade avant 1280*, Bibliologia 22, Turnhout: Brepols.

Dumbrell, W. J. (1986), 'The Theological Intention of Ezra–Nehemiah', *RTR* 45: 65–72.

––––––– (2013), *Covenant and Creation: An Old Testament Covenant Theology*, Milton Keynes: Paternoster.

Dunne, J. A. (2014), *Esther and Her Elusive God: How a Secular Story Functions as Scripture*, Eugene: Wipf & Stock.

Durham, J. I. (1987), *Exodus*, WBC 3, Waco: Word Books.

Dyck, J. E. (1998), *The Theocratic Ideology of the Chronicler*, Biblical Interpretation Series 33, Leiden: Brill.

Edwards, J. R. (2001), *The Gospel According to Mark*, PNTC, Grand Rapids: Eerdmans.

Eising, H. (1980), '*ḥayil*', *TDOT* 4: 348–355.

Embry, B. (2013), '"Redemption–Acquisition": The Marriage of Ruth as a Theological Commentary on Yahweh and Yahweh's people', *JTI* 7: 257–273.

Enns, P. (2000), *Exodus*, NIVAC, Grand Rapids: Zondervan.

Epstein, I. (ed.) (1976), *Baba Bathra*, Hebrew–English Edition of the Babylonian Talmud, new edn in 2 vols., vol. 1, London: The Soncino Press.

Eskenazi, T. C. (1988), *In an Age of Prose: A Literary Approach to Ezra–Nehemiah*, Atlanta: Scholars Press.

Eskenazi, T. C., and T. Frymer-Kensky (2011), *Ruth*, JPS Bible Commentary, Philadelphia: JPS.

Exum, J. C. (2005), *Song of Songs*, OTL, Louisville: Westminster John Knox.

Fee, G. D. (1987), *The First Epistle to the Corinthians*, NICNT, Grand Rapids: Eerdmans.

Feeley-Harnik, G. (1990), 'Naomi and Ruth: Building Up the House of David', in S. Niditch (ed.), *Text and Tradition: The Hebrew Bible and Folklore*, Atlanta: Scholars Press, 163–184.

Fensham, F. C. (1982), *The Books of Ezra and Nehemiah*, Grand Rapids: Eerdmans.

Fentress-Williams, J. (2012), *Ruth*, Abingdon OT Commentaries, Nashville: Abingdon.

Fewell, D. N., and D. M. Gunn (1990), *Compromising Redemption: Relating Characters in the Book of Ruth*, Literary Currents in Biblical Interpretation, Louisville: Westminster John Knox.

Fiddian-Qasmiyeh, E., G. Loescher, K. Long and N. Sigona (eds.) (2014), *The Oxford Handbook of Refugee and Forced Migration Studies*, Oxford: Oxford University Press.

Fisch, H. (1982), 'Ruth and the Structure of Covenant History', *VT* 32: 425–437.

Fischer, I. (2001), *Rut*, HTKAT, Freiburg im Breisgau: Herder.

Fishbane, M. (1975), *Biblical Interpretation in Ancient Israel*, Oxford: Clarendon.

Flemming, D. (2011), 'Exploring a Missional Reading of Scripture: Philippians as a Case Study', *EQ* 83: 3–18.

—— (2012), 'Revelation and the *Missio Dei*: Toward a Missional Reading of the Apocalypse', *JTI* 6: 161–178.

Fox, M. V. (2000), *Proverbs 1–9*, AB 18A, New York: Doubleday.

—— (2001a), 'Wisdom in the Joseph Story', *VT* 51: 26–41.

—— (2001b), *Character and Ideology in the Book of Esther*, 2nd edn, Grand Rapids: Eerdmans.

—— (2009), *Proverbs 10–31*, AYB 18B, New Haven: Yale University Press.

—— (2013), 'God's Answer and Job's Response', *Bib* 94: 1–23.

France, R. T. (1971), *Jesus and the Old Testament: His Application of Old Testament Passages to Himself and His Mission*, London: Tyndale.

—— (2002), *The Gospel of Mark: A Commentary on the Greek Text*, NIGTC, Grand Rapids: Eerdmans.

—— (2007), *The Gospel of Matthew*, Grand Rapids: Eerdmans.

Freedman, A. D. (2005), *God as an Absent Character in Biblical Hebrew Narrative: A Literary-Theological Study*, Studies in Biblical Literature 82, New York: Peter Lang.

Fretheim, T. E. (1984), *The Suffering of God: An Old Testament Perspective*, Philadelphia: Fortress.

—— (1991), *Exodus*, IBC, Louisville: John Knox.

Frevel, C. (ed.) (2011), *Mixed Marriages, Intermarriage and Group Identity in the Second Temple Period*, LHBOTS 547, New York: T&T Clark.

Gale, W. A. (1989), 'Ruth upon the Threshing Floor and the Sin of Gibeah: A Biblical-Theological Study', *WTJ* 51: 369–375.

Gallagher, E. L. (2014), 'The Blood from Abel to Zechariah in the History of Interpretation', *NTS* 60: 121–138.

Garland, D. E. (1999), *2 Corinthians*, Nashville: Broadman & Holman.

Garrett, D. A. (2000), *Rethinking Genesis: The Sources and Authorship of the First Book of the Pentateuch*, Fearn: Christian Focus.

Genette, G. (1988), 'The Proustian Paratexte', *SubStance: A Review of Theory and Literary Criticism* 19: 63–77.

—— (1991), 'Introduction to the Paratext', *New Literary History* 22: 261–272.

—— (1997), *Paratexts: Thresholds of Interpretation*, tr. J. E. Lewin, Cambridge: Cambridge University Press.

Gentry, P. J., and S. J. Wellum (2012), *Kingdom Through Covenant: A Biblical-Theological Understanding of the Covenants*, Wheaton: Crossway.

Gerleman, G. (1981), *Ruth, Das Hohelied*, BKAT 18, 2nd edn, Neukirchen-Vluyn: Neukirchener.

Gilbert, M. (1981), 'La place de la Loi dans la prière de Néhémie 9', in M. Carrez, J. Doré and P. Grelot (eds.), *De la Tôrah au Messie. Mélanges Henri Cazelles*, Paris: Desclée, 307–316.

Ginsburg, C. D. (1897, 1966), *Introduction to the Massoretico-Critical Edition of the Hebrew Bible*, London: Trinitarian Bible Society, repr. New York: Ktav.

Glover, N. (2009), 'Your People, My People: An Exploration of Ethnicity in Ruth', *JSOT* 33: 293–313.

Glueck, N. (1967), *Ḥesed in the Bible*, tr. A. Gottschalk, Cincinnati: The Hebrew Union College Press.

Goh, S. T. S. (2014), 'Ruth as a Superior Woman of *ḥayil*? A Comparison between Ruth and the "Capable" Woman in Proverbs 31:10–31', *JSOT* 38: 487–500.

Goldsworthy, G. (2000), *Preaching the Whole Bible as Scripture*, Grand Rapids: Eerdmans.

Goppelt, L. (1982), *Typos: The Typological Interpretation of the Old Testament in the New*, Grand Rapids: Eerdmans.

Gordon, R. P. (1995), 'A House Divided: Wisdom in Old Testament Narrative Tradition', in J. Day, R. P. Gordon and H. G. M. Williamson (eds.), *Wisdom in Ancient Israel: Essays in Honour of J. A. Emerton*, Cambridge: Cambridge University Press, 94–105.

Goswell, G. (2008), 'The Order of the Books in the Hebrew Bible', *JETS* 51: 673–688.

——— (2010), 'Keeping God out of the Book of Esther', *EQ* 82: 99–110.

——— (2011), 'The Attitude to the Persians in Ezra–Nehemiah', *TrinJ* 32: 191–203.

——— (2012a), 'The Absence of a Davidic Hope in Ezra–Nehemiah', *TrinJ* 33: 19–31.

——— (2012b), 'The Temple Theme in the Book of Daniel', *JETS* 55: 509–520.

——— (2012c), 'The Paratext of Deuteronomy', in D. Firth and P. Johnston (eds.), *Interpreting Deuteronomy: Issues and Approaches*, Nottingham: Inter-Varsity Press, 209–228.

——— (2013), 'Joshua and Kingship', *BBR* 23: 29–42.

——— (2014a), 'The Book of Ruth and the House of David', *EQ* 86: 116–129.

——— (2014b), *Ezra–Nehemiah*, EP Commentary Series, Faverdale North: Evangelical Press.

Gottwald, N. K. (1985), *The Hebrew Bible: A Socio-Literary Intro-duction*, Philadelphia: Fortress.

Gow, M. D. (1992), *The Book of Ruth: Its Structure, Theme and Purpose*, Leicester: Apollos.

—— (2000), 'Ruth', in T. D. Alexander and B. S. Rosner (eds.), *New Dictionary of Biblical Theology*, Leicester: Inter-Varsity Press, 176–178.

Green, B. (1982), 'The Plot of the Biblical Story of Ruth', *JSOT* 23: 55–68.

Greidanus, S. (1999), *Preaching Christ from the Old Testament: A Contemporary Hermeneutical Method*, Grand Rapids: Eerdmans.

Gross, C. D. (1997), 'Is There Any Interest in Nehemiah 5?', *SJOT* 11: 270–278.

Gundry, R. H. (1993), *Mark: A Commentary on His Apology for the Cross*, Grand Rapids: Eerdmans.

Habel, N. C. (1985), *The Book of Job: A Commentary*, OTL, Phila-delphia: Westminster.

Hafemann, S. J., and P. R. House (2007), *Central Themes in Biblical Theology: Mapping Unity in Diversity*, Nottingham: Apollos.

Hals, R. M. (1969), *The Theology of the Book of Ruth*, Facet Books Biblical Series 23, Philadelphia: Fortress.

—— (1976), 'Ruth', in K. Crim (ed.), *Interpreter's Dictionary of the Bible: Supplementary Volume*, Nashville: Abingdon, 758–759.

Halton, C. (2012), 'An Indecent Proposal: The Theological Core of the Book of Ruth', *SJOT* 26: 30–43.

Hamilton, J. M. (2006), 'The Glory of God in Salvation through Judgment: The Centre of Biblical Theology?', *TynB* 57: 57–84.

—— (2008), 'Was Joseph a Type of the Messiah? Tracing the Typo-logical Identification between Joseph, David, and Jesus', *SBJT* 12: 52–77.

—— (2010), *God's Glory in Salvation through Judgment: A Biblical Theology*, Wheaton: Crossway.

—— (2012), 'The Typology of David's Rise to Power: Messianic Patterns in the Book of Samuel', *SBJT* 16: 4–25.

Hamilton, V. P. (1995), *Genesis 18–50*, NICOT, Grand Rapids: Eerdmans.

Harris, R. L. (1990), 'Chronicles and the Canon in New Testament Times', *JETS* 33: 75–84.

Hartley, J. E. (1988), *The Book of Job*, NICOT, Grand Rapids: Eerdmans.

Harvey, C. D. (2003), *Finding Morality in the Diaspora? Moral Ambiguity and Transformed Morality in the Books of Esther*, BZAW 328, Berlin: Walter de Gruyter.

Havea, J., and P. H. W. Lau (eds.) (2015), *Reading Ruth in Asia*, IVBS, Atlanta: SBL Press.

Hawk, L. D. (2015), *Ruth*, AOTC 7B, Nottingham: Apollos.

Hoglund, K. G. (1992), *Achaemenid Imperial Administration in Syria-Palestine and the Missions of Ezra and Nehemiah*, Atlanta: Scholars Press.

Hollander, A. den, U. Schmid and W. Smelik (2006), *Paratext and Megatext as Channels of Jewish and Christian Traditions: The Textual Markers of Contextualization*, Jewish and Christian Perspectives Series 6, Leiden: Brill.

Holmstedt, R. D. (2010), *Ruth: A Handbook on the Hebrew Text*, Baylor Handbook on the Hebrew Bible, Waco: Baylor University Press.

Hossfeld, F.-L., and E. Zenger (2005), *Psalms 2: A Commentary on Psalms 51–100*, Hermeneia, Minneapolis: Fortress.

———— (2011), *Psalms 3: A Commentary on Psalms 101–150*, Hermeneia, Minneapolis: Fortress.

Howard Jr, D. M. (1990), 'The Case for Kingship in Deuteronomy and the Former Prophets', *WTJ* 52: 101–115.

———— (1998), 'The Case for Kingship in the Old Testament: Narrative Books and the Psalms', *TrinJ* 9: 19–35.

Hoyt, J. (2012), 'Reassessing Repentance in Judges', *BibSac* 169: 143–158.

Hubbard Jr, R. L. (1988), *The Book of Ruth*, NICOT, Grand Rapids: Eerdmans.

———— (1991), 'The *go'el* in Ancient Israel: Theological Reflections on an Israelite Tradition', *BBR* 1: 3–20.

———— (2000a), 'The Divine Redeemer: Toward a Biblical Theology of Redemption', in W. Kim et al. (eds.), *Reading the Hebrew Bible for a New Millennium: Form, Concept and Theological Perspective*, Harrisburg: Trinity Press International, 188–204.

———— (2000b), 'Redemption', in T. D. Alexander and B. S. Rosner (eds.), *New Dictionary of Biblical Theology*, Leicester: Inter-Varsity Press, 716–720.

Hummel, H. D. (1964), 'The Old Testament Basis of Typological Interpretation', *Biblical Research* 9: 38–50.

———— (1979), *The Word Becoming Flesh: An Introduction to the Origin, Purpose, and Meaning of the Old Testament*, St Louis: Concordia.

Hunsberger, G. R. (2011), 'Proposals for a Missional Hermeneutic: Mapping the Conversation', *Missiology* 39: 309–321.

Isaac, M. (2015), *From Land to Lands, from Eden to the Renewed Earth*, Carlisle: Langham Monographs.

Jacobs, L. (1991), *Structure and Form in the Babylonian Talmud*, Cambridge: Cambridge University Press.

Janzen, D. (2000), 'The "Mission" of Ezra and the Persian-Period Temple Community', *JBL* 119: 619–643.

Janzen, J. G. (1993), *Abraham and All the Families of the Earth: A Commentary on the Book of Genesis 12–50*, Grand Rapids: Eerdmans.

Japhet, S. (2006), 'People and Land in the Restoration Period', in *From the Rivers of Babylon to the Highlands of Judah: Collected Studies on the Restoration Period*, Winona Lake: Eisenbrauns, 96–116.

Jastrow, M. (1996), *A Dictionary of the Targumim, the Talmud Babli and Yerushalmi, and the Midrashic Literature*, New York: Judaica.

Jensen, P. D., and T. Payne (1997), *Guidance and the Voice of God*, 2nd edn, Sydney: Matthias Media.

Jobling, D. (1993), 'Ruth Finds a Home: Canon, Politics, Method', in J. C. Exum and D. J. A. Clines (eds.), *The New Literary Criticism and the Hebrew Bible*, JSOTSup 143, Sheffield: JSOT Press, 125–139.

Johnson, M. D. (1969), *The Purpose of the Biblical Genealogies: With Special Reference to the Setting of the Genealogies of Jesus*, SNTSMS 8, Cambridge: Cambridge University Press.

Johnson, V. L. (2009), *David in Distress: His Portrait through the Historical Psalms*, LHBOTS 505, New York: T&T Clark International.

Kaiser, W. C. (2012), *Mission in the Old Testament: Israel as a Light to the Nations*, Grand Rapids: Baker Academic.

Kalmanofsky, A. (2014), *Dangerous Sisters of the Hebrew Bible*, Minneapolis: Fortress.

Kidner, D. (1967), *Genesis: An Introduction and Commentary*, TOTC, London: Tyndale.

Klein, L. R. (2003), *From Deborah to Esther: Sexual Politics in the Hebrew Bible*, Minneapolis: Fortress.

Klink, E. W., and D. R. Lockett (2012), *Understanding Biblical Theology: A Comparison of Theory and Practice*, Grand Rapids: Zondervan.

Koorevaar, H. J. (1997), 'Die Chronik als intendierter Abschluß des alttestamentlichen Kanons', *JETh* 11: 42–76.

Koosed, J. L. (2011), *Gleaning Ruth: A Biblical Heroine and Her After-lives*, Columbia: University of South Carolina Press.

Korpel, M. C. A. (2000), 'Unit Division in the Book of Ruth: With Examples from Ruth 3', in M. C. A. Korpel and J. M. Oesch (eds.), *Delimitation Criticism: A New Tool in Biblical Scholarship*, Pericope: Scripture as Written and Read in Antiquity 1, Assen: Van Gorcum, 131–139.

——— (2001), *The Structure of the Book of Ruth*, Pericope: Scripture as Written and Read in Antiquity 2, Assen: Van Gorcum.

Korpel, M. C. A., and J. C. de Moor (2011), *The Silent God*, Leiden: Brill.

Kosmala, H. (1975), '*gāḇar*', *TDOT* 2: 367–382.

Köstenberger, A. J. (2012), 'The Present and Future of Biblical Theology', *Them* 37: 445–464.

Köstenberger, A. J., and P. T. O'Brien (2001), *Salvation to the Ends of the Earth: A Biblical Theology of Mission*, Downers Grove: InterVarsity Press.

Kraus, H.-J. (1986), *Theology of the Psalms*, tr. Keith Crim, Minneapolis: Augsburg.

——— (1989), *Psalms 60–150: A Commentary*, CC, Minneapolis: Augsburg.

Kutsko, J. F. (2000), *Between Heaven and Earth: Divine Presence and Absence in the Book of Ezekiel*, Biblical and Judaic Studies 7, Winona Lake: Eisenbrauns.

Kwakkel, G. (2010), 'Under Yahweh's Wings', in A. Labahn and P. Van Hecke (eds.), *Metaphors in the Psalms*, BETL 231, Leuven: Peeters, 141–165.

Kwon, J. (2012), 'Wisdom Incarnate? Identity and Role of '*ēšet ḥayil* ("the Valiant Woman") in Proverbs 31:10–31', *JESOT* 1: 167–188.

LaCocque, A. (1987), 'Haman in the Book of Esther', *HAR* 11: 207–221.

——— (2004), *Ruth: A Continental Commentary*, CC, tr. K. C. Hanson, Minneapolis: Fortress.

Lane, W. L. (1974), *The Gospel According to Mark*, NICNT, Grand Rapids: Eerdmans.

Lang, B. (2004), 'Women's Work, Household and Property in Two Mediterranean Societies: A Comparative Essay on Proverbs XXXI 10–31', *VT* 54: 188–207.

Lau, P. H. W. (2009), 'Gentile Incorporation into Israel in Ezra–Nehemiah?', *Bib* 90: 356–373.

——— (2011), *Identity and Ethics in the Book of Ruth: A Social Identity Approach*, BZAW 416, Berlin: Walter de Gruyter.

——— (2012), 'Back Under Authority: Towards an Evangelical Postcolonial Hermeneutic', *TynB* 63: 131–144.

——— (2012–2016a), 'Famine', in J. D. Barry et al. (eds.), *Lexham Bible Dictionary*, Bellingham, WA: Lexham Press.

——— (2012–2016b), 'Redemption', in J. D. Barry et al. (eds.), *Lexham Bible Dictionary*, Bellingham, WA: Lexham Press.

——— (2016), 'Israel and Gentiles: A Permeable Barrier?', in G. A. Yee and J. Y. H. Yieh (eds.), *Honouring the Past, Looking to the Future: Essays from the 2014 International Congress of Ethnic Chinese Biblical Scholars*, Hong Kong: Divinity School of the Chung Chi College, The Chinese University of Hong Kong, 199–215.

Lee, C.-C. (2009), '*gwym* in Genesis 35:11 and the Abrahamic Promise of Blessings for the Nations', *JETS* 52: 467–482.

LeMon, J. M. (2010), *Yahweh's Winged Form in the Psalms: Exploring Congruent Iconography and Texts*, OBO 242, Göttingen: Vandenhoeck & Ruprecht.

Levenson, J. D. (1997), *Esther*, OTL, London: SCM.

Levering, M. (2007), *Ezra and Nehemiah*, Grand Rapids: Brazos Press.

Levine, B. A. (1989), *Leviticus*, The JPS Torah Commentary, Philadelphia: JPS.

Lichtenstein, M. H. (1982), 'Chiasm and Symmetry in Proverbs 31', *CBQ* 44: 202–211.

Lim, T. H. (2013), *The Formation of the Jewish Canon*, New Haven: Yale University Press.

Linafelt, T. A. (1999), 'Ruth', in T. A. Linafelt and T. K. Beal, *Ruth, Esther*, Berit Olam, Collegeville: Liturgical.

Lipiński, E. (2001), '*'am*', *TDOT* 11: 163–177.

Lister, J. R. (2015), *The Presence of God: Its Place in the Storyline of Scripture and the Story of Our Lives*, Wheaton: Crossway.

Loader, J. A. (1978), 'Esther as a Novel with Different Levels of Meaning', *ZAW* 90: 417–421.

Longman III, T. (2001), *Song of Songs*, NICOT, Grand Rapids: Eerdmans.

——— (2014), *Psalms: An Introduction and Commentary*, TOTC 15–16, Nottingham: Inter-Varsity Press.

Lowery, R. H. (2000), *Sabbath and Jubilee*, Understanding Biblical Themes, St Louis: Chalice.

Luter, A. B., and B. C. Davis (1995), *Ruth and Esther: God Behind the Seen*, Fearn: Christian Focus.

McAmis, R. D. (2002), *Malay Muslims: The History and Challenge of Resurgent Islam in Southeast Asia*, Grand Rapids: Eerdmans.

McConville, J. G. (2002), *Deuteronomy*, AOTC, Leicester: Apollos.

McCreesh, T. P. (1985), 'Wisdom as Wife: Proverbs 31:10–31', *RB* 92: 25–46.

McIvor, J. S. (1993), *The Targum of Chronicles: Translated, with Introduction, Apparatus, and Notes*, Aramaic Bible 19, Collegeville: Liturgical Press.

McKeown, J. (2008), *Genesis*, THOTC, Grand Rapids: Eerdmans.

——— (2015), *Ruth*, THOTC, Grand Rapids: Eerdmans.

MacLachlan, G. L., and I. Reid (1994), *Framing and Interpretation*, Carlton: Melbourne University Press.

Maclean, M. (1991), 'Pretexts and Paratexts: The Art of the Peripheral', *New Literary History* 22: 273–293.

Maier, C. (1995), *Die 'fremde Frau' in Proverbien 1–9: Eine exegetische und sozialgeschichtliche Studie*, OBO 144, Freiburg, Schweiz: Universitätsverlag.

Marshall, I. H. (1970), *Luke: Historian and Theologian*, Exeter: Paternoster.

——— (1974), 'The Development of the Concept of Redemption in the New Testament', in R. J. Banks (ed.), *Reconciliation and Hope: New Testament Essays on Atonement and Eschatology Presented to L. L. Morris on His 60th Birthday*, Exeter: Paternoster, 153–169.

Martens, E. A. (1977), 'Tackling Old Testament Theology', *JETS* 20: 123–132.

Martin, O. (2015), *Bound for the Promised Land*, NSBT 34, Downers Grove: InterVarsity Press.

Matthews, V. H. (2004), *Judges and Ruth*, NCB, Cambridge: Cambridge University Press.

Mays, J. L. (1986), 'The David of the Psalms', *Int* 40: 143–155.

Meek, R. L. (2014), 'Intertextuality, Inner-Biblical Exegesis, and Inner-Biblical Allusion: The Ethics of a Methodology', *Bib* 95: 280–291.

Merrill, E. H. (1985), 'The Book of Ruth: Narration and Shared Themes', *BibSac* 142: 130–139.

Milgrom, J. (2000), *Leviticus 23–27*, AB 3B, New York: Doubleday.

Miller Jr, P. D. (1982), *Sin and Judgment in the Prophets: A Stylistic and Theological Analysis*, SBLMS 27, Chico, CA: Scholars Press.

Miller, T. (2014), *Three Versions of Esther: Their Relationship to Anti-Semitic and Feminist Critique of the Story*, Contributions to Biblical Exegesis and Theology 74, Leuven: Peeters.

Moberly, R. W. L. (2009), *The Theology of the Book of Genesis*, Cambridge: Cambridge University Press.

Moffat, D. P. (2013), *Ezra's Social Drama: Identity Formation, Marriage and Social Conflict in Ezra 9 and 10*, LHBOTS 579, New York: Bloomsbury.

Moore, C. A. (1971), *Esther*, AB 7B, Garden City, NY: Doubleday.

Moore, M. S. (2001), 'To King or Not to King: A Canonical-Historical Approach to Ruth', *BBR* 11: 27–41.

Morris, L. (1965a), *The Apostolic Preaching of the Cross*, Leicester: Inter-Varsity Press.

—— (1965b), *The Cross in the New Testament*, Exeter: Paternoster.

—— (1968), *Ruth: An Introduction and Commentary*, TOTC, Downers Grove: InterVarsity Press.

Motyer, A. (2005), *The Message of Exodus*, BST, Downers Grove: InterVarsity Press.

Muilenburg, J. (1959), 'Form and Structure of the Covenantal Formulations', *VT* 9: 347–365.

Murphy, R. W. (1998), *Proverbs*, WBC 22, Nashville: Thomas Nelson.

Murray, D. (2013), *Jesus on Every Page: 10 Simple Ways to Seek and Find Christ in the Old Testament*, Nashville: Thomas Nelson.

Murray, M. J., and D. E. Taylor (2012), 'Hiddenness', in C. V. Meister and P. Copan (eds.), *The Routledge Companion to Philosophy of Religion*, 2nd edn, London: Routledge, 368–377.

Neufeld, E. (1955), 'The Prohibition against Loans at Interest in Ancient Hebrew Laws', *HUCA* 26: 355–412.

Neumann, J., and S. Parpola (1987), 'Climatic Change and the Eleventh–Tenth-Century Eclipse of Assyria and Babylonia', *JNES* 46: 161–182.

Newsom, C. A. (1989), 'Woman and Discourse of Patriarchal Wisdom: A Study of Proverbs 1–9', in P. L. Day (ed.), *Gender and Difference in Ancient Israel*, Minneapolis: Fortress, 142–160.

Nicholson, E. W. (1965), 'The Meaning of the Expression *'am-hā'āreṣ* in the Old Testament', *JSS* 10: 59–66.

Nielsen, K. (1997), *Ruth: A Commentary*, OTL, tr. Edward Broadbridge, Louisville: Westminster John Knox.

Nu, R. (2015), 'A Reinterpretation of Levirate Marriage in Ruth 4:1–12 for Kachin Society', in J. Havea and P. H. W. Lau (eds.), *Reading Ruth in Asia*, Atlanta: SBL, 57–72.

O'Brien, P. T. (1991), *The Epistle to the Philippians*, Grand Rapids: Eerdmans.

———— (2010), *The Letter to the Hebrews*, PNTC, Grand Rapids: Eerdmans.

O'Connell, R. H. (1996), *The Rhetoric of the Book of Judges*, VTSup 63, Leiden: Brill.

Ollenburger, B. C., E. A. Martens and G. F. Hasel (eds.) (1992), *The Flowering of Old Testament Theology*, Winona Lake: Eisenbrauns.

Olley, J. W. (2014), 'Re-Versing Tradition: The Influence of Sense-Divisions in Reading the Bible Then and Now', *ABR* 62: 31–43.

Osborne, G. R. (1979), 'Type; Typology', in G. W. Bromiley (ed.), *International Standard Bible Encyclopedia*, vol. 4, Grand Rapids: Eerdmans, 930–932.

———— (2001), 'Type; Typology', in W. A. Elwell (ed.), *Evangelical Dictionary of Theology*, Grand Rapids: Baker, 1222–1223.

Oswalt, J. N. (1998), *The Book of Isaiah: Chapters 40–66*, NICOT, Grand Rapids: Eerdmans.

Ott, C., S. J. Strauss and T. C. Tennent (2010), *Encountering Theology of Mission: Biblical Foundations, Historical Developments, and Contemporary Issues*, Grand Rapids: Baker Academic.

Outler, A. C. (1980), 'The "Logic" of Canon-Making and the Tasks of Canon-Criticism', in W. E. March (ed.), *Texts and Testaments: Critical Essays on the Bible and Early Church Fathers*, San Antonio: Trinity University Press, 264–276.

Pate, C. M., J. S. Duvall, J. D. Hays et al. (2004), *The Story of Israel: A Biblical Theology*, Downers Grove: InterVarsity Press.

Patrick, D. (1977), 'The Covenant Source Code', *VT* 27: 145–157.

Payne, J. D. (2012), *Strangers Next Door: Immigration, Migration, and Mission*, Downers Grove: InterVarsity Press.

Peels, H. G. L. (2001), 'The Blood "from Abel to Zechariah" (Matthew 23:35; Luke 11:50f.) and the Canon of the Old Testament', *ZAW* 113: 583–601.

Perdue, L. G. (2000), *Proverbs*, IBC, Louisville: John Knox.

Pigott, S. M. (2002), 'Wives, Witches and Wise Women: Prophetic Heralds of Kingship in 1 and 2 Samuel', *Review and Expositor* 99: 145–173.

Pomykala, K. E. (1995), *The Davidic Dynasty Tradition in Early Judaism: Its History and Significance for Messianism*, EJL 7, Atlanta: Scholars Press.

Pope, M. H. (1977), *Song of Songs*, AB 7C, Garden City, NY: Doubleday.

Porten, B. (1978), 'The Scroll of Ruth: A Rhetorical Study', *Gratz College Annual of Jewish Studies* 7: 23–49.

Prill, T. (2008), *Global Mission on Our Doorstep: Forced Migration and the Future of the Church*, Münster: MV Wissenschaft.

Prinsloo, W. S. (1980), 'The Theology of the Book of Ruth', *VT* 30: 330–341.

Rebera, B. (1985), 'Yahweh or Boaz? Ruth 2.20 Reconsidered', *BT* 36: 317–327.

Rendtorff, R. (1985), *The Old Testament: An Introduction*, tr. John Bowden, London: SCM.

——— (1997), 'Nehemiah 9: An Important Witness of Theological Reflection', in M. Cogan, B. L. Eichler and J. H. Tigay (eds.), *Tehillah le-Moshe: Biblical and Judaic Studies in Honor of Moshe Greenberg*, Winona Lake: Eisenbrauns, 111–117.

——— (2005), 'The Psalms of David: David in the Psalms', in P. W. Flint and P. D. Miller, Jr (eds.), *The Book of Psalms: Composition and Reception*, VTSup 99, Leiden: Brill, 53–64.

Rogerson, J. W. (2010), *A Theology of the Old Testament: Cultural Memory, Communication, and Being Human*, Minneapolis: Fortress.

Rosner, B. S. (2000), 'Biblical Theology', in T. D. Alexander and B. S. Rosner (eds.), *New Dictionary of Biblical Theology*, Leicester: Inter-Varsity Press, 3–11.

Rossow, F. C. (1991), 'Literary Artistry in the Book of Ruth and Its Theological Significance', *Concordia Journal* 17: 12–19.

Rowan, P. A. (2012), *Proclaiming the Peacemaker: The Malaysian Church as an Agent of Reconciliation in a Multicultural Society*, Oxford: Regnum.

Rowley, H. H. (1965), 'The Marriage of Ruth', in *The Servant of the Lord and Other Essays on the Old Testament*, 2nd edn, Oxford: Blackwell, 169–194.

Russell, B. D. (2010), 'What Is a Missional Hermeneutic?', *Catalyst*, <http://catalystresources.org/issues/364Russell.htm>, accessed 14 August 2010.

Sailhamer, J. (1992), *The Pentateuch as Narrative: A Biblical-Theological Commentary*, Grand Rapids: Zondervan.

Sakenfeld, K. D. (1978), *The Meaning of Ḥesed in the Hebrew Bible: A New Inquiry*, HSM 17, Missoula: Scholars Press.

——— (1985), *Faithfulness in Action: Loyalty in Biblical Perspective*, OBT, Philadelphia: Fortress.

——— (1999a), *Ruth*, IBC, Louisville: John Knox.

——— (1999b), 'Ruth 4, an Image of Eschatological Hope: Journeying with a Text', in M. A. Farley and S. Jones (eds.), *Liberating*

Eschatology: Essays in Honor of Letty M. Russell, Louisville: Westminster John Knox, 55–67.

———— (2003), 'Naomi's Cry: Reflections on Ruth 1:20–21', in B. A. Strawn and N. R. Brown (eds.), *A God So Near: Essays on Old Testament Theology in Honor of Patrick D. Miller*, Winona Lake: Eisenbrauns, 129–143.

———— (2004), 'Why Perez? Reflections on David's Genealogy in Biblical Tradition', in B. F. Batto and K. L. Roberts (eds.), *David and Zion: Biblical Studies in Honor of J. J. M. Roberts*, Winona Lake: Eisenbrauns, 405–416.

Sarna, N. M. (1989), *Genesis*, Philadelphia: JPS.

Sasson, J. M. (1979), *Ruth: A New Translation with a Philological Commentary and a Formalist–Folkloric Interpretation*, Baltimore: Johns Hopkins University Press.

Satterthwaite, P. E. (1992), 'Narrative Artistry in the Composition of Judges XX 29ff.', *VT* 42: 80–89.

———— (1993), '"No King in Israel": Narrative Criticism and Judges 17–21', *TynB* 44: 75–88.

Saxegaard, K. M. (2010), *Character Complexity in the Book of Ruth*, FAT II.47, Tübingen: Mohr Siebeck.

Saysell, C. (2012), 'Deuteronomy in the Intermarriage Crises in Ezra–Nehemiah', in D. G. Firth and P. S. Johnston (eds.), *Interpreting Deuteronomy: Issues and Approaches*, Nottingham: Inter-Varsity Press, 197–208.

Scheetz, J. M. (2013), 'Ancient Witnesses, Canonical Theories, and Canonical Intertextuality', in T. Hieke (ed.), *Formen des Kanons: Studien zu Ausprägungen des biblischen Kanons von der Antike bis zum 19. Jahrhundert*, SBS 228, Stuttgart: Verlag Katholisches Bibelwerk, 12–39.

Schellenberg, J. L. (2010), 'Divine Hiddenness', in C. Taliaferro, P. Draper and P. L. Quinn (eds.), *A Companion to Philosophy of Religion*, 2nd edn, Malden, MA: Wiley-Blackwell, 509–518.

Schreiner, T. R. (1998), *Romans*, BECNT, Grand Rapids: Baker.

Schulz, R. L. (2010), 'Intertextuality, Canon, and "Undecidability": Understanding Isaiah's "New Heavens and New Earth" (Isaiah 65:17–25)', *BBR* 20: 19–38.

Scott, J. M. (1992), *Adoption as Sons of God: An Exegetical Investigation into the Background of huiothesia in the Pauline Corpus*, WUNT 2.48, Tübingen: Mohr Siebeck.

Scott, R. B. Y. (1971), *The Way of Wisdom in the Old Testament*, New York: Macmillan.

———— (1985), *Proverbs, Ecclesiastes*, AB 18, 2nd edn, New York: Doubleday.

Seitz, C. R. (2009), *The Goodly Fellowship of the Prophets: The Achievement of Association in Canon Formation*, Grand Rapids: Baker Academic.

Shepherd, D. (2001), 'Violence in the Fields? Translating, Reading, and Revising in Ruth 2', *CBQ* 63: 444–463.

Smalley, B. (1952), *The Study of the Bible in the Middle Ages*, Oxford: Basil Blackwell.

Smith, L. (1996), *Medieval Exegesis in Translation: Commentaries on the Book of Ruth*, 2nd edn, Kalamazoo: Medieval Institute Publications.

Smith-Christopher, D. L. (1994), 'The Mixed Marriage Crisis in Ezra 9–10 and Nehemiah 13: A Study of the Sociology of the Post-Exilic Judean Community', in T. C. Eskenazi and K. H. Richards (eds.), *Second Temple Studies: Volume 2, Temple Community in the Persian Period*, JSOTSup 175, Sheffield: JSOT Press, 243–256.

———— (2002), *A Biblical Theology of Exile*, Minneapolis: Fortress.

Sommer, B. D (1996), 'Exegesis, Allusion and Intertextuality in the Hebrew Bible: A Response to Lyle Eslinger', *VT* 96: 479–489.

Southwood, K. E. (2012), *Ethnicity and the Mixed Marriage Crisis in Ezra 9–10: An Anthropological Approach*, Oxford: Oxford University Press.

———— (2014), 'Will Naomi's Nation Be Ruth's Nation? Ethnic Translation as a Metaphor for Ruth's Assimilation within Judah', *Humanities* 3: 102–131.

Spellman, C. (2014), *Toward a Canon-Conscious Reading of the Bible: Exploring the History and Hermeneutics of the Canon*, New Testament Monographs 34, Sheffield: Sheffield Phoenix Press.

Stead, M. R. (2009), *The Intertextuality of Zechariah 1–8*, LHBOTS 506, New York: T&T Clark.

Stead, M. R., and G. N. Davies (2013), 'Atonement and Redemption', in M. R. Stead (ed.), *Christ Died for Our Sins: Essays on the Atonement*, Canberra: Barton Books, 35–58.

Steinberg, J. (2006), *Die Ketuvim: Ihr Aufbau und ihre Botschaft*, BBB 152, Hamburg: Philo.

Steinmann, A. E. (1999), *The Oracles of God: The Old Testament Canon*, St Louis: Concordia Academic Press.

Steussy, M. J. (1999), *David: Biblical Portraits of Power*, Columbia: University of South Carolina Press.

Stone, T. J. (2013a), *The Compilational History of the Megilloth: Canon, Contoured Intertextuality and Meaning in the Writings*, FAT II.59, Tübingen: Mohr Siebeck.

———— (2013b), 'Six Measures of Barley: Seed Symbolism in Ruth', *JSOT* 38: 189–199.

———— (2015), 'The Search for Order: The Compilational History of Ruth', in J. Steinberg and T. J. Stone with the assistance of R. M. Stone (ed.), *The Shape of the Writings*, Siphrut: Literature and Theology of the Hebrew Scriptures 16, Winona Lake: Eisenbrauns, 175–185.

Stott, J. R. W. (1968), *The Message of Galatians*, BST, Leicester: Inter-Varsity Press.

———— (1986), *The Cross of Christ*, Leicester: Inter-Varsity Press.

Stuart, D. K. (2006), *Exodus*, NAC, Nashville: Broadman & Holman.

Stuhlmueller, C. (1982), 'Psalm 22: The Deaf and Silent God of Mysticism and Liturgy', *BTB* 12: 86–90.

Sweeney, M. A. (1997), 'Davidic Polemics in the Book of Judges', *VT* 47: 517–529.

———— (2012), *Tanak: A Theological and Critical Introduction to the Jewish Bible*, Minneapolis: Fortress.

Swete, H. B. (1968), *An Introduction to the Old Testament in Greek, Appendix Containing the Letter of Aristeas*, H. St J. Thackeray (ed.), rev. R. R. Ottley, New York: Ktav.

Szlos, M. B. (2000), 'A Portrait of Power: A Literary-Critical Study of the Depiction of the Woman in Proverbs 31:10–31', *USQR* 54: 97–103.

Tannen, D. (1993), 'What Is a Frame? Surface Evidence for Underlying Expectations', in D. Tannen (ed.), *Framing in Discourse*, Oxford: Oxford University Press, 14–56.

Terrien, S. L. (1978), *The Elusive Presence: Toward a New Biblical Theology*, San Francisco: Harper & Row.

Thomas, N. J. (2002), 'Weaving the Words: The Book of Ruth as Missiologically Effective Communication', *Missiology* 30: 155–170.

Tigay, J. H. (1996), *Deuteronomy*, The JPS Torah Commentary, Philadelphia: JPS.

Trible, P. (1978), *God and the Rhetoric of Sexuality*, Philadelphia: Fortress.

———— (1982), 'A Human Comedy: The Book of Ruth', in K. R. R. Gros Louis with J. S. Ackerman (eds.), *Literary Interpretations of Biblical Narratives: Volume II*, Nashville: Abingdon, 161–190.

Trudinger, L. P. (1974), '"Eli, Eli, lama sabachthani": A Cry of Dereliction or Victory?', *JETS* 17: 235–238.

Ulrich, D. R. (2007), *From Famine to Fullness: The Gospel According to Ruth*, Phillipsburg: P&R.

Vanhoozer, K. J. (1998), *Is There a Meaning in This Text? The Bible, the Reader, and the Morality of Literary Knowledge*, Grand Rapids: Zondervan.

——— (2005), *The Drama of Doctrine: A Canonical-Linguistic Approach to Christian Theology*, Louisville: Westminster John Knox.

——— (2008), 'Introduction: What Is Theological Interpretation of the Bible?', in K. J. Vanhoozer, C. G. Bartholomew and D. J. Treier (eds.), *Theological Interpretation of the Old Testament: A Book-by-Book Survey*, Grand Rapids: Baker, 15–28.

Van Leeuwen, R. C. (1992), 'Wealth and Poverty: System and Contradiction in Proverbs', *Hebrew Studies* 33: 25–36.

Wall, R. W. (1997), *Community of the Wise: The Letter of James*, The New Testament in Context, Valley Forge: Trinity Press International.

——— (2002), 'The Acts of the Apostles', in L. E. Keck (ed.), *The New Interpreter's Bible: A Commentary in Twelve Volumes*, Vol. 10, Nashville: Abingdon, 3–368.

Walters, A. (2007), *Knowing Our Neighbour: A Study of Islam for Christians in Malaysia*, Petaling Jaya: Council of Churches of Malaysia.

Waltke, B. (2004), *The Book of Proverbs: Chapters 1–15*, NICOT, Grand Rapids: Eerdmans.

——— (2005), *The Book of Proverbs: Chapters 15–31*, NICOT, Grand Rapids: Eerdmans.

Waltke, B. K., and C. J. Fredricks (2001), *Genesis: A Commentary*, Grand Rapids: Zondervan.

Warfield, B. B. (1950), *The Person and Work of Christ*, Philadelphia: P&R.

Watts, J. W. (1992), *Psalm and Story: Inset Hymns in Hebrew Narrative*, JSOTSup 139, Sheffield: Sheffield Academic Press.

——— (2005), 'Biblical Psalms outside the Psalter', in P. W. Flint and P. D. Miller (eds.), *The Book of Psalms: Composition and Reception*, VTSup 99, Leiden: Brill, 288–309.

Webb, B. G. (1996), *The Message of Isaiah*, Leicester: Inter-Varsity Press.

——— (2000), *Five Festal Garments*, NSBT 10, Leicester: Apollos.

————— (2012), *The Book of Judges*, NICOT, Grand Rapids: Eerdmans.

Weinfeld, M. (1996), 'Ruth, Book of', in *Encyclopaedia Judaica*, Jerusalem: Keter.

Wenham, G. J. (1979), *Leviticus*, NICOT, Grand Rapids: Eerdmans.

————— (1981), *Numbers*, TOTC, Leicester: Inter-Varsity Press.

————— (1987), *Genesis 1–15*, WBC 1, Waco: Word Books.

————— (1994), *Genesis 16–50*, WBC 2, Dallas: Word Books.

————— (1997), 'The Gap between Law and Ethics in the Bible', *JJS* 48: 17–29.

————— (2000), *Story as Torah: Reading the Old Testament Ethically*, Edinburgh: T&T Clark.

Whybray, R. N. (1968), *The Succession Narrative: A Study of II Sam. 9–20 and I Kings 1 and 2*, SBT 2/9, London: SCM.

————— (1994), *The Composition of the Book of Proverbs*, JSOTSup 168, Sheffield: Sheffield Academic Press.

Wilch, J. R. (2006), *Ruth: A Theological Exposition of Sacred Scripture*, CC, St Louis: Concordia.

Williamson, H. G. M. (1985), *Ezra, Nehemiah*, Waco: Word.

Williamson, P. R. (2000), *Abraham, Israel and the Nations: The Patriarchal Promise and Its Covenantal Development*, JSOTSup 315, Sheffield: Sheffield Academic Press.

————— (2007), *Sealed with an Oath: Covenant in God's Unfolding Purpose*, NSBT 23, Downers Grove: InterVarsity Press.

Wilson, G. H. (1992), 'The Shape of the Book of Psalms', *Int* 46: 129–142.

Wilson, L. (2008), 'Job', in K. J. Vanhoozer, C. G. Bartholomew and D. J. Treier (eds.), *Theological Interpretation of the Old Testament: A Book-by-Book Survey*, Grand Rapids: Baker, 148–156.

————— (2015), *Job*, THOTC, Grand Rapids: Eerdmans.

Wilson, R. R. (1977), *Genealogy and History in the Biblical World*, New Haven: Yale University Press.

————— (1984), *Sociological Approaches to the Old Testament*, Philadelphia: Fortress.

Wolde, E. van (1997), *Ruth and Naomi*, London: SCM.

Wolfe, L. M. (2011), *Ruth, Esther, Song of Songs, and Judith*, Eugene: Cascade.

Wolfenson, L. B. (1924), 'Implications of the Place of the Book of Ruth in Editions, Manuscripts, and Canon of the Old Testament', *HUCA* 1: 151–178.

Wolters, A. (1988), 'Proverbs XXXI 10–31 as Heroic Hymn: A Form-Critical Analysis', *VT* 38: 446–457.

—— (2001), *The Song of the Valiant Woman: Studies in the Interpretation of Proverbs 31:10–31*, Carlisle: Paternoster.

Wong, G. T. K. (2006), *Compositional Strategy of the Book of Judges: An Inductive, Rhetorical Study*, VTSup 111, Leiden: Brill.

Wright, C. J. H. (2004), 'Implications of Conversion in the Old Testament and the New', *International Bulletin of Missionary Research* 28: 14–19.

—— (2006), *The Mission of God: Unlocking the Bible's Grand Narrative*, Downers Grove: InterVarsity Press.

—— (2011), '"Prophet to the Nations": Missional Reflections on the Book of Jeremiah', in J. A. Grant, A. Lo and G. J. Wenham (eds.), *A God of Faithfulness: Essays in Honour of J. Gordon McConville on His 60th Birthday*, LHBOTS 531, New York: T&T Clark, 112–129.

Wright, N. T. (1991), 'How Can the Bible Be Authoritative?', *Vox Evangelica* 21: 7–29.

Würthwein, E. (1969), *Die fünf Megilloth*, HAT 18, 2nd edn, Tübingen: Mohr Siebeck.

Yoder, C. R. (2001), *Wisdom as a Woman of Substance: A Socio-economic Reading of Proverbs 1–9 and 31:10–31*, BZAW 304, Berlin: Walter de Gruyter.

—— (2003), 'The Woman of Substance (*'ēšet ḥayil*): A Socio-economic Reading of Proverbs 31:10–31', *JBL* 122: 427–447.

Young, A. (2013), 'Expats Volunteering to Teach Refugee Children', *ExpatGo Malaysia*, <http://www.expatgomalaysia.com/article/1111/expats-volunteering-to-teach-refugee-children>, accessed 31 May 2013.

Younger, K. L. (2002), *Judges and Ruth*, NIVAC, Grand Rapids: Zondervan.

Zakovitch, Y. (1999), *Das Buch Rut: Ein jüdischer Kommentar: Mit einem Geleitwort von Erich Zenger*, SBS 177, Stuttgart: Verlag Katholisches Bibelwerk.

Zevit, Z. (2005), 'Dating Ruth: Legal, Linguistic and Historical Observations', *ZAW* 117: 574–600.

Index of authors

Childs, B. S., 69, 162
Chisholm Jr, R. B., 71
Ciampa, R. E., 6
Clark, G. R., 128
Clifford, R. J., 48, 49
Clines, D. J., 11, 124
Cohen, M., 33
Collins, C. J., 20
Cooper, A., 54
Craigie, P. C., 124
Creach, J. F. D., 60
Cross, F. M., 34, 133

Darr, K. P., 89
Daube, D., 40
Davies, E. W., 155
Davies, G. N., 129
Davies, J. A., 144, 145
Davis, B. C., 89
Davis, D. R., 95
Davis, E. F., 45
Dell, K. J., 50
Dempster, S., 2, 23, 55, 56
Donahue, J. R., 115
Donaldson, L. E., 28
Driver, S. R., 33
Duguid, I. M., 105, 113
Dukan, M., 40
Dumbrell, W. J., 14, 18, 145
Dunne, J. A., 101
Durham, J. I., 125, 133, 145
Duvall, J. S., 6
Dyck, J. E., 25

Edwards, J. R., 130
Eising, H., 44
Embry, B., 125
Enns, P., 109
Epstein, I., 53
Eskenazi, T. C., 6, 8, 9, 14, 22, 32,
  33, 48, 71, 89, 107
Exum, J. C., 97

Fee, G. D., 127
Feeley-Harnik, G., 32

Fensham, F. C., 12
Fentress-Williams, J., 16, 23
Fewell, D. N., 50
Fiddian-Qasmiyeh, E., 86
Fisch, H., 27
Fischer, I., 41
Fishbane, M., 10
Flemming, D., 142
Fox, M. V., 45, 46, 47, 49, 50, 97,
  99, 111
France, R. T., 85, 131, 136, 137,
  139
Fredricks, C. J., 28, 73, 74, 144
Freedman, A. D., 101
Freedman, D. N., 83
Fretheim, T. E., 90, 126, 133, 145
Frevel, C., 9
Frymer-Kensky, T., 6, 8, 9, 22, 32,
  33, 48, 71, 89, 107

Gale, W. A., 24
Gallagher, E. L., 57
Garland, D. E., 84
Garrett, D. A., 72
Genette, G., 37
Gentry, P. J., 144
Gerleman, G., 27
Gilbert, M., 16
Ginsburg, C. D., 39, 40
Gladd, B. L., 139
Glover, N., 47
Glueck, N., 33
Goh, S. T. S., 42, 44
Goheen, M. W., 143
Goldsworthy, G., 3
Goppelt, L., 138
Goswell, G., 11, 14, 16, 18, 21, 23,
  25, 59, 97
Gottwald, N. K., 64, 65
Gow, M. D., 5, 31, 104
Green, B., 80
Greidanus, S., 136
Gross, C. D., 12
Gundry, R. H., 131
Gunn, D. M., 50

194

Index of Scripture references

Index of ancient sources

Titles in this series:

An index of Scripture references for all the volumes may be found at
http://www.thegospelcoalition.org/resources/nsbt